D0531284

# CRIME PREVENTION

# CRIME PREVENTION

## A CRITICAL INTRODUCTION

## KAREN EVANS

Los Angeles | London | New Delhi
Singapore | Washington DC

© Karen Evans 2011

First published 2011

Apart from any fair dealing for the purposes of research or
private study, or criticism or review, as permitted under the
Copyright, Designs and Patents Act, 1988, this publication
may be reproduced, stored or transmitted in any form, or by
any means, only with the prior permission in writing of the
publishers, or in the case of reprographic reproduction, in
accordance with the terms of licences issued by the Copyright
Licensing Agency. Enquiries concerning reproduction outside
those terms should be sent to the publishers.

SAGE Publications Ltd
1 Oliver's Yard
55 City Road
London EC1Y 1SP

SAGE Publications Inc.
2455 Teller Road
Thousand Oaks, California 91320

SAGE Publications India Pvt Ltd
B 1/I 1 Mohan Cooperative Industrial Area
Mathura Road
New Delhi 110 044

SAGE Publications Asia-Pacific Pte Ltd
33 Pekin Street #02-01
Far East Square
Singapore 048763

**British Library Cataloguing in Publication data**

A catalogue record for this book is available from the British Library

ISBN 978-1-84787-067-4
ISBN 978-1-84787-068-1 (pbk)

**Library of Congress Control Number: 2010929204**

Typeset by C&M Digitals (P) Ltd, Chennai, India
Printed by CPI Antony Rowe, Chippenham, Wiltshire
Printed on paper from sustainable resources

MIX
Paper from
responsible sources
FSC
www.fsc.org    FSC® C013604

# Contents

# Introduction

Much previous work on crime prevention has remained quite narrowly focused and limited to a discussion of the prevention and management of those crimes which are perceived to affect 'ordinary people' going about their daily business, addressing what Shaftoe (2004) has termed 'locational crimes' and ignoring or marginalising those crimes which appear more removed from our everyday lives. This book however, following from the work of such authors as Crawford, Gilling and Hughes, is concerned with the political nature of crime prevention, subjecting its normative frameworks to critical attention. It contends that crime prevention practices cannot be understood when divorced from the political contexts and ideological frameworks and theories which create and sustain them. To this end the following chapters subject crime prevention policies in the UK, and in particular the New Labour project on preventing crime, to a close and critical scrutiny. In doing so, the book reveals the intensely ideological nature of the 'fight against crime' and how this has played out in recent decades to form the crime prevention and control landscape which we currently see before us. It reveals that major transformations have taken place in the practice of law and justice in Britain, some of which have been much debated and critiqued, but others which have slowly, subtly but irredeemably affected our relationship to the law and the forces of the state.

It has become generally accepted over recent years that crime and its control serve a number of political ends. This has been highlighted and discussed in the academic literature most recently in terms of the discussion around the governance of security and safety (Crawford 2002, Garland 2001, Hughes and Edwards 2002, Johnston and Shearing 2003) and by the major political players in Britain, who, for the last thirty years, have embraced a crime agenda and given it particular prominence in their party policies and pronouncements. During this period their increasingly politicised agenda has developed in range and scope. Thirty years ago the prevention of crime was predominantly localised and based at the level of neighbourhood and street but this can no longer be said to be the case. As the story outlined in this volume unfolds, the focus on the local and the community is not replaced, but is joined by bigger questions of 'race', migration, war and human rights. The agenda of crime prevention and control at the local level has been clearly impacted by wider national and super-national issues and a truly 'glocalised' (Hughes 2007) agenda has developed in which practices formed and delivered at the local level influence and are in turn influenced by practices formed within national and global arenas. Today, for example, one cannot discuss race-hate crimes at the local level without reference to international state agendas, war-mongering, Islamophobia and the increasing numbers of insecure and unsafe nation-states across the globe. Community safety, previously a concern to address local economic and social conditions as a partnership between local state and community actors, has become professionalised and driven by requirements to reduce 'signal' crimes and to manage risks defined at a national level and delivered through top-down structures and strategies. The net of control has been cast wider to encompass numerous arenas which were not previously considered crime matters and redefined them as such. As a result crime prevention practices have found their way into a whole range of social policy issues and the number and range of 'suspect' populations has grown.

As social control and discipline has been further dispersed and state functions passed over to the private sector these practices have also leaked into many commercial and market-organisations which are much harder to hold to account. In our dealings with the state, public and private sector organisations we are all now subjected to risk assessments and impacted by policies created to manage criminality, whether we are forced to undergo finger-printing and full body-scans at airports or to submit evidence of nationality and residence when opening a bank account or delivering a seminar at a university. How this has happened, how the prevention of crime has moved from a localised and specialised activity to encompass a whole range of practices which threaten human rights and privacies can only be understood in the context of political and ideological drivers of change. This book aims, through a close reading of the New Labour project in the UK in its particularity, to uncover some of the wider forces, political perspectives and engrained ideologies which have driven this significant move. What has happened in the UK in this specific period has a broader significance and affects landscapes of crime control outside of these national boundaries and will continue to have effect beyond the current period. The construction of 'problems' and 'risks' which have been evident within UK policy are also becoming more evident across Europe and many advanced capitalist economies and the economic and social circumstances within which such ideas flourish are present outside UK borders and worsening in depth. So the solutions to these 'problems' presented across different nation-states, I would argue, are likely also to coalesce.

This book consists of nine substantive chapters each of which aims to explore one facet of the crime prevention agenda as it has been presented largely in the UK context, and then offers a conclusion which brings together the themes that have become prominent and made clearer throughout this step-by-step analysis. While each chapter can be read on its own as a synthesis of policy and direction in that particular policy area, the directions and themes presented in each are closely linked to the rest and the trajectory of change which has occurred over the last thirty years can only be really understood when the book is read as a whole.

Changing policing agendas and the increasing privatisation of policing services which has taken place alongside the granting of further powers to police officers are introduced and discussed throughout the volume. The transformations which have taken place in this area are so closely linked to wider changes in policy and practices that they could not be discussed in a standalone chapter. Chapter 1 outlines the state of affairs in crime prevention as it was understood by theorists in the twentieth century and covers the different perspectives which competed with each other as crime prevention grew as a subject for academics and policy-makers in the last half of that century. The resulting legacy of the debates and discussions which took place forms the basis for an understanding of the ascendancy of a reactionary and de-radicalised approach to crime prevention which was never seriously countered by the New Labour project. Chapter 2 demonstrates how the seemingly radical and progressive approach taken by the Blair government of 1997 rapidly demonstrated its ideological commitment to policies inspired by an attachment to neo-liberal economic discourses. It charts how, while giving limited space to projects to combat and reverse social exclusion, the government could not detach itself from the old ideas of individual responsibility, cultural deficit and blaming so beloved of previous administrations. Chapter 3 considers how the communitarian ideals which informed much of New Labour's thinking justified government shifting from playing the role of provider to that of enabler and thenceforth to enforcer. Couched in terms of a giving up of state power to the individual and the community the eventual outcome of the embracing of communitarian ideals resulted in a moral authoritarian approach to community which demanded individual and collective responsibility but which closely prescribed the terms in which this responsibilisation was to be permitted. Chapter 4 continues to chart the rise of the authoritarian agenda looking at New Labour's flagship legislation on crime and the agenda set by the provisions of the Crime and Disorder Act 1998. Beyond this obvious turn to intrusive measures of social control, however, the chapter demonstrates how this agenda was forced downwards through the use of managerial tools and a centralisation of criminal justice policies and practices. In so doing any remaining radical voices and alternative perspectives were gradually squeezed out of the debate. Chapters 5 to 8 explore contradictions and inconsistencies in policy aimed at young people, minority and migrant populations and the tensions between welfare and criminalising discourses are presented. These discussions reveal the extent to which the control agenda came to pervade social interventions in what were perceived to be 'problem' areas. Criminalising discourses and practices tended to construct these groups as an 'enemy within' and government policy towards them became heavily tinged with social control, risk management, monitoring and surveillance. As the state produced a particular knowledge of these groups based on discourses of separation and difference these were reproduced within local communities, cities and regions producing fractures and segregation within them while at the same time community cohesion and mutual respect were preached from above.

Chapter 8 details ways in which Labour's Respect Agenda, although ostensibly concerned with rebuilding trust in policing and justice systems actually served to undermine the rule of law and due process with the extension of many summary police powers and demonstrated a withdrawal of trust in community by government. Chapter 9 continues this theme explaining how, under New Labour minor transgressive acts could be redefined as crime and dealt with accordingly, ratcheting up the response to more serious infringements of the law. At the same time the over-policing and targeting of certain groups was more in evidence; fears of urban youth were reformulated in political and media panics around urban youth gangs and black culture and political protestors redefined as 'domestic extremists'. The concluding chapter summarises many of the consequences of governing through crime and fear, of placing responsibilities before rights and of extending social controls outside of previously accepted boundaries.

As I complete this introduction in May 2010 the New Labour project in Britain appears to have reached its end and a coalition of Conservative and Liberal Democrats have taken charge of government and divided out ministerial offices among these two parties. While much has been promised in terms of 'change' in the terms and perspectives of the new government formation the manifestos and promises of the two governing parties do not offer much hope for a different thinking on crime and its prevention to emerge. True there is a commitment in the coalition document to reverse the erosion of civil liberties which has taken place under the previous Labour administrations. It is promised that plans for ID cards and biometric passports will be scrapped and intrusive databases collecting and storing personal information will be scaled down. However, so many consistencies can also be detected with the attitudes and perspectives which have shaped the trajectory of policy around crime prevention and social control over the last decades that there is much cause to believe that crime prevention policy will continue in the current vein. Deep cuts in welfare provision will create the conditions under which social provision will be further privatised, local authorities' ability to provide for its local populace will remain seriously eroded and there will be further calls for the individual and family to extricate themselves from dependence on the state and to build independent structures of support. The refrain of 'Broken Britain', taken up with some zeal by Conservative leadership and echoed by their partners in government will ensure that attention will continue to be drawn away from the state and its inability to achieve security for its population and that the singling out of suspect populations and the blaming of groups who are seen to lie outside accepted boundaries of behaviour will continue apace.

# 1

# Crime prevention in the twentieth century

The problem of crime has become much more complex in recent years. Rates of reported crime have appeared to stabilise but reports of some crimes are still increasing; changes in social relationships and technological breakthroughs have allowed new forms of crime to emerge; national security has emerged as a key priority and the fear of crime has become as important a measure of well-being as the experience of crime itself. The reduction of crime and the promotion of security have become key political priorities while at the same time the terrain on which crime is 'fought' has been anything other than stable. The economic cycle has seen slump turn to boom and back again; significant cultural changes have radically altered social norms and values; global changes have impacted on life-styles and eroded the ability of nation-states to regulate their citizens and new forms of social harm, such as climate change, have been identified which have yet to enter the lexicon of crime and criminality. In attempting to understand and explore the impact of these changes, the discipline of criminology has had to develop much more sophisticated theoretical insights and tools with which to examine current trends and to predict future developments.

The study of crime, of crime prevention and of safety is a very different concern today than it was three decades ago when a British prime minister first swept into power on a 'law and order' ticket. The Conservative party, led by Margaret Thatcher, used the problem of crime, policing and order as a tool to aid their election to government, introducing a significant political agenda which is still current today (Reiner 2007). Looking back on those days, the Conservatives' agenda on crime seems crudely fashioned and peculiarly naïve. Crime was caused by permissive social relations, a liberal agenda in education and a legacy of the welfare state which offered a something-for-nothing culture (this refrain was later taken up by subsequent Labour administrations). Through Thatcher's terms of office (she resigned in 1990 to be replaced by John Major until Labour took office in 1997) to the turn of the century the problem of crime was largely perceived as a domestic concern by government, academics and policy-makers alike and was tackled accordingly. Yet by the time Labour had won their second consecutive election in 2001 the problem of crime was taking on a distinctly different flavour and was beginning to be linked to strong globalising and transnational forces. New enemies needed to be fought with new weapons and the Labour government set about constructing a modern crime prevention framework fit for twenty-first century crime. In truth, however, and as outlined in subsequent chapters, the legacy of Thatcher's neo-liberal political project informed a great deal of new Labour's thinking.

This chapter will look more closely at some of the key transformations which have underpinned the shifting agenda of crime prevention in western democracies from the early 1970s when crime first became a political issue in the UK to the point at which New Labour took office. The chapter will relate the political turn in crime prevention to a series of changes which first became apparent within the United States but which soon began to affect other western liberal democracies. In doing so I do not wish to ignore the vast majority of the world's population which has lived under a different set of political and material experiences, but for the purpose of this work it is necessary to take a more western-centric view in order to highlight the particular preoccupations which have beset and upset the affluent 'west' and which have driven their particular policies and perspectives on the prevention of crime. While the preoccupation with crime remained a problem for domestic policy and primarily an issue of the internal workings of the nation-state, the crime policies of the western nations did not overly affect the world outside. However, as will be uncovered in later chapters, as the problem of crime 'globalised', this can no longer be said to be the case.

## The politicisation of crime

Although crime rates had been rising since the mid-1950s they did not become a party political issue until the early 1970s when a Conservative government under Edward Heath expressed its commitment to establishing 'law and order' across the UK (Waiton 2006). The 'crimes' and disorder which Heath's government faced were profoundly political as well as social in nature. Growing civil rights movements (such as lesbian and gay activism, black power and feminism) were organising to challenge old-established ways and to push more progressive agendas on to the state and law-makers. Trade union militancy was at its height with the miners' strikes of 1972 and 1974 in particular attributed with playing a major part in the eventual downfall of Heath's government. Both Heath and Thatcher, as newly elected leader of the opposition in 1974, turned to the law and order agenda partly to counter growing political unrest but also as a consequence of growing social unrest which the economic crisis of the 1970s had thrown into the mix. In doing so they disrupted a cross-party consensus which had stressed rehabilitation rather than retribution and a welfare rather than crudely punitive approach to offenders

(Garland 2001: 34–9). Under Conservative leadership formal social control mechanisms were championed as the way to bring disordered populations into line. The story of the 'authoritarian turn' in state responses to crime, as demonstrated by the adoption of more aggressive policing styles in particular, has been skilfully told by Hall et al. (1978) in *Policing the Crisis*. This heavy-handed response to crime was allied to a racialisation of the crime agenda whereby inner-city youth, i.e. young black males, were targeted as 'the enemies within', blamed for disrupting peaceful Britain through their enjoyment of a 'strange' and 'alien' culture (Hall et al. 1978).

A heavy-handed and 'military style' of policing black youth persisted into the early 1980s when a number of inner-city neighbourhoods exploded into violence in 1981 (Cowell et al. 1982) and again to a lesser extent in 1984. The free rein which had been given to the police to patrol de-industrialised neighbourhoods, to stop and search predominantly black youth but also more generally the poor and the unemployed victims of Thatcher's neo-liberal economic and social policies, was partially halted by the findings of the Scarman Report. Lord Scarman had been charged with chairing an enquiry into the violent outbursts in Brixton, London in 1981. While falling short of accusing the police of institutional racism Scarman called for a greater community input into policing strategies and for the police to build closer links to local authorities and neighbourhood organisations. A patchy framework of police and community consultation groups was set up so that different organisations and individuals could comment on policing priorities and practices in their local area (Fielding 1991: 172).

While on the one hand policing after Scarman moved slowly towards a more consensual style in which some attempts were made to rebuild shattered police–community relations, the formal mechanisms of social control were once more brought down heavily in the policing of the miners' strike which lasted a full twelve months from March 1984. Police forces were brought in to mining areas to restrict the movement of miners out of their villages, to prevent the demonstration of solidarity between pits, to break up picket lines and to ensure that strike-breakers could get in to work. Those active in the solidarity movement for the miners will remember the images of uniformed police waving ten pound notes at miners brought to penury by months of strike action. Their behaviour demonstrated quite clearly how the government could, and did, use the police and the law for their own political ends.

Successive Conservative and Labour governments from the 1970s to the 1990s gradually reached a consensus over the need to utilise crime and its prevention as a political tool. All this was done in the name of bringing order back in to streets, communities and, at times, even working class organisations. This move to incorporate the prevention of crime into the remit of the state brought with it a level of central intervention into the organisation and control of neighbourhood and locality. As we will see throughout this work, this interventionist stance has certainly not diminished although in changing political and economic climates direct provision of crime prevention measures has been partially passed on to private

providers. The changing nature of social provision was both ideologically motivated and driven by fiscal considerations. As the welfare state came under attack
consequent to the rise and then the domination of neo-liberal perspectives in
government, swingeing budgetary cuts signalled an end to the state as the ultimate
provider of public services (Fabricant and Burqhardt 1992). While the government continues to 'steer' crime prevention policy setting its direction through the
creation of policy and directing resources, it has allowed other organisations, both
public and private to 'row' the boat and act as the deliverers of services on the
ground (Osborne and Gaebler 1992).

## The growth of the crime prevention industry

The backdrop to an increased interest in crime prevention policy and practices
was the increase in recorded crime evident in much of the west during the latter
half of the twentieth century. Debate rages as to the accuracy of crime statistics
and how useful they might be in comparing changes in offending over time and
between different nations – not only do the recording practices *within* national
boundaries change over time but there are also major differences *between* the
recording practices of different nation-states and definitions which different
national crime control agencies use to identify and categorise actions as particular
forms of crime. Despite these problems and difficulties, however, the extent and
nature of recorded crime is a useful starting point as these statistics shape how the
problem of crime is perceived and defined. It is to recorded crime statistics that
governments and professionals turn when justifying new directions in policy and
practice or proposing and designing solutions to the problem of crime.

Recorded crime data for the UK shows a fairly stable level of crime since police
records began in 1876 up until the 1930s. After this point recorded crime began
to slowly rise until the Second World War. After another brief period of stability,
crime rates start on a more steeply rising trajectory from the mid-1950s. The general trend remains on this steep incline until its peak in 1995 after which crime
rates begin to drop significantly for the next ten years, after which this fall levels
out (Home Office 2009). In 1981 Britain introduced the self-report victimisation
survey imported from the United States which became the British Crime Survey.
This had no good news to tell, estimating in its first report in 1982, that the actual
incidence of crime was four times that recorded through police records (Safe
Neighbourhoods Unit 1986). This prolonged increase in recorded crime has been
partly attributed to growing affluence in the west and the shift to a consumer-
oriented capitalism which has meant that there are many more opportunities to
commit crime while at the same time societal changes have meant that informal
social controls which might have deterred the commission of crime have broken
down (Bottoms and Wiles 1992). Whatever the reasons, Britain experienced
roughly four decades of steeply rising rates of recorded crime and so steep was this

increase that the ten years between 1981 and 1991 saw a doubling in recorded crime rates.

## Inequalities in the distribution of crime and crime prevention

Nationally recorded crime rates can only reveal so much about the nature and extent of crime within any particular country and can tell us little about how crime is distributed within national boundaries. As the 43 police forces of England and Wales recorded and published their crime data on a force-wide basis allowing some scope for comparing crime rates across force areas, this crude comparative tool could not distinguish differential crime rates within their regions. Furthermore, it was not until the first tranche of data from the British Crime Survey (BCS) that rates of crime across different areas could be directly compared. The British criminologist, Tim Hope, conducted secondary analysis of BCS data in 1994 which uncovered a striking relationship concerning victimisation in different areas which had hitherto lain undetected. Hope split the BCS data into ten groups (deciles) ranging from low to high-crime areas. He found that 'a gradual increase [in incidence of victimisation] across the majority of areas is dwarfed by the exponential increase in victimisation experienced in the minority of high-rate areas' (Hope 1996: 4). To put it more simply, areas with the highest rates of crime were suffering vastly more than any other areas – for property crime they suffered 25 times that of the second lowest area and twice the rate of the next highest area and for crimes against the person the highest crime areas suffered 76 times more crime than that suffered in the third lowest area and four times more than the next highest area. Crime was found to be highly concentrated amongst a minority of the population – those living in 'low status urban areas of poor quality housing with above average concentrations of children, teenagers and young adults alongside a preponderance of single-adult households' (Hope 1996: 7). Confounding previous expectations it seemed that the poorest populations were most at risk of becoming victims of crime.

Compounding this problem of the concentration of crime within certain areas, Farrell and Pease (1993) discovered another key element to victimisation – that those who are victimised once are more likely to be so again. They named this phenomenon 'repeat victimisation' and their research was extremely influential in targeting crime prevention projects on those who had already had experience of crime. The Kirkholt Burglary Project served as an exemplar for this type of targeted crime prevention. Those households which had been burgled were offered a whole raft of security measures for their home as well as the practice of 'cocooning', that is social ties were strengthened with immediately adjacent houses putting in place informal surveillance measures over the burgled property. In their evaluation of the Kirkholt project, Farrell and Pease detected a significant drop in rates of burglary as well as a reduced fear of crime in the area. Farrell, Pease and

Hope's work led to a targeting of interventions to reduce crime which Hope warned, although effective, might in the end prove to be socially-divisive – suggesting that low crime neighbourhoods might resent the extra money spent on high-crime neighbourhoods or that high-crime areas might be type-cast as 'land-scapes of fear' (Taylor 1995) beyond redemption and lying outside normal values and moralities.

The targeting of crime prevention policies came of age with the use of Geographical Information Systems, developed in the 1990s, to map the incidence of crime within local areas and regions. The occurrence of each crime could be plotted on a street map and crime 'hotspots' identified which revealed the streets, parks or even buildings where particular crimes were concentrated. These crime maps were constructed and held by the police but were shared with local author-ities where strong partnerships had been established between the two organisa-tions. With the advent of the Crime and Disorder Audits and Partnerships required by the Crime and Disorder Act of 1998 (more of this in Chapter 2) crime maps were more widely used and shared and formed the basis for many more closely targeted interventions (Hirschfield et al. 2001). Through these proc-esses the 'problem of crime' became more closely linked to problematic areas.

## The fear of crime

Growing public concern and attention to the increase in crime rates has meant that crime is now perceived as a major social problem. Very few people can have escaped any kind of victimisation and fewer will know of no one who has been a victim of crime.[1] This shared experience of crime and its effects has led to an increasing fear of crime adding to a crisis in 'ontological security' among the popu-lations of the west (Giddens 1990). This crisis is not solely related to a fear of crime but links into numerous social changes which people have lived through in recent decades. Some of these changes, especially when linked to increased prosperity and opportunity that a rising economy can bring, will have been positive and strength-ening influences but present too are many risks associated with living in present-day consumer capitalism: the loss of security in employment; rapidly changing social relationships; the need to compete against others to get ahead and the expe-rience of facing a longer working life in difficult and changing circumstances. Added in recent years have been concerns of more global significance relating for example to the realities of climate change, almost constant wars, the impacts of economic and banking collapse and loss of many taken-for-granted certainties in life. All this has led sociologists to comment on the high risks associated with living under late capitalism and the increasing lack of control which individuals have over forces more powerful than themselves which can impact very negatively on their current and future plans (Beck 1992). Giddens (1984) has suggested that late modernity swept away old knowledge systems and behaviours based on long-standing traditions and social relationships and that in their stead we are forced to constantly reinvent ourselves anew, acquiring information relevant to our present circumstances. In addition this information must be constantly replaced as the environments in which we function and in which we make personal decisions remain volatile and changeable. We are left not knowing who or what to trust and under such stress the fear of crime can take on unimaginable proportions (Evans et al. 1996). Why, it is asked, when crime has been falling for an extended period, does the fear of crime not diminish? Are we the 'worried well' (Farall et al. 2009)? The fear of crime, however, can act as a proxy for many other fears linked to lack of economic stability, control over our futures and undermining of established knowledge bases which are certainly not diminishing and are most probably on the increase. In addition once victimised the damage that this experience can wreak on an individual and their close friends and family may shatter what little sense of security that they possess and victimisation may not be easily or rapidly overcome.

It could be argued that it does not suit the governing bodies and organisations of social control to accept the true nature of our fears which are amorphous, ever-present and growing in stature and range. After all there is no easy way to control the volatile economic and social forces of neo-liberal capitalism once they have been unleashed and largely left unregulated. Instead it is easier for government and law-makers to identify one or more social groups or 'types' which can function as the endpoint of our fears, anger and frustrations. In the United States in the 1960s and 1970s the black, inner-city poor were framed in this way – and to a great extent still are – but still more 'dangerous others' have been constructed and join them in this category. In Britain 'black inner-cities' have been used to this end, especially in the 1970s, and were joined from the 1980s and 1990s by the, often white, indigenous 'underclass' and in the latter years of the twentieth century by migrants and asylum seekers and then, around the turn of the century, with the rise of Islamophobia this became the fate of Muslim populations worldwide (Fekete 2009).

## What has been tried in crime prevention?

### Offender-centred strategies

The oldest strategies to prevent crime are centred on the offender themselves. The criminal justice system was formulated to deter offenders through conviction and punishment ensuring that the victim of crime receives justice but is also constrained in their behaviour. Incarceration was considered in liberal terms as offering a space in which to rehabilitate the individual, allowing the prisoner time to reflect on their behaviour and gain the support necessary to improve their future prospects. In more progressive and modern criminal justice systems imprisonment is considered a last resort and punishment and rehabilitation take place within community settings, including measures such as contact with probation, diversion from crime and, more recently, including restorative work to begin to make good some of the damage caused by offending. All of these strategies are based on the belief that the cause of offending behaviour lies within the individual. Barring the use of life sentences or the death penalty, these are measures which also suggest that a person can be persuaded to behave differently or can be supported in different ways to help them desist from committing crime in the future.

There are many diverse theories which attempt to explain why the individual commits crime. Pre-modern understandings suggested that crimes might be committed by people who were in some way possessed by evil forces which had to be driven from them through the use of extreme physical punishments, sited on the possessed body and designed to drive the possessor out. With the advent of more enlightened ways of thinking, classical criminology, following the works of Jeremy Bentham and Cesare Beccaria, considered the 'criminal' to be a rational actor possessing free will who could be deterred from crime through a system of punishments 'fitted' to the crime in their level of severity and the individual's loss of freedoms. With the development of positivist and science-based explanations for human behaviours, popular in the nineteenth century, classical criminology's explanations were challenged by a view that individual pathology led to criminality with, in the late nineteenth century, the Italian criminologist Lombroso famously proposing that people might be born criminal due to genetic predisposition (Gibson and Hahn-Rafter 2006).

A medical and psychological approach to criminality prevailed until the middle of the twentieth century under which it was proposed that offending could ultimately be treated by utilising medical knowledge. Only after the introduction of social welfare provision following the Second World War did the state step in to provide medical models of treatment as a part of its commitment to offer support to those in need and fostering a 'correctionalist penal-welfare' stance (Garland 1994 in Hughes 1998: 43). In 1974, however, research based in the United States (Martinson 1974) claimed that there was little evidence to demonstrate the efficacy of such treatment-based practice, this model of crime prevention was perceived as fundamentally flawed and that in truth 'nothing works'. His work fuelled and was often quoted by the proponents of an already growing anti-welfare agenda which spawned a return to the philosophy of deterrence and punishment which had preceded welfarism.

## Right realism and situational crime prevention

With the collapse of the 'correctionalist penal-welfare' stance and with it the idea that people could be changed and helped out of their offending, alternative measures for controlling crime had to be sought. While a 'punitive turn' proved popular it was a reactive approach which had most impact and intervention after an offence had been committed and an offender caught rather than proactively focusing on stopping crime being committed in the first place. Police detection rates, however, are notoriously low, at around 24 per cent of recorded crimes in the 1970s and falling to around 20 per cent by the end of the 1990s (*Daily Telegraph* 2001a) and the search to find methods by which to prevent crime could not be abandoned. Policy-makers turned to more practical and less idealistic solutions to the prevention of crime, embracing instead what has been termed 'right realism'. Rejecting explanations of crime which looked to economic and social structures as major factors in shaping criminality, this approach, drawing on routine activities theory (Cohen and Felson 1979), focused instead on disrupting the conditions in which crimes could occur – the coming together of potential offenders, opportunities for crime and the absence of a capable guardian to protect the target of crime – and seeking to control crime and criminality rather than to eliminate them. Thus a long-standing support, continuing to this day, for situational crime prevention measures was born (see for example the work of Ronald Clarke, Gloria Laycock, and J.Q. Wilson). Crime prevention measures adopted as a consequence of this approach were based on the principles of cost–benefit analysis and considered the offender as a rational, calculating individual who would weigh up the costs and consequences of being caught with the rewards and benefits achieved through the commission of crime (Akers 1990, Clarke and Cornish 1985). The practice of 'target-hardening' grew out of this work in order to limit the opportunities for crime to take place. It proposed that where a crime is seen as more difficult or risky to commit then this reduces the attractiveness of the criminal act and the potential offender will turn away from it. So potential targets were protected or made physically harder to attack – cars were built with integrated alarm systems, windows locked and shuttered and open spaces fenced and gated in order to deter offenders.

In the 1970s a perspective emerged which considered the impact which physical environment could have on the offender and urban environments themselves were studied as places which appeared criminogenic (Bottoms and Wiles 1992: 11). Researchers looked for ways in which various urban environments could be adapted and controlled so that they were less conducive to crime. In the United States, Oscar Newman's (1972) work on 'defensible spaces' proved particularly influential, followed in 1985 by British academic Alice Coleman's complement to Newman's work on 'designing out crime'. Both Newman and Coleman argued that the physical layout of areas could be manipulated in order to lessen crime in the neighbourhood. Newman argued that residents would be more prepared to defend and watch over their own private spaces than they would public spaces. Coleman applied Newman's theories to the built environment typically found in Britain to argue that poorly designed environments could actually instil and normalise criminogenic responses in young people routinely subjected to them. As a result of their work local authorities set about a large-scale redesign of their estates; houses and flats were given private gardens to the front and back and communal spaces were removed or given extra security measures. Public areas were fenced off and gated to render them semi-private and lighting and lines of sight across estates were improved. During the 1970s government funds were set aside for the improvement of local authority housing estates under Estate Action, Safe Neighbourhoods and Urban Aid programmes. Any problems of crime and vandalism were more closely monitored and addressed. The practice of 'designing out crime' has become widespread and is now routinely practised in both public and privatised spaces. It is as prevalent in commercial areas as in residential – shop fronts are shuttered over night, anti-ram-raid bollards fitted in front of shop windows and the commercial transaction itself is secured in ways which were unimaginable twenty years ago.

Perhaps one of the most widely cited and influential, though also highly critiqued (see Kinsey et al. 1986, Matthews 1992), articles written on crime prevention and which adopts a right realist perspective is that which was laid out in Wilson and Kelling's 'Broken Windows' thesis in 1982. Wilson and Kelling argued that signs of disorder and incivility will, if unchecked, accumulate to such an extent that they foster feelings of fear and abandonment in local neighbourhoods and lead to spiralling crime rates. Their work led to a crackdown on any signifiers of disorder, not only windows left broken and graffiti daubed on walls but also on the people considered to create unease within an area. In New York this influenced a new aggressive policing style, 'zero tolerance policing' which, under the guidance of Police Commissioner William Bratton from 1994, led to a 'tough on crime' stance in which people begging, sleeping rough or drinking alcohol in public places were routinely, and sometimes aggressively, removed.

The designing of urban environments to increase safety and security has largely taken a specialist approach which offers technical solutions to what could be considered social problems but which in doing so not only fundamentally changes the physical aspect of places but impacts on social practices as well. In the hunt for solutions to the problem of crime the developing technology around Closed Circuit Television systems (CCTV) has played a major role in 'social ordering practices' according to Coleman (2004), particularly since the early 1990s. According to McCahill and Norris (2002), between 1992 and 2002 over a quarter of a billion pounds was spent on cameras with an estimated additional three billion for their maintenance. Cameras are used as signifiers of guardianship in an area, but also have increasingly been used to control the behaviour of the young, the poor and the homeless, in fact anyone standing outside of what are considered to be 'acceptable' social values. An architecture of security has been constructed across the country which in recent years has included anti-terrorist measures which 'harden' so-called vulnerable areas against terrorist attack. The highly visible measures have created more securitised environments, such as private shopping malls which have all the requisite 'secure-by-design' features offering a veneer of safety, security and affluence suggesting that the world is not a dangerous place, as long as money and technology can be thrown at the problem.

Situational crime prevention measures have been criticised for doing nothing to address the root causes of crime and offending. As a consequence, it is argued, they cannot reduce overall rates of crime but can only displace it, either to places where security measures are not in place or to different forms and methods of crime, although this is hotly denied and contested by the proponents of such measures who argue that the wider benefits of situational crime prevention out-weigh any initial recorded displacement (McLennan and Whitworth 2008). It has also been suggested that physical barriers and security measures can prove to be socially divisive (Bottoms and Wiles 1992), can contribute to an increased fear of crime and construct a fortress mentality which can negatively impact on people's sense of well-being (Home Office 1993: 65). Perhaps the key criti-cism, however, is that these measures rest on certain assumptions about human behaviour – that offenders are driven by rational calculations and also that people respond differently to public and private spaces. It represents, furthermore, a fundamentally pessimistic perspective which suggests that crime will always exist and that the best that can be done is to protect the 'innocent victim'. It presumes, thereby, that crime is committed by outsiders and that communities of the innocent are vulnerable to predatory individuals. It presumes too that crime takes place in public places and limits crime reduction to those crimes where targets can be hardened – crimes which take place in private places, in the boardrooms, in the home and crimes against the person are marginalised. It is a technicist and administrative perspective which, while partial and flawed, suited the Home Office search to find relatively easy and quick fixes to rising rates of crime (Maguire 2004).

While academic criminology moved towards a more sociological analysis and a 'new criminology' (Taylor et al. 1973) embracing developing theoretical inputs using Marxist and Interpretivist perspectives, and a 'left realist' response to the right realism presented by conventional criminology (Lea and Young 1984, Matthews and Young 1992), the Home Office interest remained linked to 'a new and pragmatic "administrative criminology" emerging out of the ashes of positiv-ism ... with an emphasis on surveillance, control and containment' (Bottoms and Wiles 1995: 4). These two strands of criminology remain in direct opposition but it was right realism which drove the crime prevention agenda. The situational approach to crime prevention has become highly favoured and institutionalised within government and policy-making circles and widely accepted as an effective defence against crime (Laycock and Clarke 2001) despite a continued increase in crime rates recorded throughout the 1980s and early 1990s. So the Home Office Crime Prevention Committee, set up in 1967, became a Standing Con-ference on Crime Prevention in 1987 and later spawned the Crime Prevention Unit and the Home Office Research and Planning Unit. These organisations con-tinued throughout these decades to support and later to publish empirical research on crime prevention activities which were generally highly technicist in nature – focusing on the criminal act rather than the actor and concentrating on situational crime prevention. The discipline of Crime Science grew out of this perspective at the turn of the twenty-first century (Smith and Tilley 2005) and the opening of the Jill Dando Institute of Crime Science within University College London in 2001.

Despite criticisms of the situational crime prevention which have labelled it as fundamentally pessimistic and, as Wilson acknowledges, concerned only with 'moderate gains' rather than 'utopian goals', situational crime prevention is seen as a practical, immediate and relatively low-cost solution to crime with measurable outcomes. This is contrasted to social crime prevention measures which are considered expensive to maintain over the long-term and indeterminate in their results. Crawford has argued, however, that the inexorable rise of situational crime prevention is more related to a political perspective which emphasises individual responsibility for both the commission of crime and its prevention and which rejects any measures based on collective and social responses. He argues that:

> The installation of governments committed to a neo-liberal ideology – emphasising the free market, a minimal state and individual free choice and responsibility – dovetailed with and promoted criminological ideas which shared the same basic propositions. As a consequence, the spread of situational crime prevention needs to be understood as connected to the political programmes with which it is aligned. (Crawford 1998: 65)

## Social crime prevention

In contrast to situational crime prevention measures social crime prevention considers the causes of criminality to be rooted within social formations and intervenes in the social world of the individual to attempt to divert them from offending. Social crime prevention is mainly concerned with strengthening the social bonds which tie individuals to normative groups and values with the expectation that this will make offending against these groups less likely and will equip the individual with a moral code which will steer them towards more positive goals and aspirations. It does not identify the causes of criminality within the individual's pathology but looks at how social structures can influence rates of crime. Social crime prevention is therefore more aligned to social policy interventions in schools, housing, employment and services to children, young people and families.

The first identification of social structure as contributing to the problem of crime came with the work of the Chicago School of sociologists in the early twentieth century. They identified the newly emerging urban landscapes of America with socially disorganised neighbourhoods, weak social ties and an absence of shared values, norms and expectations as key to understanding the high rates of offending found within them. Building neighbourhood projects, family support and youth schemes were perceived as important factors in reducing people's propensity to commit crime. Social crime prevention was later linked to Hirschi's control theory, which explained why people conform to social expectations, Merton's strain theory, which pointed to the disjuncture between legitimate aspirations and the lack of opportunities available to residents of disadvantaged neighbourhoods as a key motivational factor behind their offending, and to the work of Cloward and Ohlin on the ways in which young people adapt to their limiting social environments (Crawford 1998: 104–7).

Social crime prevention has tended to concentrate on youthful offending behaviours in the belief that it is the poor socialisation of the young which leads to their disproportionate involvement in crime. As a result, many of the social interventions placed into local neighbourhoods to deter crime are youth-focused and designed to prevent the early onset of offending. These interventions have also been targeted at the poorest communities in the belief that it is within these places that lack of legitimate opportunities are most keenly felt (Hope and Shaw 1988). This targeting of crime prevention initiatives to neighbourhoods and individuals grappling with the multiple problems of poverty, exclusion and lack of opportunity has led to 'risk-based' interventions through which specific 'risk factors' are identified which when present in an individual's particular circumstances might increase their propensity to commit crime, or might mean that they are less able to desist from crime once involved. Risk-based interventions have been built around a growing body of developmental criminology (Farrington 2006) and research into criminal careers such as that conducted by The Cambridge Study of Delinquent Development since the early 1960s (Farrington et al. 2006). The identification of 'risk' factors and the targeting of interventions towards those most 'at risk' has become a more accepted way to build social policy measures in recent years and has contributed to a policy focus on 'risky' and 'troubled' youth (see Chapter 5 for a fuller discussion).

In earlier periods social crime prevention measures, while targeted at specific populations, did not write off entire social groups as criminogenic, but accepted that individuals within impoverished and marginalised neighbourhoods adapt differently to their lack of opportunities, with crime as only one possible adaptation – strains and conflicts also leading to mental health problems, self-harming and withdrawal from social life and civic institutions. However, in the late 1980s and 1990s the 'discovery' of an underclass in Britain (Murray 1990) moved discussion much closer to a condemnation of entire neighbourhoods, communities and social groupings as being particularly prone to crime and outside 'normal' group behaviours. This has gone hand in hand with what Knepper (2007) refers to as a 'criminalisation of social policy' whereby funding for social intervention projects becomes dependent on crime prevention outcomes rather than seen as a social good in its own right. Social crime prevention has remained 'the poor man' within crime prevention for many years (Crawford 1998). Funding has been directed at those measures which can be seen to result in direct and measurable outcomes and much social crime prevention has been criticised as remaining unproven as an effective crime prevention measure (Cornish and Clarke 1986). The general with-drawal of social policy and welfare provision from many neighbourhoods has also severely limited funding to such projects.

## Community-based crime prevention

The targeting of particular 'high-crime neighbourhoods' for both situational and social crime prevention measures has focused attention on why specific communities appear to need more intervention than others. A number of schemes were designed to intervene directly into what became seen as 'problem neighbourhoods' in Britain from the 1980s. The Safe Neighbourhoods Unit set up by NACRO[2] from 1980 provided both situational and social crime prevention measures to areas vulnerable to crime. NACRO proposed and developed services individually tailored to neighbourhoods, services for victims, more links between police and communities and a meaningful community input into the design of services (Bright 1991). Priority Estates Projects were developed by the then Department of the Environment (DoE) from 1979 to improve unpopular local authority housing estates and City Action Teams were set up in the mid-1980s to support local crime prevention initiatives where these were linked to employment and training with home security improvements and business security schemes often provided by a local workforce. The then Department for Trade and Industry (DTI) set up its Inner City Task Forces from 1988 which were managed by the DoE from 1992. The Five Towns Initiative in 1986, followed by Safer Cities in 1988 set out to build local partnerships to reduce crime and the fear of crime and to create cities and towns where both the local economy and community could prosper (Tilley 1993). These initiatives were required to produce audits of crime, to set up information systems to manage data on crime and to build community committees with representation from all interested groups, including residents, to plan crime reduction and implement services to victims of crimes. Crime Concern, set up in 1989 as a publicly funded non-governmental organisation with charity status but with initial funding from the Home Office, championed the idea of Neighbourhood Watch schemes and local community Crime Prevention Panels.

Research in the 1990s further underlined the importance of approaches which tailor crime prevention activities to local community dynamics. Foster and Hope published evaluations of two Priority Estates Projects (PEP) in Hull (Foster and Hope 1993, Hope and Foster 1992). They found that improvements to the fabric of the estates alone was insufficient to bring down crime – one estate had a particular problem with young people which after the PEP project appeared allevi-ated in one area of the estate but exacerbated in another; the other had a largely demoralised community which could not respond positively to the changes taking place. Hope argued for 'Holistic, consistent, community-based policies' which are 'properly designed and highly-resourced' (Hope 1995: 33).

Community crime prevention brought together a number of approaches; a developing left realist trend within criminology which exhorted crime prevention practitioners to take locality seriously and to consider a local area's particular problems, environment and available community resources; a commitment to involve the different elements of community in crime prevention agendas and the utilisation of a combination of situational and social measures. Community crime prevention fostered a multi-agency approach which set out to measure, evaluate and test various crime prevention measures and their effects. These various projects and initiatives formed the basis of what was to become a more fully community-oriented approach to crime prevention and what was to become known as 'community safety'.

## The 'cultural turn' in crime prevention policies

It is interesting to note that the early examples of community-based crime pre-vention were not initially developed through the Home Office or with crime prevention as their main focus of activity. These were initiatives of the DoE or the DTI which set out concerns for local environmental improvements or to increase the availability of job opportunities in marginalised and de-industrialised neigh-bourhoods. The link with crime prevention was predicated on the idea that impoverishment – both environmental and financial – contributed to increased rates of offending and that the solution lay in bettering the quality of life and opportunities for the residents of marginal places. Crime was considered a func-tion of a 'new poverty' (Hope 1996) resulting from de-industrialisation, unem-ployment, loss of financial and social opportunities which were visited on neighbourhoods through external forces outside their control and that the with-drawal of public services and funding to many areas had resulted in the abandon-ing of troubled neighbourhoods. At some point in the 1980s, however, fuelled by the resurgence of a right-wing, neo-liberal agenda promoted by Thatcher and her supporters in government, the focus moved away from a concern with the struc-tural conditions which led to distressed and struggling communities and moved to a discussion of their dysfunctionality. This cultural turn in crime policy was con-servative in the extreme and looked to place the blame for crime at the doors of the offender, blaming 'bad parenting and wicked individuals' for a rise in crime while denying the link between unemployment, deprivation and offending (Ferguson 1994). From this point the focus of community crime prevention inter-ventions moved towards a perspective which perceived community as having broken down in high crime neighbourhoods and which consequently argued for a strengthening of the internal mechanisms of community to allow resilience to crime and criminality to develop. The question of who should take responsibility for this state of affairs and begin to put it right was high on the political agenda.

# Who is responsible for preventing crime – from state to privatised crime control

## The state

From the end of the Second World War, Britain built a post-war interventionist state wherein the welfare of the individual was considered a collective responsibility to be managed by the state through education for all, free health-care and benefits to the poor and out-of-work. Within this welfarist approach the protection of individuals from crime was slower to materialise as a function of the state but this idea began to gradually gain in prominence. Crime prevention was initially seen as the responsibility of the public police force rather than of any other institutions of the state. The first such force, instigated in London in 1829 was instructed by the then Home Secretary that the prevention of crime was their principal object (Bottoms and Wiles 1995: 2). Indeed, according to Bottoms and Wiles 'so successful were the new public police that they remained for about 120 years the dominant form of official crime prevention, and exercised an ideological hegemony over how crime prevention was to be provided in modern Britain' (1995: 2). Indeed, the police acted as the sole providers of crime prevention practices until the mid-twentieth century when their dominance in this field began to be challenged by a growing number of security companies, firms supplying private security personnel and private firms developing security technologies. The demand for commercial security services grew as crime and fear of crime appeared to increase, crime prevention remained, however, a mainly public concern and the police did not share this role or the information that they had on the occurrences of crime, with other organisations.

By the 1950s most police forces had at least one crime prevention officer with the crime prevention responsibilities of the police written into statute under the Police Act of 1964. However, in truth, the crime prevention officer was often of low status and his or her work not afforded a great deal of significance. Their work was largely spent on advising individuals and businesses on effective situational crime prevention measures which could be implemented to reduce the opportunities for crime (Johnston et al. 1993). Crime prevention within the police began to gain in status and importance only from the late 1960s when the Home Office began to take an interest in crime prevention as an activity which it should support and further develop. However, the Home Office was exercised by research which showed policing to be less effective than had been presumed and looked for ways to supplement the police role.

## The community

From the early 1980s a process of 'demonopolisation' (Garland 2001) of crime prevention practice began to be put in place. In January 1984 the government issued Home Office Circular 8/84 for distribution to every local authority in which it was made clear that henceforth crime was to be considered as the responsibility of the whole community. This was a significant moment in the development of crime prevention which has shaped the development of the discipline ever since. This move to involve 'community' in crime prevention, however, was always double-edged. On the one hand it took the consideration of the prevention of crime away from being the sole reserve of the police and thereby afforded it the chance to become something more progressive and socially-oriented than it had previously been, but on the other hand it could also be viewed as part of the Conservative government's move to 'responsibilise' (Garland 2001) individuals and their families and to take crime prevention out of the remit of the central state and local government. After all this was a government which was committed to rolling back state and welfare provision and to cut back on public services wherever possible. Stanley Cohen (1985) saw in these moves a 'dispersal of discipline' whereby the practice of maintaining social order was gradually passed outwards and downwards to involve an unprecedented range of actors.

In the first instance it has always been perceived as the responsibility of the individual to prevent their own victimisation. This accepted wisdom, however, creates its own inequalities as those groups most vulnerable to victimisation have had to take on the burden of protecting themselves from harm. Women, for example, have long curtailed their own freedoms in order to protect themselves from personal assaults and harm. Other groups, however, due to their vulnerable position in society may be unable to take their own preventive measures and may be victimised by the very people who are expected to be their protectors. Children in particular are placed in an ambivalent position; on the one hand it has been assumed that as especially vulnerable they would enjoy the protection of adults and indeed very little advice has historically been offered to children and young people on how to keep themselves safe. On the other hand young people have been considered the perpetrators of much harm too and the phrase 'young people at risk' has come to suggest to the majority that they are at risk of becoming offenders rather than victims. Furthermore, as we have seen above, it is often those with the least ability to pay for requisite protection who are most at risk of victimisation, both for property crime and violence against the person.

From 1982 Neighbourhood Watch (NW) schemes were introduced in Britain and heralded as a new frontier in the fight against crime (Bennett 1988). They were described as 'a network of public spirited members of the community, who observe what is going on in their own neighbourhood and report suspicious activity to the police. Drawing on ideas of civic engagement and community, groups of neighbours were encouraged to take responsibility for their own protection – although in partnership with the public police. In simple terms the 'citizen becomes the "eyes and ears" of the police' (Metropolitan Police Department 1983: 1 in Bennett 1988). Neighbourhood Watch Schemes were considered a great success (Bennett et al. 2008) although it has been acknowledged that they have always been easier to maintain in low-crime neighbourhoods (Laycock and Tiley undated) and were followed by Pubwatch, Shopwatch and other similar projects. By the early 1990s there were estimated to be 115,000 NW schemes covering more than 5 million homes (*Guardian* 6 April 1994). At this point they seem to have reached their peak for in 2009 the NW website was still reporting similar coverage. Crime Concern was initially funded to manage these schemes which married informal surveillance with community-building.

From the mid-1990s, however, the responsibility of the individual to protect themselves from crime took on a new and potentially alarming turn. Beginning with Conservative Home Secretary Michael Howard suggesting in 1994 that civic-minded citizens should complement the policing function by patrolling their own streets (*Independent* 1994), then fuelled by concern that the public police could not protect the 'good citizen' from coming to harm, debates raged concerning the right of the individual to protect and defend themselves from harm. These debates surfaced again in 1999 after a Norfolk farmer was jailed for the murder of a young burglar on his premises (*Independent* 2000). It was at the time that NW schemes were at their height, that Howard envisaged that they could be extended to include community crime prevention patrols. The suggestion that NW schemes should contribute to this more formal crime prevention role proved to be contentious. Howard was not supported by the police who were concerned that the unregulated use of citizens on patrol could easily deteriorate into vigilantism and provide more problems than it would solve. In 2000 the populist tabloid *News of the World* instigated a campaign of naming and shaming those convicted of molesting children suggesting that communities should organise against paedophiles in their midst; it was reported that in one neighbourhood this even led to an attack on a local paediatrician's office (BBC News 2000a). This media 'campaign' seemed to have been targeted as much at the 'liberal establishment' which insisted on keeping the details of the convicted away from the public as it was directed at promoting self-policing but it nevertheless spawned a great deal of discussion as to when action against an offender was a crime or merely protection of the victim where state powers to intervene were severely curbed.

NW schemes were predicated on the assumption that the threat to people's sense of well-being was always external and in this assumption there lay a fundamental flaw for in reality many high-crime communities held within them the perpetrators of crime (Walklate and Evans 1999). Yet in some ways too, NW schemes appeared to appeal to the more optimistic, they suggested that the residents of the majority of neighbourhoods could work together to bring about positive changes. With the perceived success of initiatives such as Neighbourhood Watch, Shopwatch, Pubwatch and so forth and the closer involvement of communities in crime prevention the stage was set for further developments in this regard. In 1986 the first 'community safety' units were set up by a number of London councils, closely followed by other left-leaning Labour councils in other parts of the country. Community Safety was championed by these councils for a number of progressive reasons. The community safety perspective linked crime with wider social problems and suggested that crime cannot be solved without a consideration of these problems. The community safety approach took the focus away from individualised crime prevention measures and suggested collective solutions were both possible and necessary. It was an approach too which took consideration of the prevention of crime away from being the sole preserve of the police and also of the Home Office, acknowledging that other levels and types of expertise could be located within local authorities, voluntary organisations and within the experience of residents living with the fear and reality of crime on the ground. It 'broaden[ed] the concept of crime prevention from its rather narrow associations with the police, security technology and control, in order to encompass the wider issues of protection and the role of the local authority in the creation of safe environments' (Bright 1987: 49). As a consequence, the adoption of the agenda of community safety served in many ways as a resistance to the agenda proposed by a right-wing, neo-liberal Conservative government which increasingly blamed individuals for their plight and exhorted them to take their own remedial actions.

By the early 1990s, the community safety agenda was gaining more ground and was endorsed by the Home Office Standing Conference on Crime Prevention through its Morgan Report *Safer Communities: the Local Delivery of Crime Prevention through the Partnership Approach* published in 1991. The recommendations of the Morgan Report were not adopted wholesale, however, and in particular its recommendation that local authorities rather than the police should be held statutorily responsible for the delivery of crime prevention and community safety strategies. While the Conservative government was keen to push a partnership approach to crime prevention work it was not keen to give more responsibility to local authorities at a time when its overall political perspective was based on a running down of local authorities and their welfare responsibilities. It was not until a new Labour government and its 1998 Crime and Disorder Act that local authorities were given a statutory responsibility for crime prevention work and then only in partnership with, rather than as a replacement for, the police. Nevertheless, Tilley has suggested that the push for partnership working had, by the early 1990s, succeeded in 'promoting institutionalisation of attention to crime at local level' (Tilley 1993: 55). In later chapters we will see how successive Labour governments after 1997 put in place what has been termed a new 'community governance' of crime prevention and security. It led to the promise that crime prevention practices would become democratically accountable and move out of the politicised realm of state controlled agendas (Johnston and Shearing 2003, Hughes 2007). Community governance, however, has also been perceived more cynically as a method for managing community input into crime prevention practice which largely ignores what the community wants but co-opts them into pre-formed government agendas (Crawford 1997, Hope 2001).

## The private sector and the privatisation of crime prevention

With the 'cultural turn' in crime prevention in the 1990s the focus turned again to the criminality of individuals and their communities. The move to multi-agency and partnership working which had promised so much in terms of a re-embedding of collective practices in crime prevention work was accompanied by a return to an individualising rhetoric which blamed collapsing communities on individual actors, their selfishness and greed and adherence to a 'something for nothing' culture. Problems of crime and social exclusion were no longer cast as resulting from the withdrawal of the state from social provision but seen as arising as a consequence of the withdrawal of the individual from forms of civic life and civil society. As this perspective gained in ascendancy, attitudinal change became the key to social improvement. Responsibility for the reduction of crime turned once again away from the state and towards those individuals and communities affected. Rather than an approach which helped individuals struggling to cope with structural disadvantages, a zero tolerance of behaviour deemed 'problematic', became the order of the day (Burney 2005: 25–7). The notion that social problems should be identified and responded to as public matters was replaced with a belief that the various private realms must look after themselves. Initially challenged by Labour, both in opposition and in office, this became the thrust of many policy directions subsequent to Labour's election victory in 1997, as we will see in later chapters.

The privatisation of crime prevention has continued apace in recent years. Not only have new and privately funded organisations grown up to take up crime reduction as their mission, and some also to gain profit from this necessary activity, but public organisations have seen their functions passed over to private or semi-private organisations. This new 'privatised prudentialism' (O'Malley 1992) has even gone so far as to affect policing services across Britain. There has been a growth of private security firms and semi-privatised community safety officers and wardens working alongside the formally-constituted police services which can no longer be said to be the main line of defence against crime but only one in a line of many. The criminal justice system has also been partially privatised with increasing numbers of voluntary and private companies providing youth services, diversionary activities and working with offenders. The prison service too has seen various private security concerns delivering services such as the transportation of prisoners and the building and staffing of prisons and detention centres.

## Professionalisation of crime prevention

In 1995 Jon Bright, Director of Field Operations for Crime Concern, presented a paper to the British Society of Criminology's annual conference. His presence at the conference, his first visit, signified a developing working relationship between academia and crime prevention practitioners. His presentation to the conference called for a clearer conceptual framework for the practice of crime prevention. 'There is little agreement' he opined 'about how [crime] should be tackled. Public and political debate is at an appallingly low level. We cannot agree how much there is, how seriously it should be viewed, how it is caused, how it might be prevented or who should lead on prevention' (Bright 1995: 1). There is, he added, 'no widely accepted body of knowledge of what works and how it should be implemented' (Bright 1995: 2). Bright considered crime prevention to be in its 'early modern period', characterised by incoherent approaches, belief in certain approaches without the requirement for evidence, experimentalism and a scatter-gun approach to solving problems. He suggested that a body of knowledge and expertise should be drawn together, that good practice should be disseminated nationally and that clear plans and strategies should be drawn up and implemented across the regions to co-ordinate crime prevention activities.

Bright's concern was shared by a growing body of crime prevention practitioners (see Tilley 1994) and reflected the movement of crime prevention from being a specialist subject within criminology, policy and policing to becoming a growing professional concern. As crime prevention moved from the sole practice of the police and was included in the remit of many agencies, from educationalists to planners, the newly involved professionals needed a framework of action, training and guidance on how to move forward with this new responsibility. It also, more cynically, fitted the needs of organisations like Crime Concern to deliver this expertise and training to a burgeoning crime prevention workforce. With the election of a Labour government in 1997 committed to continue and extend the role of multi-agency crime prevention partnerships, the blueprint for action drawn up by Crime Concern was adopted to be passed down to the newly created Crime and Disorder Reduction Partnerships (CDRPs) as the methods which they should follow to reduce crime in their areas (see Chapter 2). Hence, the pattern of crime audit: identification of priorities for action; appraisal of different options; setting of clear objectives, methods, outputs and outcomes followed by the monitoring of performance and clear evaluation of outcomes and practices, became the normative framework in which CDRPs operated.

The move to professionalise and to standardise crime prevention practices moved them away from a consideration of the complex and multi-faceted nature of crime and criminality which had characterised the academic discipline of criminology from the 1960s onwards. A body of research which had stressed the importance of locating practices in reducing crime within the specific dynamics of community and locality was also lost as projects which had been proven to have some beneficial impact in one area were taken 'off the shelf' and applied in other neighbourhoods. This 'modernisation' of crime prevention meant that to spend time on what Bright termed the 'rather fruitless search' (1995: 6) for what causes crime was abandoned and replaced with a purely outcome-based measure of success – the 'what works' paradigm of crime prevention whereby the measurable reduction of crime superseded all other considerations rose to prominence. This trend has reached its current apogee in the development of 'crime science' and the launch in 2001 of the London-based Jill Dando Institute of Crime Science which seeks to apply the most advanced scientific techniques to crime prevention and detection.

Ideological and technological developments have driven crime prevention into new directions since the mid-1980s. As we have seen, the collection and management of information on crime has become much more sophisticated in recent decades. The development of software that can map crime onto geographical areas on a street-by-street basis and the collection of more sensitive and accurate data on crime and victimisation has meant that a new paradigm of 'crime management' could begin to move into the ascendancy. Under this perspective what can be proved and demonstrated to be true takes precedence over other forms of knowledge. Subjective forms of knowledge, that which is gleaned from experience, hunches, in-depth understandings which may grow organically but which cannot be objectively proved are downgraded. However, as Crawford (1998) has pointed out, the prevention of an event is always difficult to demonstrate and the range of tools which could be used to address the crime problem became narrower with the aim of crime prevention projects redefined as that which could lead to demonstrable, and thereby more immediate, outcomes. Interventions designed to bring about more long-term attitudinal changes, to increase the resilience of young people to resist negative influences in their life, to educate and train for long-term life success, have been less in evidence as funds for such projects have been less forthcoming. As we will see in later chapters the fact that the managerialist approach emphasises and foregrounds outcomes has also been used to direct policy and practice on the ground. When funding is dependent on particular outputs organisations are forced to work in specific ways to achieve those specified outcomes and to continue to receive much-needed funding.

## Concluding comments

This chapter has followed the changing directions of crime prevention theory and policy since it first emerged as a concern for criminologists and politicians alike. It has demonstrated that many of today's 'common-sense' and taken-for-granted assumptions around how to prevent crime are actually heavily contested. There have been closely fought debates concerning how best to approach the problem of crime and its prevention which have taken place on a shifting terrain, while the rise of crime as an item on the political agenda has given these debates added prominence. Over the next chapters the changing face of crime prevention in more recent times will be closely followed and the contribution of New Labour policies to crime will be studied in some detail. This current chapter has covered a great deal of ground and thereby left much underexplored, however it sets the context, politically and theoretically for the trajectory upon which New Labour was set in 1997 and which has been more widely adopted throughout the west in recent years. It is a starting point from which much that was radical and progressive in crime prevention was somehow lost and in which the management of crime and neo-liberal approaches to its reduction had clearly gained, and remained in, the ascendancy.

### FURTHER READING

Crawford, A. (1998) *Crime Prevention and Community Safety: Politics, Policies and Practices*. London: Longman.

Matthews, R. (1992) 'Replacing "broken windows": crime incivilities and urban change', in R. Matthews and J. Young (eds), *Issues in Realist Criminology*. London: Sage.

### NOTES

1  In 2007 a crime and safety survey published by the European Commission (van Dyk et al. 2007) found Britons and the Irish were more likely than residents of any other European country to fall victim to the ten most widely reported crimes.

2  Then still titled the National Association for the Care and Resettlement of Offenders.

# 2

# Joining up to the New Labour agenda

The continuities between the policies and practices of New Labour and the Conservative governments which they replaced are, looking back, quite clear to see, so it is easy to forget with what euphoria the end of 17 years of Conservative government was met in May 1997. Following an overwhelming Conservative defeat on 1 May the next day's newspapers were full of photographs of grim-faced former Cabinet ministers and backbenchers at the moment that they faced their very public fall from grace. While there was not exactly partying in the streets, those 43 per cent who voted Labour and others who played some part in the Conservative Party's downfall went about their business the next day with more of a spring in their step, a wider smile on their face and a sense of relief that it was all really over. There was a sense of anticipation, a feeling that there were new, more progressive, paths to follow and a curiosity as to how a Labour government would act in office after all its years in opposition. As the Labour Party manifesto *New Labour because Britain deserves better* promised, 'The vision is one of national renewal, a country with drive, purpose and energy' (Labour Party 1997). The New Labour talk was of 'one nation' government, in marked contrast to previous Conservative administrations, which would as Blair proclaimed as he entered Downing Street as Prime Minister on 2 May, govern 'for all its people' (BBC News 1997).

## Discovering social exclusion

When in August 1997, less than four months after their general election victory, Peter Mandelson, then a Minister without Portfolio in the newly formed government and a close ally of Tony Blair, announced the arrival of a new government body to investigate and explore ways to tackle the problem of social exclusion in Britain, it seemed as if this new way of thinking and acting was about to come to fruition. The Social Exclusion Unit (SEU) was seen as defining the difference between Conservative and Labour. It promised a distinct departure from the *laissez-faire* attitude which had contributed to the creation of a poverty ridden 'underclass' in society and moved the ruling philosophy towards intervention in society and a recognition that government control and power could and should be used to take steps to improve people's lives. As Blair declared on launching the unit, 'The Social Exclusion Unit will yield results over months and years not days, but its purpose is central to the values and ambitions of the new Government. Its role reflects a new mood in the country and the values of a new Government' (Cabinet Office 1997).

The Social Exclusion Unit was to demonstrate this new approach in a number of ways. Eighteen Policy Action Teams were formed which included a diversity of voices. Academics, renowned experts and representatives of significant organisations joined policy-makers and government officials to collect evidence and hammer out recommendations to government to help alleviate problems which had been building up under previous political administrations. This on its own appeared a radical departure, but there were a number of other aspects to its work, explored below, which further demonstrated a commitment to change.

## Terminology

Use of the very specific term *social exclusion* signalled a departure from the ideology and rhetoric of a Conservative party which had long used the value-laden term 'the underclass' to refer to the long-term unemployed, those categorised as underachieving and those with persistent and often serious social and/or health problems (Long and Bramham 2006: 133). This new term was perceived to be more progressive suggesting exclusion was not chosen but conferred on particular groups. Less condemnatory in its tone and in its recognition that deprivation was multi-layered it also suggested that there were no simple, quick-fix solutions to complex and deep-seated problems affecting society.

## The importance of social policy

At this early point in the New Labour administration, social exclusion was explained as resulting not from the actions of feckless individuals, but from a failure in social policy which had abandoned a significant minority of the population to live and to bring up their families in degenerated and workless areas with ineffective and inefficient social provision. In contrast to previous Conservative administrations, the Labour government stressed the need for intervention as the key to successful integrative outcomes. Social exclusion 'was conceived as an intractable and multifaceted entity that would require a sustained multi-agency response' (Coaffee and Deas 2008: 171) and which would require more creative thinking and policy responses than had hitherto been made available.

## Recognising the scale and depth of exclusion

The scale of the problem of social exclusion was recognised as affecting literally millions of people. The Social Exclusion Unit released figures which showed there to be five million individuals living in families where no one of working age was in employment and three million living on the worst 1,300 housing estates in Britain (SEU 1998). This recognition of how deeply social exclusion was experienced within British society pointed to the existence of a deep-seated and collective problem which indicated the necessity for social rather than individual solutions to the problem at hand.

## A failure of government

New Labour talked of the need to carry out a root and branch reappraisal of state provision, not only as to which services were to be provided but in the ways through which government departments worked to offer their services. The piecemeal pattern of previous interventions in poverty-stricken areas was to be replaced with a more considered, effective and efficient linking up of services to focus provision on all aspects of need. The new perspective of 'joined-up working' was coined at this time whereby all relevant agencies were to work together to tackle extant problems which were linked to, and which fed, each other and were required to consider the effects of their actions on each other's work (SEU 1998: 34). The team overseeing the SEU, for example, included representatives from various government departments including representatives of local government, Education and Employment, the Department for the Environment, Transport and the Regions, the Department of Social Security and the Home Office.[1]

## The shift to intervention

Instead of dealing with problems once they had already arisen, the SEU saw the importance of intervening to prevent problems from occurring in the first place and thereby shifting resources from problem-management to problem-prevention (*Guardian* 1997a). Previous governments were criticised not only for implementing policies which adversely affected impoverished communities but also for sitting back while communities disintegrated under their watch, only intervening when problems had already spiralled out of control.

## Involving communities

In his foreword to the first SEU report *Bringing Britain Together* (SEU 1998), Blair criticised previous attempts at the regeneration of Britain's 'problem' areas as having being characterised by 'a tendency to parachute solutions in from outside, rather than engaging local communities. Too much', he went on to write, 'has been imposed from above, when experience shows that success depends on communities themselves having the power and taking the responsibility to make things better' (SEU 1998: 7). John Prescott, then deputy prime minister, went on to criticise the amount of funds which had been spent on consultancies and glossy brochures under the Conservatives and pledged that the Social Exclusion Unit would work *with* communities in order to help them to solve their own problems (*The Times* 1997).

The SEU was charged with developing a long-term comprehensive approach to the myriad of problems present within excluded neighbourhoods. At this early point in their administration the government acknowledged that it did not have all the solutions at its fingertips. As leader of a new government, made up of politicians who had been in opposition for many years, Blair displayed some humility in his insistence that, 'We don't believe that Whitehall knows best. We need practical experience. We need the insights of people who have worked at the sharp end' (Cabinet Office 1997). To this end the 18 Policy Action Teams (PATs) were put together – each to research and report back on a different aspect of social exclusion. The government claimed to have involved over 400 people in these teams and to have consulted 'thousands more' (SEU 2001: 8).

So for many reasons the Social Exclusion Unit seemed to herald a departure from previous administrations and to set up a new and distinctive way of working. The move to an interventionist stance seemed to envision a more welfare-oriented model of care. In an interview in March 1998 Jack Straw, then Home Secretary reiterated:

> I think there's a good chance that there will emerge from all this in 10 years' time a society in which class divisions are much less marked. We will hopefully have a combination of the best of the States and the Netherlands, where the searing class divisions in our society are no longer noticeable. You won't have these estates where the casualties of the past 18 years have been dumped. (*New Statesman* 1998)

## This is the Third Way...

In the previous quoted passage Straw cited the United States, along with the Netherlands as providing examples of social policy which could be emulated in New Labour's policy-making. In referencing both neo-liberal and social democratic governments as providers of good practice Straw demonstrated the governing party's commitment to the 'Third Way' – a political philosophy which was to steer a centrist course by borrowing from free market as well as social democratic thinking. Indeed, this context is everything and the formation of the Social Exclusion

Unit, although heralded as a breakthrough in government thinking, was only one part of a series of policy pronouncements. A variety of government-led taskforces were set up immediately after the election to consider policies around other related areas – on youth justice, school standards, welfare-to-work and on tax and benefits. The accompanying government rhetoric was somewhat less inclusionary in its vision and less of a departure from previous Conservative thinking. Instead government minister after government minister declared their firm commitment to spending restraint, no increases in welfare benefits and a pledge to keep taxation low. In announcing the SEU, Mandelson reiterated these pledges suggesting that there would be little extra money available to carry out the unit's recommendations and then only when economic circumstances allowed for it. Furthermore, he used his speech to pay tribute to the former Conservative Prime Minister, and arch neo-liberal Margaret Thatcher, for her determination in driving political agendas forward. This was a statement which was clearly antagonistic to those trying to distance themselves from her approach, and suggested an admiration for a politician who was generally seen as presiding over policies which had economically and socially divided the nation and contributed to its growing population of urban and rural poor. Mandelson's tribute to Thatcher also strongly suggested that New Labour was prepared to push their agenda through in the face of any criticism, echoing Margaret Thatcher's infamous mantra 'There is no alternative'.[2] Mandelson's tribute then was generally seen as an attack on the party's more welfare-oriented traditional supporters some of whom had already called for increased taxes to pay for policies which would lift significant numbers out of poverty. In the end the SEU was launched with only £200 million which was found from Lottery money and used to fund after-school clubs as part of an initiative to tackle truancy in secondary schools (*Scotland on Sunday* 1997).

Perhaps most tellingly the launch of the Social Exclusion Unit in December 1997[3] took place at a time of backbench revolt against plans to cut benefits to lone parents who had lost or had resigned from employment. The policy was a legacy of the previous Conservative government which Labour did nothing to reverse. The irony of presiding over £395 million cuts to benefits at the same time as the opening of a unit to tackle poverty and exclusion was not lost on the 120 MPs who signed a letter to the then Chancellor Gordon Brown urging him to abandon the cuts. The depth of opposition to the move was underscored by rumours that four parliamentary private secretaries were prepared to resign over the issue. These seemingly contradictory approaches, however, were justified by government spokespersons from Blair downwards. Labour's particular approach to tackling exclusion was explained by the government's strong attachment to a 'Third Way' philosophy. The 'Third Way' was a rejection of both *laissez-faire* 'sink or swim' capitalism and also of 'socialist' policies which argued for the redistribution of wealth. Instead the 'modern', twenty-first century way was supposed to tread a middle ground. Economic security was to be brought on the back of technological innovation, competitive enterprise and the foregrounding of education. Social security was said to arise from enabling rather than providing governments, encouraging communities and civic institutions to play a greater part in expanded structures of governance and allowing the market to play a role in the provision of much-needed services (DLC 1998).

Critique of the Social Exclusion Unit came from a number of quarters. There were those, such as former Labour deputy leader Roy Hattersley, along with representatives from the Liberal Democrat and Scottish National Parties, the multi-denominational group Church Action on Poverty and Director of the Scottish Low Pay Unit who argued for policies which would oversee a redistribution of income and an immediate improvement in benefits. They commented on the SEU's limited remit and called for real action to alleviate mass poverty and inequality across the UK. In October 1997 shortly after the Labour government's annual conference, their first since taking over the reins of power, 56 prominent UK sociology and social policy academics signed a letter to the *Financial Times* in which they criticised Labour's push to make work, education and training a condition of benefits (*Scotsman* 1997). The economist Will Hutton later argued that the government should 'recognise that income inequality and sheer poverty – not inequality of opportunity – are important sources of social injustice that require redress' and that 'unless action is taken to address urban and economic decay then any policy on social exclusion or improving public health standards is stillborn' (*Observer* 1998).

## Whatever happened to the Social Exclusion Unit?

The more progressive agenda of the Social Exclusion Unit very soon began to give way to Labour's Third Way philosophy. Each of the seemingly more progressive and creative aspects of the SEU's agenda, described above, were corrupted in different ways.

## Terminology: from underclass to the 'cultural deficit'

In choosing the terms derived from a perspective of social exclusion rather than an agenda based on the eradication of poverty, the government could more easily segue into a discourse based around cultural rather than financial exclusion. This allowed a range of policies to develop which were built around changing people's attitudes and actions without first lifting them out of poverty. Tackling worklessness and truancy became the main focus of the SEU. As Harriet Harman, the then Secretary of State for Social Security opined at the launch of the Centre for Analysis for Social Exclusion (CASE):[4] 'Work is the only route to sustained financial independence. But it is also much more. Work is not just about earning a living. It is a way of life' (*Independent* 1997b). The subtext of her speech was, of course, that worklessness is also a way of life – rather than something imposed on a person through economic circumstance, lack of education or training, or an employment market which discriminates against certain individuals and groups. This recourse to cultural explanations resurfaced in government rhetoric more strongly in subsequent years and was used to explain the continued existence of all sorts of problems faced by individuals – not only poverty but also crime, homelessness and patterns of migration and was not far removed from previous discourses of the underclass.

It was not only an *individual's* cultural deficit which was seen to lead to the problems of social exclusion, organisational cultures were put under scrutiny too. Financial incentives, as well as more punitive measures, were used as a route to bring about a variety of cultural changes deemed necessary. In March 1998, for example, the Commons Education and Employment Select Committee suggested that schools should receive a financial bonus for helping disruptive children gain qualifications and that they should lose money for each permanent exclusion (*Independent* 1998a). The serious issue of disruptive and excluded pupils was thus perceived as a matter which could be put right through a short-term financial fix, the attitude or policy of the school being at fault rather than seeing truancy as the consequence of a more deep-seated and complex predicament.

## From social intervention to individual responsibilisation

It is a small step from accepting the argument that social exclusion is culturally ingrained towards focusing on and targeting those individuals who are seen as perpetuating and transmitting that culture and the main proponents of New Labour stepped almost seamlessly into this mode of thinking. Mandelson typified this approach in a speech reported on 3 February 1998[5] when he likened New Labour's approach to that which lay behind that of the charity The Big Issue.[6] In this speech Mandelson clearly stated the government's belief that the giving of welfare led to a culture of dependency and that Labour's approach would be one of 'lifting the dead hand of dependency and offering instead a helping hand, extending opportunity to those previously denied it' (*Scotsman* 1998). Those who did not grasp this hand were perceived as workshy, lazy or unconcerned and thereby partly or wholly to blame for their plight. Consider the words of David Blunkett, the then Education and Employment Secretary who blamed the 'intolerable behaviour' of 'lazy and ignorant parents' for many of the 'problems of underachievement and indiscipline' exhibited by their children. 'While poverty early on in life makes a great difference to the opportunities available later on' he opined 'it is the poverty of expectation and dedication which is the deciding factor' in their children's demise (*Guardian* 1998d). This took government policy very far from its pledge to eradicate poverty and towards a culture of individual blame and responsibility. Furthermore, the 'helping hand' if spurned threatened ever more punitive sanctions – parents could be fined up to £1,000 if their children persistently missed school and schools would be 'named and shamed' if they expelled too many pupils. Social problems were no longer perceived as a failure of social policy but became instead a failure of the individual or organisation to grasp the vision offered by the New Labour philosophy.

## Scale and depth of exclusion: who is in genuine need?

When the Social Exclusion Unit was launched it was acknowledged that the previous 17 years of Conservative government had left behind a legacy of deprivation which was intensely concentrated within 44 local authority areas. These 'very poor neighbourhoods' were said to number several thousand although estimates varied depending upon the criteria used (SEU 1998: 13). Millions were living and growing up in extreme poverty, however the government's refusal to take the welfare path and increase benefits to the unemployed and low paid meant that the poor had to 'help provide for themselves where they can do so' (Mandelson 1998). Government discourse began to focus on 'those in genuine need' (Mandelson 1998) so dividing the poor into the authentic and the bogus.[7] Anxiety over the intractable and concentrated nature of deprivation described in various SEU documents soon morphed into a concern that individuals within deprived neighbourhoods, or even whole communities, were not doing enough to help themselves. As well as concentrating on those 'in genuine need' the SEU also focused its attention towards identification of the most vulnerable within a locality so that by the time the unit published its 2001 report *Preventing Social Exclusion*, a reflection on the Unit's previous four years' work, its stated focus was now on much smaller groups of those at disproportionate risk. In its 2004 report *Breaking the Cycle* the SEU concentrated its focus on 'the most disadvantaged' (SEU 2004: 6). As a result, it adopted a 'client-centred approach' (SEU 2004: 7) which identified and targeted the most troublesome individuals in a neighbourhood. Such targeting and individualising of social troubles had neatly taken the government's agenda away from taking millions out of poverty and towards working with a more manageable group of perhaps thousands.

## A failure of government: joined up working and the governance of crime

The SEU was eager to promote partnership working and to move beyond a piecemeal approach to multi-faceted social problems. Yet in linking a range of interventions together certain dominant themes emerged as the drivers for social policy. Muncie (2000), Crawford (2002) and Gilling (2007) have all discussed the effects of a subsequent 'criminalisation of social policy'. As the agenda around crime reduction dominated political discourses then interventions had to be justified in terms of their crime reduction outcomes and attracted funding on this basis. Simon (1997) and Stenson and Edwards (2003) further described the emergence of a new mode of 'governance through crime' where the threat of crime and victimisation drove policy developments in all areas from housing through to health. All other approaches were subsumed under this totalising discourse and lost ground under an onslaught of objectives related to the reduction of crime. The consequences of this dominant discourse are discussed in later chapters, in relation for example to the government's response to the perceived growth in gang cultures where any approach other than treating youth gangs as a problem of crime was roundly rejected or ignored for many years. So those partnerships which were created were subsumed under the dominant rubric of crime reduction. At the same time those researching in the area have questioned whether the government's efforts to break down the silo mentality and to ensure 'joined-up' thinking across departmental boundaries was ever really achieved (Coaffee and Deas 2008).

## From prevention to reduction: a retrogressive move

Each of the Policy Action Teams charged with researching aspects of exclusion and suggesting alternative policy formations was asked to propose any preventive measures which could be taken to ensure that, once the current targets of policy were lifted out of social exclusion, others would not fall into the same trap. This prevention was not always couched in altruistic terms as Mandelson underlined in his speech to the *Big Issue* in 1998: 'If we can shift resources from picking up the costs of problems to preventing them, there will be a dividend for everyone' (*Scotsman* 1998). However Gilling (2007) has carefully outlined how, in the area of crime – which dominated much of New Labour thinking – the prevention of crime soon gave way to the less radical emphasis on the reduction of crime and this will be further explored below.

## Community and partnership: doing it the New Labour way

Despite New Labour's pledge to involve local people and communities in decision-making in ways which were unprecedented and previously unimagined, the New Labour administration has been criticised for being one of the most authoritarian governments ever to take office. Partly this criticism has stemmed from a view that the government does not listen and has, as Mandelson predicted, been willing to drive through its ideological agenda in the face of any criticism. However, there are other reasons why the promise to involve communities in policy-making became particularly difficult to deliver. Labour's much criticised managerialist interventions and 'audit culture' play their part here. As we shall see in later chapters, much of Labour's governing strategy has been to steer from the centre and to 'hand down' goals, policy objectives and targets to local authorities and community level organisations for delivery (Follett 2006: 102). This left little room for discussion of local priorities to emerge and even less space for local communities to get their voices heard in the mad dash to achieve the targets set from above. In addition New Labour appeared to have little conception as to how varied communities are and how fractured and divided they may be internally (Measor 2006, Walklate and Evans 1999) so when government policy-makers talked of engaging 'the whole community' (Mandelson and Liddle 1996: 19) this betrayed a certain naïvety and lack of knowledge as to how communities are actually organised. The results of this are explored in more detail in Chapter 3.

## The demise of the SEU

The Social Exclusion Unit was initially characterised as 'one of the most prestigious in Whitehall' (*Independent* 1997a), based in the Cabinet Office, involving senior civil servants and reporting directly to the Number Ten Policy Unit. However, by May 2002 the SEU was moved into the Office of the Deputy Prime Minister (ODPM) under the control of John Prescott. Rather than working directly to the Prime Minister the Unit was subsequently expected to link to other aspects of the ODPM's work. The move could be interpreted as a downgrading of the Unit, moving it away from the attention of the New Labour leadership and under the wing of the more marginalised and 'old Labour' Prescott. Later, in 2006, the office of Social Exclusion Minister was formed within the Cabinet Office. While this might have been seen to signal a continued level of support for the Unit's work, one year later and nine years after its inception the Unit was wound up, replaced by a Social Exclusion Taskforce whose remit was to work with hard to reach groups such as children in care, teenagers at risk of pregnancy and people with mental health problems. The much wider remit with which the SEU was initially tasked which expressly acknowledged the deep-seated and damaging effects of poverty on a generation of UK citizens, had by this time been firmly cast aside to reveal a much narrower focus on particular 'problem groups', outlining once again New Labour's shift away from the collective and social and towards an individualised and privatised route out of exclusion. According to BBC reports at the time the Unit's demise was a function of 'tussles over funding and the arrival of Mr Blair's "respect agenda", which covers much of the same territory' (BBC 2006) but it had been apparent for some time that New Labour had left behind any earlier promises that it would change the landscape of poverty and deprivation in England through progressive social interventions.

## Social exclusion and crime

Right from its inception the Social Exclusion Unit was linked with the prevention of crime. In a brief speech launching the unit Blair referred to the problem of crime numerous times (Cabinet Office 1997). He spoke of 'crime-ridden estates', pensioners afraid to leave their houses, blighted lives in which shared values break down, and young truants starting on a slippery slope leading to drugs and criminality. The initial priorities of the SEU, however, highlighted prior even to the submission of reports and evidence by the various Policy Action Teams, were to combat worklessness and to reduce truancy. Worklessness was to be addressed through 'welfare-to-work' schemes while truancy was linked to other issues such as drug use and bullying. Very quickly, indeed by January 1998, anti-truancy policies became more firmly established within an anti-crime agenda. In this month the Metropolitan Police released statistics which revealed that children aged between 10 and 16 years of age were responsible for 40 per cent of all street robberies and a third of car thefts and burglaries in London. Furthermore, they revealed that most of these offences took place during school hours. In the same month the Basic Skills Agency published a report on low educational attainment among offenders aged between 17 and 25 years of age. Their data showed that nearly half of those who took part in the research could not write their name and address or give more than two pieces of information about themselves without making mistakes. These issues were referred directly to the SEU for action. The SEU in turn fed these concerns into the Crime and Disorder Bill which was before Parliament at the time and which was amended to recommend that the police be given increased powers to arrest truants and take them back to school.[8] Additionally, parenting orders which could be used to require parents to take steps to make their children attend school were also included in the subsequent 1998 Act.

It became impossible to separate the problems of crime and social exclusion in the government's thinking as the two were so often linked in government discourses. As Blair reiterated, 'Everyone knows that the problems of social exclusion – of failure at school, joblessness, crime – are woven together when you get down to the level of the individual's daily life, or the life of a housing estate' (Cabinet Office 1997).

The 'joined-up' agenda to which the government was clearly committed reflected its concern that seemingly disparate problems faced by individuals in socially excluded neighbourhoods were in reality closely linked. However, it soon became clear that of all the issues faced by residents of socially excluded areas, it was to be the twin problems of worklessness and crime which were to dominate future policy agendas and which were to occupy a prominent place in the government's thinking.

## The administrative solution to tackling crime

Labour had clearly set out its new perspective regarding crime in its 1997 election manifesto:

> On crime, we believe in personal responsibility and in punishing crime, but also tackling its underlying causes – so, tough on crime, tough on the causes of crime,

different from the Labour approach of the past and the Tory policy of today. (Labour Party 1997)

The 1997 manifesto was unclear as to how the *causes* of crime would be tackled, apart from a somewhat vague commitment to 'attack the causes of crime by our measures to relieve social deprivation' (Labour Party 1997), but a raft of clear objectives for dealing with the consequences of crime *were* spelt out. Labour would:

- fast-track punishment for persistent young offenders aiming to halve the time it takes persistent juvenile offenders to come to court;
- reform the Crown Prosecution Service so that more criminals would be convicted;
- place more police on the beat and free them from much paperwork and bureaucracy;
- crack down on petty crimes and neighbourhood disorder;
- instigate a fresh parliamentary vote to ban all handguns.

Much of the manifesto's treatment of crime focused on the problem of youth crime.[9] As we will see in Chapter 5, crime committed by the young exercised a great deal of the first and subsequent terms of the Labour government and their 1997 manifesto clearly signalled their future intent in this area. Much of the thinking behind this section of the manifesto was written in reference to an Audit Commission document published in 1996 entitled *Misspent Youth*. This report focused on the extent of offending by young people, arguing that the processes employed for dealing with young offenders, from initial detection of their crimes to sentencing within the courts, was in need of some attention and updating – in New Labour jargon 'modernising'. The report was concerned with the costs of dealing with crime committed by young people and sought to reduce an estimated one billion pounds spent on detecting, processing and dealing with young offenders each year, to cut the bureaucracy and paperwork associated with police arrests of young people and to divert some of the resources employed in dealing with young offenders in the courts towards a more preventive model. To this end the report recommended a 'caution-plus' programme whereby, if appropriate, young offenders were diverted away from court, subject to a police caution but also required to undergo some kind of programme to address their problem behaviour.

While *Misspent Youth* was primarily an audit of the criminal justice system questioning whether it represented 'value for money' (Pitts 2001) in November 1997, the Home Office White Paper (1997b) *No More Excuses: A New Approach to Tackling Youth Crime in England and Wales* looked more like a wholescale attack on criminal justice professionals and the welfare ethos which had developed within some parts of the youth justice system generally over the previous decades (Goldson 2000). With little evidence to back up his position the then Home Secretary, Jack Straw, wrote in his preface to this Paper:

An excuse culture has developed within the youth justice system. It excuses itself for its inefficiency, and too often excuses the young offenders before it, implying that they cannot help their behaviour because of their social circumstances. Rarely are they confronted with their behaviour and helped to take more personal responsibility for their actions. The system allows them to go on wrecking their own lives as well as disrupting their families and communities. (Home Office 1997b)

In writing this preface, Straw referenced the Audit Commission's 1996 report and Labour's election manifesto commitment to halve the time taken to process young offenders through the courts. Rather than considering the funding, staffing or procedural mechanisms which might be holding up the efficient functioning of the system however, he embarked on the vilification of an entire profession and pledged to implement a 'root and branch reform of the youth justice system' (Home Office 1997b). This strategy of 'penal populism' (Pitts 2001: 39) reflected New Labour's tendency to ensure that 'the problem is reduced from one of social structure to one of social administration' (Pitts 2001: 136).

Straw went on to outline some key ideas which were to continue to shape government policy in the area of youth crime:

- that the aim of the youth justice system would be the prevention of offending and enshrining this in statute;
- that offenders, and their parents should face up to their offending behaviour and take responsibility for it;
- there would be earlier, more effective intervention when young people first offend;
- partnership between all youth justice agencies would deliver a better, faster system.

These ideas informed the Crime and Disorder Act 1988 which came on to the statute books in the UK after receiving royal assent in July of that year.

## The Crime and Disorder Act 1998

The Crime and Disorder Act of 1998 might better have been entitled the Youth Crime and Disorder Act as its main aim appeared to be reform of systems of youth justice. The consequence of these reforms and discussion of the youth justice system is more specifically dealt with in Chapter 5; here we look at some of the main tenets of this legislation and how the Act changed crime prevention practice at the national and at the local level.

New legislation around crime and crime prevention was eagerly awaited after the general election in 1997. In opposition Labour had argued for the implementation of the Morgan Report,[10] discussed in Chapter 1, and had seemed to champion the perspective of community safety. Many local authorities were hoping to be given a more central role in crime prevention and community safety work and had already started to take their work around crime prevention seriously in their regeneration agendas, working more closely with the police as a result. It was also assumed that the approach of community safety rather than crude crime prevention would become the expected direction of the state's response to crime (Pitts and Hope 1997). In the first of these expectations local practitioners were not disappointed, but it is questionable whether the second was achieved in any sustainable way.

The first key point to notice in the Act is its name. By adding 'disorder' to the 'problem' of crime the government was signalling a substantially new approach and a casting wide of the crime prevention net. It was now not only the breaking of criminal laws to which the government was addressing its attention but also the wider problem of disruptive and troublesome behaviour. Just what was meant by 'disorder' and by whom it might be considered a nuisance was not addressed. Nevertheless it is not surprising that the problem of youth disorder was incorporated into legislation at this time. As McLaughlin (2002) has outlined, it was widely considered that in previous decades there had been a breakdown of community and a 'crisis of the social' across Britain (McLaughlin 2002: 85–8) through which lawlessness, criminality and anti-social behaviour had become normalised within many communities peopled by 'the underclass'.[11] This belief in the increase of such behaviour had become so ingrained in popular thinking and in political rhetoric (by both Conservative and Labour politicians) that this had become 'the dominant discourse' (Hughes 2007: 112) and would have to be seen to be dealt with. Of course the 'problem' of disorderly youth is not a new one. Indeed, it has a long history and has re-emerged as a political problem at a number of different periods over the last two hundred years (Cohen 1980, Davies 1992, Pearson 1983). Whether the extent of such problems is currently largely 'invented' and exaggerated (Hughes 2007) or whether anti-social behaviour is experienced as a major and limiting condition of living in marginal areas remains a moot point for criminology. In popular discourse, however, something needed to be done about the problem of 'feral youth'. New Labour, learning from left realist criminology before it, recognised that working class communities, already under so much stress from unemployment, rundown housing, poor schools and underfunded public services, were also those most at risk from the consequences of fractured communities. Indeed, many were calling out for help in controlling crime and re-establishing a lost social order (Walklate and Evans 1999) and it was here that Labour hoped to make a mark.

## New Labour's new orders

The Crime and Disorder Act began with the introduction in law of a whole raft of new 'orders' aiming to control and contain 'problem' behaviour. Anti-social behaviour orders, sex offender orders, parenting orders and child safety orders were all introduced by this legislation, adding significant new powers to the police repertoire and extending some of these to local government. Using these powers courts could, amongst other measures, place severe restrictions on individuals' behaviour, require them to participate in remedial programmes and place conditions on their participation in public arenas. The Act also required local government to act on the 'problem', to record personal details and closely monitor those reported as involved in anti-social behaviour and some criminal acts. This was a significant departure from their previous duties, widening the remit of local government into areas that had hitherto been the sole responsibility of the police and arguably significantly changing the relationship between citizen and local government.[12] Only sex offender orders were kept strictly within the jurisdiction of the police authorities.

## Defining and working with 'anti-social behaviour'

Anti-social behaviour was defined, quite loosely, as behaviour 'that caused or was likely to cause harassment, alarm or distress to one or more persons not of the same household'.[13] An application to court for an order to curb such behaviour could be made by 'a relevant authority' – either the local council or any chief officer of police responsible for the area in which the nuisance occurred. Anti-social behaviour orders, soon referred to as 'asbos', would be made through a magistrates' court and in order to 'protect persons in the local government area [or adjoining area if the police or council in that area agreed] in which the harassment, alarm or distress was caused or was likely to be caused from further anti-social acts' and to ensure that similar behaviour was not repeated by the person to whom the order was applied. 'Asbos' were to last for a minimum of two years and no maximum time period was specified. If the 'asbo' were to be breached within that time then this could lead to six months' imprisonment or a fine, or both, and while the behaviour leading to the 'asbo' was considered a civil matter, breach of such an order was to be a criminal offence.

The Crime and Disorder Act was heavily criticised (see Ashworth et al. 1998, Jones 2001, Plowden 1999). Indeed, the then Director of the Howard League, Frances Crook, was quoted as saying, 'These proposals are potentially the most insidious attack on civil liberties this century. This legislation could be used in a highly discriminatory way against anyone who is different or non-conformist' (House of Commons 1998). A number of difficulties with these measures to tackle anti-social behaviour were highlighted, including the following, which demonstrate some of the dangers in issuing these orders as well as the disproportionate punishments that can be issued using the legislation:

- Anti-social behaviour itself was very loosely defined and determining whether or not it has occurred depends very much on the interpretation of very contested terms to what can be quite ambiguous behaviour (Campbell 2002).
- The Act blurred a fundamental distinction between civil and criminal acts and had the consequence of 'defining deviancy up' (Burney 2002).

- Different individuals or indeed communities may have different expectations of neighbours and/or tolerance of different behaviours, however this legislation did not allow for the local context of any individual action to be taken into account (Walklate and Evans 1999).[14]
- The individual accused may not have *intended* to cause harassment, alarm or distress, but an 'asbo' could still be granted even if no intent was present and the behaviour was unintentionally problematic or even where the harassment, alarm or distress was a result of a misinterpretation of someone's actions.
- Anti-social behaviour can be deemed to have resulted when one individual harasses, alarms or distresses only one other. This leaves disputes between individuals open to this charge. Complaints against individuals can be malicious – for example racist in intent – but there are no safeguards against malicious complaints being taken seriously under this legislation (House of Commons 1998).
- Research leading up the 1998 Act was much concerned with the problem of 'nuisance neighbours'. In such disputes it can sometime be difficult to separate 'perpetrator' from 'victim', however the 'asbo' legislation suggests the issues would be quite clear-cut.
- 'Asbos' are issued under civil law and dealt with by a magistrates' court so no criminal standards of proof are needed. Criminal offences have to be proved beyond reasonable doubt, while guilt in civil matters can be decided on the balance of probabilities. Since 'asbos' can be issued on this lower standard of proof they have been considered as possibly breaching human rights (Office of the Commissioner for Human Rights 2005).
- Breach of an 'asbo' can be considered a criminal offence with possible prison sentence attached. This has left the possibility that an individual could be imprisoned as a result of behaviour which was not initially considered serious enough to be a criminal matter. This in turn has been criticised by the European Commission for Human Rights.
- 'Asbos' can limit any behaviour of an individual which is considered to be a nuisance and also to place geographical restrictions on that behaviour – they have prohibited people from riding bikes, taking particular bus routes, entering shopping centres and in one much-cited occasion a woman who had attempted suicide on a number of occasions was prohibited from going near railway lines, rivers, bridges or multi-storey car parks (Hewitt 2007).
- There is no upper time limit on an 'asbo' – they can, and have been, granted for a lifetime.

## The monitoring of children

The Crime and Disorder Act's emphasis on curbing any troublesome behaviour by young people also led to a number of measures which charged responsible adults with the close monitoring of children and young people. 'Asbos' could be applied to anyone of 10 years or older (16 in Scotland). For anyone *under* this age the legislation provided the child safety order, administered by the family court system. These orders could also be applied for by a local government if a child committed an act, or it was thought that they might commit an act, which would have been considered an offence if the child was of an age that they could be considered criminally responsible. Child safety orders could also be granted if a child contravened a curfew notice (of which more later) or acted in a manner defined as anti-social (but see the problems with definition above). Child safety orders were not intended to be as long-term as 'asbos'. They can *require* a child to comply with its stipulations but usually for a maximum of only three months unless there are exceptional circumstances and then they can be applied for for up to twelve months. Child safety orders can also place children under the care or supervision of a social worker or member of a youth offending team. Parenting orders could be issued to those responsible for any child or young person who had been taken to court under the Crime and Disorder Act. It was possible for the court to issue the parents or guardian of a child in court with a parenting order requiring the adult responsible for their care to attend counselling or guidance sessions or to conform to any other requirements which the court laid down for them. Any breach of the order by the parent or guardian could result in a fine. This was a new step in the blaming of, and enforcing responsibility onto, adults for the behaviour of children under their care leading as Arthur (2005: 241) has argued to the 'criminalisation of inadequate parenting'.

While the gamut of orders which were put together under the 1998 Act were designed to curb the behaviour of individuals who had been identified as involved, or potentially involved, in problematic behaviour, the Local Child Curfew Scheme, also made law under this Act, was of an entirely different order. This allowed local authorities to impose a blanket ban on the presence of any unaccompanied child under ten in a specified public place at a specified time (initially between the hours of 9pm and 8am) for a period of up to one month. Any child breaking this curfew could be picked up by the police and taken home or to a 'place of safety' if taking the child home was deemed to be inappropriate. The police were mandated to inform the relevant local authority of any breach of curfew within 48 hours of the breach taking place. These curfews could be applied whether or not the child was engaged in any unlawful or 'anti-social' activity. Curfew orders had only ever previously been applicable to those in contact with the criminal justice system and who were subject to monitoring within the community. Their extension to people not even suspected of offending and without reference to the criminal justice system reinforced Frances Crook's worries that a particular morality was being imposed from above and that anyone not complying with its requirements, or living life under different normative moral and social codes, could be severely penalised as a result. In addition and equally controversially, children of school age suspected of truanting could be removed by the police to a designated place of safety. Both the curfew and the truancy clauses of the Act extended police control over young people's movements, allowing them to potentially stop, question and detain children who had not committed any criminal offence. Interventions in young people's lives which might previously have been seen as lying under the auspices of the welfare agencies was now made a police matter – another consequence of the criminalisation of social policy issues. Even clothing choices could be monitored and controlled. The 1998 Act allowed the police to remove and seize 'any item which the constable reasonably believes that person is wearing wholly or mainly for the purpose of concealing his [sic] identity' making refusal to give up any such clothing to the police an arrestable offence. This was generally seen to be a tool in the police armoury to curb the behaviour of the infamous 'hoodie' and the fashion of young people to wear hoods low over their faces whatever the weather. This style, adopted by many young males, which admittedly apes the concealing of faces by those who do have criminal intent, was completely outlawed in a number of places such as some shopping centres as though all adopting it were somehow cut from the same (criminal) cloth.

## The monitoring of offenders

Alongside the closer monitoring of non-offenders, those who were arrested and charged could be subject to even closer scrutiny. Drug Treatment and Testing Orders were introduced by the legislation as a community sentence for any offenders over the age of 16 (reduced to 14 in 2003). Those found to be misusing drugs could be offered treatment for their drug use which would also involve regular tests establishing their drug-free status, as well as regular reviews by the court to check up on their progress. Any breach of the order would mean a return to court and resentencing. These orders suggested that 'drug-dependent offenders can be successfully "coerced" into treatment as they pass through the criminal justice process' (Hough et al. 2003: 1). Reparation Orders, in a similar vein, coerced offenders into making some sort of supervised amends for their actions. The detention and training order (DTO), justified as a measure to ensure that custody for children was a constructive experience with an appropriate focus on education and training in reality 'represents a very substantial increase in the custodial powers of the youth court and a loosening of the conditions which must be met before custodial orders can be imposed on children aged 12–14 years' (Bateman 2001: 36), while the introduction of reprimands for a first, and final warnings for a subsequent offence, regulated and proscribed in law the young offender's path to more serious penalties and appearance before court.

There were a number of other clauses in the 1998 Act which were significant in criminal justice practice. The law was changed on racially aggravated offences which placed these in a more serious category of offence and, perhaps most significant of all, was the removal of the presumption in law that a child under 14 years of age is incapable of understanding the criminal nature of their actions – in legal terms 'Abolition of rebuttable presumption that a child is doli incapax'. This in effect meant that a child of ten or over could be held *criminally* responsible for his or her actions. This very significant change to the law was placed halfway through the Act under a 'Miscellaneous' section but was perhaps one of the most far-reaching and garnered much debate and criticism (Bandali 1998). These changes will be further explored in Chapters 5 and 6.

## Joining up crime and disorder strategies

The Crime and Disorder Act placed local councils alongside the police as the authorities responsible for devising and implementing strategies to reduce crime in their local areas. In a move straight out of the Morgan Report, police and local authorities were tasked to work together to prepare and publish audits of crime and disorder every three years, to devise crime and disorder reduction targets and to constantly measure performance against these set objectives. In addition local authorities were given the statutory duty to consider the crime and disorder implications of every part of their work. Crime and Disorder Reduction Partnerships, explored more fully in later chapters, sought to bring together representatives from a range of welfare, health, education, housing and criminal justice agencies to work closely together to meet crime reduction targets and to share information and combine strategies. The removal of the boundaries – the joining up – of crime with other social policy and welfare issues meant that in the first instance it was the crime agenda that was the focus of their partnership work.

## Concluding comments

This chapter has carefully unpicked and examined some of the major early policy responses of New Labour which were developed in order to prevent and reduce the extent of criminal offending. We have seen how the more progressive aspects of New Labour thinking were gradually eroded and have become in danger of being overwhelmed under the onslaught of more powerful and conservative forces. This has not happened in an easily traced and linear fashion, nor has it simply been a question of a clear struggle between progressives and conservatives within the governing party, although at the very start of New Labour's term of office the fiercely fought debate concerning the future of welfare in Britain contained some of these characteristics. Largely it has occurred as a consequence of the contradictions in 'Third Way' ideology – the philosophy which was deemed necessary to make Labour electable and which meant that in office they would remain fiscally 'prudent' and that increased taxation to fund welfare programmes was absolutely ruled out. In effect the incoming government left themselves with very little room to manoeuvre financially while ideologically they were wedded to a politics of 'responsibilisation' described by Garland in his well-received and much referenced 2001 work *The Culture of Control*. The drive to 'responsibilise' individuals, to force them to see the error of their ways and to change their negative behaviours, infuses the text of Straw's *No More Excuses* (Home Office 1997b) both explicitly and implicitly and is absolutely apparent in the various penalties and orders of the Crime and Disorder Act.

Despite, and at the same time as, their work to prevent social exclusion, systems of crime control were put in place which extended control over personal behaviour, severely limited what the law deemed as acceptable behaviour and increased the punishment for any transgressions. Despite the government's early rhetoric around combating social exclusion, the powers which they handed out to police and local authorities did not create a system of justice which understood the very real social problems and poverty – of finance and spirit – which had been created throughout Britain in the preceding decades. It looked instead to quick-fix solutions to deep-seated social problems (Young 1999). Instead of looking to handle such issues with tact, sensitivity and a long-term view of change it put in place crude, over-bearing and top-down remedies. For Garland contemporary crime control in the UK and the USA is shaped by the need to meet very immediate and practical problems associated with high rates of crime but also to address the many risks, insecurities and problems of social order which adherence to a neoliberal politics of the market brings in its wake. There is, of course an alternative. Much European criminology during the 1980s and 1990s shows that a different system of criminal justice and crime control is possible. Pitts' work on responses to youth crime in France gives useful examples of how different political traditions and a state committed to creative interventions within marginalised neighbourhoods has led there to attempts to include disaffected youth in social and political initiatives to bring about change (Pitts and Hope 1997, Pitts 2001). However the governmental politics of the USA and UK have been dominated by social conservatism and right-wing and neo-liberal government projects. There is some evidence that this moral, authoritarian, punitive and populist form of government may currently be gaining ascendancy in other liberal democracies and shaping a more exclusionary set to politics therein.[15]

There is another aspect to Labour's 'Third Way' approach which we have started to examine in this chapter and which will be further explored in the next. As Gilling (2007) outlines, once complex, difficult and contradictory social problems become 'joined-up' to a clear-cut objective to reduce crime, the latter becomes the dominant partner. Figures on crimes recorded and offenders detected are constantly collected and updated making the objective of crime reduction measurable and easy to translate into political priorities. The complex and overlapping factors which can lead to criminal offending, however, are much more difficult to capture in media-friendly sound-bites and discussions of the support and care needs of young offenders and their families are perceived as unpopular (Jamieson 2006) and potential vote-losers. While using punitive sanctions to intervene in already damaged families may well be counter-productive (Arthur

2005) crime and punishment is seen as an easier discourse to engage with than that of care and support and to campaign on the former agenda does not require the wholesale political and social change which would be needed to seriously engage with the latter.

As organisations as different as social services, social housing providers, educational establishments, health and youth work agencies became increasingly involved, through partnerships with agencies of crime control, so their work was dragged closer to the crime reduction agenda as it was being reformulated by New Labour. The use of sanctions, punishment and the criminal law, and a zero tolerance of behaviour cast as 'anti-social' became a dominant theme with which partnership organisations had to contend. While anathema to some, the punitive and zero tolerance turn seemed to gel quite readily with others (see Cowan et al. 2001 on the growing links between social housing provision and policing), the growing discourse of social control became further dispersed (Cohen 1985) and impacted on the work of an unprecedented range of agencies.

## FURTHER READING

Levitas, R. (2005) *The Inclusive Society? Social Exclusion and New Labour.* Basingstoke: Macmillan.

Pitts, J. (2001) *The New Politics of Youth Crime: Discipline or Solidarity.* Lyme Regis: Russell House Publishing.

## NOTES

1   At its launch the Social Exclusion Unit also included a number of non-government personnel from Crime Concern, Kent police; the public and community affairs section of the NatWest Group; the independent think-tank Demos; an assistant director of social services at Hammersmith and Fulham council; an assistant chief probation officer in Inner London and the chief executive of the Church Urban Fund.

2   As explained by Google's The Phrase Finder: 'This is the mantra chanted by "dries" during the prime ministerial reign of Margaret Thatcher, by which they demonstrated their belief that free-market capitalism was the only possible economic theory. It was said so often amongst them that it was shortened to TINA. The hard-right Thatcherites called themselves "dries" to demonstrate their opposition to the "wets", i.e. the One-Nation Tories whom Thatcher despised. Wet was the public school nickname for any boy who showed any sign of caring for his fellow beings.' http://www.phrases.org.uk/meanings/376000.html (accessed 25.07.08).

3   It was launched in Scotland in January 1998.

4   The launch of the SEU coincided with that of this new research unit within the London School of Economics. CASE was set up to explore and analyse elements of social exclusion.

5   This speech, offered to the Annual General Meeting of the organisation – The Big Issue – was designed to answer criticism of the government's plans for welfare reforms which had garnered much opposition from within and outside the Labour Party. The reforms included cuts to benefits for single parents.

6  The *Big Issue* magazine was founded in 1991 during the previous Conservative administration. Its founder believed that the key to solving the problem of homelessness lay in
   helping people to help themselves. By selling *Big Issue* newspapers on the streets the
   homeless were given an alternative to begging.
7  This tactic was also employed to separate out the 'bogus' from the 'genuine' asylum
   seeker and this will be further explored in Chapter 6.
8  This was already possible in Scotland.
9  Criminologists have long pointed out the problems of demonising youth by concentrating
   on their behaviours above all other groups and their arguments can be followed in a
   number of publications. See, for example, the ongoing work of Barry Goldson, John
   Muncie and John Pitts. Criminologists have also demonstrated the lack of attention
   which successive governments have placed on more serious crimes, especially those
   committed by business and the state. For recent work in this area turn to the writings of
   Steve Tombs and Dave Whyte.
10 See House of Commons Hansard Debates 8 December 1995 (pt 6) Col 627.
11 For an often-quoted (and by many critiqued) thesis on this 'underclass' in Britain see the
   work of Murray (1990 and passim).
12 The Housing Act of 1996 had already allowed local authorities to monitor anti-social
   behaviour in limited ways. It had introduced Introductory Tenancies which allowed the
   speedy eviction of tenants of local authority properties if they exhibited anti-social behaviour within the first twelve months of their tenancy period. Almost half decided against
   their use (The Crime and Disorder Bill 1998: 14).
13 In Scotland the terms of an anti-social behaviour order differed slightly, for example the
   term 'harassment' was omitted at this point and it was stipulated that the behaviour had
   to have occurred on more than one occasion.
14 The author lived in a street in Salford with no back gardens where it was usual on a warm
   summer night to take armchairs into the street and sit drinking with neighbours into the
   small hours. Rather than be considered problematic behaviour it was deemed quite anti-
   social if neighbours did not join in!
15 Political parties espousing the politics of neo-liberalism have gained renewed popularity
   in Australia and New Zealand and in 2009 elections to the European Parliament
   returned an unprecedented number of right leaning (and some extreme-right) MEPs and
   McAra (2008) has written that the criminal justice 'architecture' of post-devolution
   Scotland has abandoned its previous penal-welfarism and turned more readily to the
   punitive populism, public protection and risk management of the rest of the British Isles.

# 3

# Crime and community: from communitarianism to the management of crime

'Community' has long been invoked as a positive tool by and through which crime prevention practices could be better developed and sustained in the longer term. Sociological analyses of crime and community from the 1930s to the present day have revealed how patterns of crime differ from neighbourhood to neighbourhood and the study of the local dynamics of crime and social control reveal important clues as to how crime can be best tackled in particular areas (Evans 1997, Hope 2001, Hope and Foster 1992, Hope and Hough 1988, Hope and Shaw 1988, Walklate and Evans 1999). As we have seen in Chapter 1, the strength of locally-based interventions rooted within communities affected by crime and fear of crime, were later adopted within the perspective of community safety and the approach that all organisations, enterprises and individuals in a neighbourhood should work together to ensure change for the better. By the mid-1990s this agenda had been incorporated into many towns and cities across Britain and local community safety partnerships were making positive contributions to local interventions around crime, safety and economic regeneration.

## New Labour's communitarian agenda

As Labour came to office in 1997 it brought with it a particular commitment to community involvement in governance, drawing inspiration from the communitarian philosophy espoused by the US sociologist Amitai Etzioni. Etzioni's interpretation of communitarianism had come into prominence in the US under the Democratic administration of Clinton and appeared on initial glance as though it might offer more of a progressive than punitive approach when applied to local crime control, however it took on, as we will later see, a 'moralistic and rightist' tone (Hughes 2007: 15). New Labour's version of communitarianism was also closely allied to their Third Way philosophy. Their adviser in the practice of this approach was the UK academic and sociologist Giddens who wrote:

> The cause of so many political and social ills ... is the civic decline that is evidenced in the weakening sense of solidarity in some local communities and urban neighbourhoods, high levels of crime, and the break-up of marriages and families. (Giddens 1998: 78)

New Labour in government set out to combat this disintegration of society through a re-embedding of community values and organisation at neighbourhood level. They envisaged neighbourhoods which were largely self-regulating, held in check through informal social controls and to some degree independent of the state, requiring minimal intervention from above. In practice this would mean reliance on strong civic institutions, from the more personally oriented such as the family and neighbourhood associations, through to functioning and effective local governance at the micro-level such as police–community consultative groups and local community safety and crime reduction steering groups – linked with local state providers in education, housing and health among others. New Labour hoped to achieve this vision by engaging and then involving individuals at these different levels. This, it hoped, would lead to a resurgence of civic feeling and belonging, a new-found confidence in community and a re-connection to lost moral values flowing from a more collective consciousness, shared understandings and future goals.

## The stakeholder society

Labour claimed to be moving towards a 'stakeholder society', using an approach drawn from Third Way economics in which it is argued that modern and democratic enterprises should give every employee a stake in the running of their business and thereby a share in its success. In Blair's political philosophy each individual would be given a 'stake' in the running of civic institutions but in turn they must first and foremost *participate* in local civic life. In return for their participation in local community and governance the individual would receive the benefits of a more responsive and informed local governmentality. In this new social contract the central state must relinquish certain of its powers to the periphery so that, at the local level, individuals would feel that they were being consulted and listened to and that they were developing a 'stake' in the political arena by which they could really make a positive improvement to their lives. Only then could community re-emerge as a strong and significant area of social life and as a force which could be galvanised in the pursuit of a safer and less troubled society. In moving towards this approach Blair was signalling a break from the previous Conservative governments' appeal to community. John Major, Conservative Prime Minister from 1990 to 1997, had presided over a 'back to basics' approach to community, harking back to a mythical golden age in which Britain had been at ease within itself and community life flourished without recourse to the state. New Labour's approach, however, was to build community afresh for the twenty-first century setting out a mutually beneficial pact between state and community, whereby each needs the other's expertise and resources.

## From provider to enabler

In setting out this differing appeal to community, however, New Labour was not only attacking the policies of previous governments – but was also laying down a marker against the 'something for nothing' culture which they suggested pervaded society. In this way New Labour's communitarian approach was also 'Tony Blair's rebuff to Old Labour' (Driver and Martell 1997: 28) and within its process of 'modernisation' was the intention 'to distance the party from its social democratic past' (ibid: 33). As Hughes has outlined, communitarianism places 'A strong and recurrent emphasis ... on duties and responsibilities to the wider society rather than freedoms and rights for the individual' (2007: 20). So while distinguishing Labour from the hyper-individualism of Conservativism, and appealing to the social and collaborative essence of humanity, it was clearly intended that the individual had to give in order to receive something back – a better life was to be achieved through participation not through expectation. This pact was to apply, not only in local civic life but also in the economy; rewards were to be gained through participation in the labour force and in the creation of wealth not through systems of welfare benefits and state handouts. As Gordon Brown, then Chancellor of the Exchequer opined in his first annual budget speech after Labour took office:

> Unemployment blights not just individuals' lives, but whole communities. So we need a 'new deal' for communities which recognises that the answer to social exclusion is economic opportunity ... And I say to those who can work: this is our 'new deal'. Your responsibility is to seek work. My guarantee is that if you work, work will pay. (*Guardian* 1998c)

Brown's speech clearly set out the philosophy which ran throughout the New Labour government and which as David Blunkett, when Education and Employment Secretary, later put it, set out a new relationship between the state and the individual whereby 'Government should be there to support and encourage people to help themselves but not to attempt to do everything for them' (Smithers and Woodward 2001). Government had therefore shifted from its former role as a provider to its new role as an 'enabler' (Keith 2004) and as Roger Smith explained it, 'the Government has committed itself to *enable* [my emphasis] individuals and communities to achieve their aspirations, but only if they, at the same time, are willing to honour their social responsibilities' (2001: 23).

Communitarianism replaced what were perceived as the old, paternalistic, philosophies whereby the power held by the state is used to shape the life of the individual at a local level. Instead community and neighbourhood-led organisations are supported in order that they can take a more significant role in setting local priorities and actions. It signalled a move away from government which is state-centred and centrally-prescribed towards a system of local governance through which power is devolved downwards and outwards towards the margins. As a condition of this power shift, however, local organisations, the voluntary sector, community groups and all those agencies which make up civil society are charged with taking responsibility for what happens in their locality – almost as a moral duty. It is a move away from a mentality of 'the state knows best' but it is also a clear break from democratic socialist values which perceived the state as the provider and carer for the many. Indeed, the emphasis it places on local rather than central governance and the championing of 'civil society' above state agencies has increasingly led to a marginalisation of local state providers and to the privatisation of much local service delivery (Lavalette and Ferguson 2007).

## From 'enabler' to 'enforcer'?

The communitarian approach espoused by New Labour contained many contradictions and this could be seen in sharp relief once it was translated into policy on the ground. On the one hand the communitarian agenda aspired to a progressive devolution of power and responsibility to the local level, but on the other hand it has been described as 'morally prescriptive, conservative and individual' (Driver and Martell 1997: 27). As the inspiration of communitarianism was translated into the political and policy agenda it became apparent that individuals were expected to conform to notions of 'the good society' which were centrally prescribed with little room for local determination. This 'moral authoritarian communitarianist' stance adopted by government (Hughes 1996) set certain approved expectations, standards and moral values and rejected all others. Furthermore, the burden of action was firmly placed on individuals, their families and communities to intervene in areas which were previously seen as the responsibility of the state alone with the growing threat that services would be withdrawn to those individuals who did not take on this responsibility to 'help themselves'. As we will see, the government increasingly adopted managerialist and coercive measures to ensure conformity to prescribed goals. At the same time, however, certain areas of governance which profoundly affected the terrain in which local communities and citizens operated remained the sole preserve of the state – the setting of local spending limits, of local service delivery goals and targets, of setting criminal and civil sanctions – severely limiting the power of local organisations to follow their own agendas.

## Communitarianism and the maintenance of order

As far as the maintenance of law and order was concerned communitarian ideals suggested that 'Social compliance ... derives primarily from informal controls built into everyday relations' (Hughes 1996: 20) and communitarianism and the Third Way philosophies espoused by New Labour set out to achieve 'a reordering of the relationship between the community and the state and the transfer of significant social control functions, together with the creation of new control mechanisms, to the community' (James and James 2001: 225). It was envisaged that communities should by and large police themselves through the imposition of a clear moral framework and adherence to a particular set of social values while stronger links would also be built between policing professionals and the communities which they served. As James and James go on to argue, 'the communitarian philosophies of New Labour are having the effect, at least in part, of incorporating the family and the community into the social control mechanisms of the state' (2001: 225). Severe recriminations were suggested for those who stepped outside the normative framework – public shaming as a tool to warn offenders of the social approbation their actions generate, random drug and alcohol testing and, as Etzioni intimated, acceptance of technically flawed evidence in court if this leads to the conviction of the 'real criminal' (see Hughes 1996: 22–3) – all measures which we will see in later chapters were taken up to some extent over the subsequent decade.

While the stakeholder agenda and Third Way ideologies were driven down to local community level, to profoundly affect the lives of the ordinary working-class citizen, they were never applied upwards to foster change in the organisation of the economic and corporate life of Britain although the stakeholder agenda was originally mooted precisely in order to democratise, 'modernise' and set limits to the excesses of this section of society (Spangenburg 2001). Indeed, at the corporate level the government approach was to set preferred goals and expectations but rarely to enforce. As Driver and Martell point out, while New Labour considered legal sanction to be the most appropriate method for ensuring individual compliance with the law, when it came to corporate responsibility more generally 'persuasion and voluntary agreements are regarded as more effective' (1997: 43). It appeared that the governing authorities were more comfortable investing trust and empathy in the business community than within working class and troubled neighbourhoods.

## New Deal for Communities

After their election to government in 1997, New Labour was keen to put their communitarian perspective into effect. Not long after the Social Exclusion Unit (SEU) was launched in 1997 the government announced the New Deal for

Communities (NDC) which was launched in 1999. NDC concentrated funding in selected neighbourhoods considered some of the poorest in England and Wales and is an example of what is generally termed an 'area-based initiative' (ABI). Indeed, NDC was heralded by Sheffield Hallam University researchers as 'one of the most important ABIs ever launched in England' (CRESR 2005: 5). Although in opposition Labour had signalled its intention to move away from ABIs, which they criticised as divisive and unable to bring about the large-scale change which was needed to take effect across British society, soon after taking office 39 areas were invited to apply for funds to kick-start regeneration locally – initially 17 in the first round in 1998 and another 22 just one year later. Funding for these schemes was made available for ten years and in that time the government hoped to see positive outcomes for these neighbourhoods in the areas of community development and engagement; improving housing and the physical environment; health and education; reducing worklessness and the fear and experience of crime. Following its communitarian agenda, themes of community involvement and partnership working were prominent within the programme and each NDC area was to be run by a board which included representatives from the community as well as the key agencies delivering services to that community.

## Innovative and Third Way?

Although yet another area-based programme, NDC was hailed as experimental and innovative in character. It was envisaged that the areas chosen to receive NDC funding would act as 'pathfinders' or pilot projects and that they would be allowed some leeway to evolve creative and innovative solutions which would later act as exemplars for other areas. NDC was not all about funding and was supposed to give added value to those neighbourhoods in which it was applied through the initiative's intention to fully engage the community, implement close joint working through the management of partnership boards and to allow 'a strong degree of local flexibility and freedoms' (Lawless 2004: 383) to steer regeneration towards local concerns and problems.

New Labour had signalled its intention to look at social problems through a different 'lens' and, following their Third Way philosophy, to adopt a modern, progressive approach to its social interventions. However, area-based initiatives themselves were not an innovative departure from earlier regeneration projects, indeed Lawless (2004) identifies their emergence over 35 years ago. However, Third Way and communitarian approaches promised an ideological break from the socially divisive measures adopted by previous Conservative administrations. The preceding Conservative governments had introduced two new funding mechanisms for urban regeneration in the 1980s. The first was that area-based regeneration should be accessed through competition between local authorities for a limited pot of resources and the second was that private sector funding must be levered in to any bids for such funding. Starting with the 1987 Safer Cities programme all regeneration programmes were based on funding regimes which required local authorities to put in place urban coalitions involving public and private sector bodies. These Urban Development Corporations (UDCs) became the key delivery agents of urban regeneration. Although local authorities were also involved in the coalitions, the move to encourage such a decisive degree of private sector involvement was generally regarded as a quasi-privatisation of regeneration work and another attempt by the then Thatcher-led government to weaken the hold of the public sector in local areas. The UDCs were dominated by business interests and brought many practices from the private sector into regeneration work (Taylor et al. 1996). They would, for example, use private consultants to produce expensive bid documents arguing the case for the funding of their area above all others. For every winner in these competitions there were obviously losers, disappointed authorities, neighbourhoods and communities which had lost out to the successful bidders.

The UDCs' approach had been heavily criticised by Labour Party in opposition and its New Deal was supposedly premised on a different set of funding and bidding criteria. One of the first departures of the NDC initiative was the removal of the competitive bidding process. Those areas which were to benefit from NDC funding were identified through alternative means in an attempt to ensure that the worst areas received funding rather than the most experienced bidders. This obviously left a large number of the 3,000–5,000 struggling neighbourhoods identified by the Social Exclusion Unit in England and Wales (SEU 1998) without recourse to such monies so that the targeted element of regeneration funding had not been removed in practice. In the absence of the competitive bid documents which in the past would have included a range of area indicators and targets for improvement, all the NDC partnership bodies were initially tasked to produce reports which laid out the key economic and social data for the area and outlined possible regeneration plans. Each NDC area was required to prepare a delivery plan setting out the area's problems and how these might be addressed. The projects were then evaluated and checked as to whether their targets had been reached.

## Have NDC's made a difference locally?

At the time of writing the ten-year phase of NDC had not yet been fully evaluated. In 2008, however, the report of Phase 2 of its interim evaluation found that the largest area of spending for NDCs was on physical regeneration (at around 27 per cent of all funds), 11 per cent had been spent on crime and disorder reduction and another 11 per cent on improving health outcomes (CRESR 2008: 9). Between 1999 and 2006 the government had spent £1.54 billion in these areas and reports showed that funding had been used to support 'a wide range of outputs across the Programme including, over 400 improved community facilities, 40 more police officers, 120 improved schools, more than 300 business start-ups, almost 18,000 new or improved dwellings, and more than 150 new neighbourhood level wardens' (CRESR 2008: 11). This interim report praised the NDC areas for focusing on effecting local solutions for local problems and identified the longer-term funding of the projects as having allowed new relationships to bed in and a strategic overview to develop.

Each NDC area blended regeneration of the physical environment (in the regeneration jargon – place-based outcomes) with more social interventions (person-based outcomes) but to differing degrees depending on the issues which were perceived to be locally relevant. Nevertheless this second evaluation report acknowledged that, some six to seven years into the initiative place-based outcomes, including more positive perceptions of the neighbourhood and reducing fear of crime, were outperforming the person-based such as improvements in health and numbers in paid work. However, despite the increased funding, regeneration personnel and policies active within these areas, the second phase of the interim evaluation found no statistical evidence that the NDC areas had improved any more than other similar areas which had not been subject to the same funding and management over the same period.

## 'Modernising' local government

Of course in the ten years of NDC other neighbourhoods were not left to their own devices without extra funding or policy initiatives. A whole host of different initiatives, some attracting increased funding, others diverting existing resources to new areas were implemented across the different regions and countries of Britain so that not one could be said to be unaffected by government interventions and ideas. Indeed, Gilling has criticised the government for excessive 'initiativitis' (2007: 185) during this period.

The New Deal for Communities followed on from the government's commitment to tackle social exclusion in a 'joined-up' way. The intractable nature of social exclusion was recognised in the government's insistence that the pathfinder areas should engage in joint working across departmental areas in all of its key thematic priorities of worklessness, health, education, crime, housing and the physical environment (Coaffee and Deas 2008: 171) linking services which had hitherto been firmly entrenched within what were termed their own distinct service delivery 'silos'. The government hoped that through this methodology lessons learned from the New Deal would inform future 'joined up' working across all local authority areas and services and that such innovation would eventually become normal practice. As this new way of conceptualising problems and working together was 'rolled out' across the country and the NDC model became 'mainstreamed', there would be little further need for pilot projects and neighbourhood-based interventions.

Shortly after the NDC programme was announced came news that many areas would qualify for funding for a number of 'special action zones' which would be focused around the separate themes of education, health and employment and each of which would attract increased funding for these services. So Health Action Zones, Employment Action Zones and Education Action Zones were set up in different areas, some overlapping and covering the same neighbourhoods and each was charged with ensuring community representation and partnership working. But the 'initiativitis' did not end here.

## Steering from the centre through Local Strategic Partnerships

In September 2000 the Neighbourhood Renewal Unit was set up in the then Department for the Environment, Transport and the Regions. It developed a National Strategy for Neighbourhood Renewal for the 88 most deprived local authority areas in England. This Unit put in place Local Strategic Partnerships (LSPs) which were set up to facilitate 'joined-up' working at the local level. They attracted extra resources from a Neighbourhood Renewal Fund and a Community Empowerment Fund in order that the public, private, community and voluntary sectors could work together to meet local needs. Each LSP was to prepare and implement a Local Neighbourhood Renewal Strategy to pinpoint the local areas most in need and to improve employment opportunities, regenerate the physical environment and reduce crime as well as working to improve education, health and housing. LSPs could set up and run services at neighbourhood level through Neighbourhood Managers with their own devolved budgets and money from local 'Community Chests'. By this point local systems of partnership and governance in some of the poorest areas of Britain had become very complex indeed giving rise to some concern that their residents may have been over-consulted and suffering from partnership overload (Lawless 2004).[1]

From an initial reading of the policy documents associated with these many initiatives it would seem that the radical objective of devolving power to the regional, local and neighbourhood level had indeed commenced. In reality, however, a great deal of the work of LSPs, rather than being left to local people and organisations to decide, was specifically mapped out in advance of their implementation. The government's guidance notes to aid the setting up of LSPs, for example, set clear objectives and established local authorities as the bodies responsible for initially setting them up and monitoring their success (DETR 2001). As Gilling has aptly demonstrated, local government found itself very closely steered from the centre and unable to deviate from the clear delivery and performance targets set centrally. As the lead organisation in LSPs, the local authority officers involved in the partnerships would have been acutely aware of this necessity to deliver to these previously stated objectives. A number of LSPs were also chosen to work to Public Service Agreements, service delivery programmes which had to be agreed with government offices and in which further targets were laid down for authorities to achieve over particular time periods. To complicate matters further Local Area Agreements were introduced in 2004 and updated in 2007. These purported to further devolve power to the localities and away from central government but with the ever-increasing setting of performance targets and managerialist interventions in the affairs of local government and service providers which have been outlined by many commentators over the past decade it is difficult to detect any substantial relinquishing of power to localities on the ground (Coaffee and Deas 2008, Crawford 2001, Power 1997, Stoker 2004). Indeed, as Hughes concludes, 'communitarian participation, never mind community leadership, remains a lofty and often righteous aspiration that is very rarely realized in practice in the work of partnerships' (2007: 64).

## Local government and the crime reduction agenda

As we have seen in the previous chapter, the Crime and Disorder Act of 1998 fundamentally changed the relationship of local authorities to crime reduction work. Many had already become deeply involved in the prevention of crime and in developing community safety work while Labour was the party of opposition. In making the reduction of crime and disorder a statutory responsibility of local government, the 1998 Act placed the reality of these local authorities' interventions into law as a statutory requirement. This was a triumph for local councils who had become increasingly marginalised during previous Conservative administrations (Gilling 2001: 112) but which could now feel that their work was being taken seriously.

Prior to the 1998 Act local authorities did not routinely set aside funds for community safety work from their mainstream budgets. Much of the work that was carried out in this area was financed through European funding such as URBAN and regeneration programmes funded through initiatives such as the Single Regeneration Budget and Capital Challenge – which were subject to a competitive bidding process. This meant that community safety work was generally tied to specific areas or projects which had been able to attract such specialised funding. After the Act all local authorities, working together with the relevant police service as equal partners, had to put in place a strategy for reducing crime and disorder and the misuse of drugs across the whole of their area. This strategy had to be informed by an audit of crime and disorder which reviewed levels and patterns of crime and analysed the data collected. Their findings were to be widely published and consulted upon. From this consultation a strategy for reducing crime and disorder had to be formulated – with clear objectives including short- and long-term targets. The police and local councils, 'the responsible authorities', were required to invite other relevant bodies, such as the health and fire services as well as educators, social landlords and probation to work with them on this audit and strategy which had to be constantly reviewed and renewed every three years. In addition all local authorities were now required by law to consider the crime and disorder implications of all the work which they carried out and to do all that they reasonably could to prevent crime. This 'joining up', at least as far as crime and disorder were concerned, was designed to prevent any one department putting in place practices which might inadvertently or otherwise increase the crime statistics. So for example, education authorities would have to review their policies on school exclusions, since the link between offending and truancy had already been made.

The statutory obligations put in place by the 1998 Act changed the landscape of crime prevention and community safety almost overnight and strengthened the hand of local governments (Gilling 2001: 115). Some local authority areas already had community safety partnerships in place and many had already made close links between their regeneration work and crime prevention (Hancock 2001) but none had covered the whole of their service delivery area or looked so comprehensively at the crime and disorder implications of all their work. Other local authorities were more or less starting from scratch. Crime and Disorder Reduction Partnerships (CDRPs), or Community Safety Partnerships (CSPs) as they are sometimes known (in Wales they are always CSPs), had to be set up and begin joint working on delivering an audit, consultation and strategy as soon as possible and government guidelines set out the parameters of the work to be covered by the emerging partnerships. These guidelines gave little autonomy to the local partnerships; instead the political requirement that crime and disorder be reduced was so strongly articulated that crime reduction targets were forced downwards onto local neighbourhoods. If the political priority was youth crime and substance misuse, for example, then this had to be seen to be reduced in all localities – never mind what the local community saw as its own priority. This is less the government as 'enabler' and more as 'enforcer'.

The background to this supposedly innovative, new mode of governance and self-regulation (Crawford 1997) was a managerialist, performance-driven model driven by central government and imposed on the local deliverers of services. Government documents driving and guiding work with local communities were riven with contradictions, on the one hand celebrating the expertise and abilities of those outside government and pushing for the building of ever stronger community organisations with the powers to govern locally, while at the same time they allowed only the narrowest of spaces within which these communities could operate. The *Guidance for Crime and Disorder Reduction Partnerships and Community Safety Partnerships* published in 2007 is an example of this approach which was replicated across so many documents produced by government departments and the Audit Commission among others. In the interests of improving performance and increasing effectiveness of CDRPs the guidance required and 'expects' a whole host of structures to be set up, conditions to be met and objectives to be aimed for. Then, somewhat naïvely or disingenuously it suggests that 'Beyond the statutory requirements, partnerships have the flexibility to deliver in their own way' (Home Office 2007a: 4).

## Police and the crime reduction agenda

The police, the other 'responsible authority' within the CDRP, were equally subject to the increasing managerialisation of public services (McLaughlin 2007: 182–7). They too were now subject to performance targets and were more closely managed from the Home Office. After 1997, McLaughlin argues:

> The first new Labour administration (1997 to 2001) refined the centralizing logics of the existing legislative framework to ensure that police force and police authority efforts were directed to realizing both Whitehall defined 'best value' and crime reduction targets. (2007: 184)

The Home Office began to compare the performance of different forces on volume crimes such as residential burglary, the policing of drugs and crimes involving violence and placed the detection of these offences as a priority for the police. The police were also subjected to new effectiveness and efficiency measures which meant that their work was subject to audit on both. After 2001 and the appointment of David Blunkett as Home Secretary, the operational independence of the police was further undermined as Blunkett made his agenda clear in the setting up of a Police Standards Unit (PSU), in 2001 and the Police Reform Act (PRA) in 2002 (McLaughlin 2007). The PSU, as a result of its remit to assess the performance of all forces in England and Wales and to ensure that they followed 'best practice', in effect promoted both the standardisation of policing practices and an evidence-based 'what works' agenda which further limited the operational decisions which local forces could make. Through the PSU's obligation to refer forces which were giving some cause for concern to the Home Secretary for direct intervention, the government had ensured that it had an effective bite with which to force change on the police. The PRA further extended the power of the centre over what were quasi-independent forces. This Act set out the requirement for the police to follow a centrally set National Policing Plan and policing codes of practice. Despite their initial opposition to many of these centralising moves the police were now statutorily required to follow orders from above and they too had lost much of their regional and local autonomy.

## Community engagement: for what and at which level?

It became increasingly difficult for local and community partners within CDRPs to ensure that their agendas were established as equally legitimate – especially if they deviated from centrally-held concerns. Research has demonstrated that local communities can be incredibly innovative and resilient in resisting force from the centre (Cooper 2004) especially when they are supported by local and regional authorities less wedded to central government objectives (Hughes 2007). Ultimately, however, community-led organisations are the least powerful of partnership members (Mulgan 2003) and the spaces which they are able to carve out for themselves and their own priorities can only be found in the chinks of the central government's armour. At the level of community it became increasingly difficult to resist centrally-imposed demands for to do so meant to risk losing access to available funding streams and to the support and guidance which accompanied the government's agenda. It also risked the alienation and continued marginalisation of resistant groups and communities from those who continued to hold both the purse-strings and the power to withdraw official mechanisms of support.

Involving the community in any kind of policy-making process is fraught with difficulties and raises as many questions as it answers. Khan (1998: 35–7) identified a number of questions pertinent to the government's decision to involve community in policy design and implementation. He asked local government officials to consider:

- What are your aims and what are you prepared to give in order to achieve them?
- Why do you want to consult in the first place?
- At what stage in the policy process do you want to consult?
- Who do you intend to consult?
- What methods for public involvement will be utilised?

Some of these questions were easier to answer than others. It seems apparent from government documents outlining their agenda for NDCs and new forms of local governance that it was believed that community involvement would bring about a more targeted and sustained regeneration practice and that, rather than seeing community involvement as one part of a process which was led by more formally-based organisations such as local regeneration bodies, the government was keen to ensure that it infused all crime reduction and regeneration work. The National Strategy for Neighbourhood Renewal, for example, clearly states:

> The Strategy recognises that sustainable renewal can only be achieved if it has community ownership. Full community involvement, starting where the Community is, and with its priorities, is as important as improving public services. Moving to this position will be a long-term process and will entail change in all sectors and agencies and for individuals. (SEU 2001: 71)

It was envisaged that community representatives would make up a large proportion of the management boards running each of the NDCs and there was to be a concerted effort to consult hard-to-reach communities and to reassure these groups that their views would be taken into consideration. So in answer to Khan's questions the government felt that in order to achieve sustainable regeneration in some of the most deprived neighbourhoods in Britain it was necessary to ensure that local concerns were fully integrated into their strategy for change, that local people should play a full part in the management of regeneration, that all communities – even hard-to-reach groups – must feel included and that this should be an integral and ongoing process throughout the period of New Deal and beyond into local government mechanisms more generally. In addition the government was to 'give' to communities by making funding more accessible to locally-based community organisations and putting around £2 billion into the worst performing neighbourhoods over a ten-year period. This approach certainly indicated that the government was committed to involving the community in ways hitherto unseen. As I wrote in 2002 concerning the setting up of CDRPs:

> The particular rhetoric which has accompanied this move, and which has been perceived as driving policy in this direction, strongly suggests that crime should no longer be dealt with by 'expert' agencies and individuals alone but that the involvement of community-based organisations and individuals who are, after all, closer to the experiences of victimisation are better placed to find solutions. (Evans 2002: 12)

Indeed, in 2003 David Blunkett authored a pamphlet entitled *Active Citizens, Strong Communities: Progressing Civil Renewal* in which he set out his vision for the regeneration of civic pride and his agenda for action in this area. In this he restates the significance of local knowledge and expertise suggesting that this is absolutely essential to the success of interventions at the local level. Communities' expertise lies, for Blunkett, in their situated knowledge and experience of day-to-day life in their neighbourhood. Communities, he writes, 'have the networks, the knowledge, the sense of what is actually possible, and the ability to make solutions stick' (Home Office Communication Directorate 2003: 3). Indeed, he restated a number of times within the booklet the importance of the state's role in guiding and giving support to local communities. The pamphlet's message is steeped in 'the Third Way' ideology and in its rejection of too much state intervention but also stresses the importance of not leaving communities to cope by themselves. It is strong in its vision of an enabling and supportive state working alongside an engaged and participating civic polis.

To bring about this crucial partnership between state and citizen Blunkett suggests that:

There are three crucial ingredients:

- Active Citizenship: citizens should be given more opportunities and support to become actively involved in defining and tackling the problems of their communities and improving their quality of life.

- Strengthened Communities: communities should be helped to form and sustain their own organisations, bringing people together to deal with their common concerns.
- Partnership in Meeting Public Needs: public bodies, within the established democratic framework, should involve citizens and communities more effectively in improving the planning and delivery of public services.

(Home Office Communication Directorate 2003: 3)

Around this visionary statement of intent he exposes what he considers to be the reality of community life. In his call to build communities built on respect, mutuality, solidarity and tolerance where people take responsibility for their own lives he exposes his belief that he considers these values to be currently lacking. Indeed, Blunkett paints a picture of cynical and disinterested communities which shirk their responsibilities and civic duties and which are led by consumerist values and the demand for instant gratification. Hughes notes this tendency for communities to be framed in both negative and positive terms – as he puts it as both the breeders of and the prophylactic against crime and disorder (Hughes 2007: 110). Indeed, it is interesting to note that a section of Blunkett's treatise on active citizenship specifically links civil renewal to these law and order issues – to the work of the Home Office on the reform of the police and the need to work within CDRPs to reduce crime and anti-social behaviour. The active citizen, he suggests, would be involved in their local Neighbourhood Watch scheme, a Special Constable and/or engaged with systems of community-based criminal justice.

That so much of Blunkett's discussion of active citizenship is linked to the policy around preventing offending is testament to how central the crime agenda became within the government's focus on community involvement. However, this focus on the effect of offending within communities, together with Blunkett's somewhat dystopian view of community as fragmented, mistrusting and crime-ridden, severely impinged on the promise to deliver on a vision of positive, community-centred and local, governance. It is time now to look at the second part of Khan's first question which is crucial to this process. He asks 'what are you prepared to give?' to achieve community involvement. From the research to date it appears that the government was actually prepared to 'give', to concede, very little.

## Whom do we trust?

One of the first priorities for building partnership working and to engage communities within an agenda for change is to sustain or to build mutually trusting relationships between partners. However, centrally the government developed a number of policies which might be considered destructive of any trust which might have been in existence.

Five years into NDC Paul Lawless, while heading up the national consortium undertaking the government-funded evaluation of NDC uncovered a shocking level of distrust in both the local council and NDC partnerships among residents in many of the NDC areas. Only around an average of 40 per cent of respondents offered 'a great deal' or a 'fair amount' of trust in their local councils and only slightly more in their NDC partnerships. Levels of trust in these bodies appeared to be affected by local conditions in that they varied widely from 62 per cent of those surveyed in Sunderland offering 'a great deal' or a 'fair amount' of trust, to only 18 per cent in Walsall (Lawless 2004: 388–9). As Lawless iterates:

> None of this should be seen as at all surprising … These are disadvantaged areas where there has often been a steady deterioration in economic opportunities and social infrastructure. Partly as result, residents tend to lose a degree of trust in local institutions. (2004: 388)

As Lawless implies, and Misztal has previously outlined, trust has to be earned and any intervention in the areas most affected by neo-liberal economic and social policies which degenerated as a result of consistent neglect needed to be mindful of this fact. While the Labour election manifesto for 1997 explicitly acknowledged that after eighteen years of Conservative government 'People *are* cynical about politics and distrustful of political promises' (Labour Party 1997; emphasis in original) there followed nothing in subsequent New Labour literature which recognised that trusting relationships had to be carefully rebuilt. It is as if New Labour expected their new political broom to sweep such old feelings of mistrust away; after all, they were not the Conservatives. However, in neighbourhoods which had long seen their needs ignored, opportunities limited and aspirations thwarted by those charged to consider the best future for the country it is hardly surprising that their residents did not wholeheartedly embrace the new incumbents in power.[2] In addition many were situated in local council areas in which the Labour Party had held the majority of councillors for some time and some of the local conditions of suspicion and mistrust of politicians would have been forged between local residents and sitting Labour councillors. Offering trust in the organs of local politics and the vision of the New Labour government was by no means automatic. However, as Gilling and others have observed, trust is a key concept in the motivation to build sustained, co-operative relationships and networks (Evans 2004, Gilling 2007, Misztal 1996) and without it there can be no real and sustained partnership.

## Who does the government trust?

In the early period of New Labour there was hope that this time things would be different, that communities would be listened to and that finally a government was in place that was committed to local action and which valued and encouraged input from local people. It is worth quoting Foley and Martin in full, for their early analysis of NDC typifies this optimistic assessment. They wrote that:

> Previous initiatives have been criticised for the way in which competition for funding and the tight deadlines for submission of bids have militated against genuine community involvement. Statutory agencies have often taken the lead in preparing bids, with communities being brought in at a much later stage to help implement plans over which they have little or no influence. Under the New Deal for Communities the competitive element has been eliminated and the chances of genuine community involvement from the outset have been increased by allowing longer lead-in times in which to develop bids and by the provision of funding to support the development of proposals. Moreover, unlike previous policies, outputs can be specified at different stages over a maximum of ten years rather than having to be defined at the outset. Partnerships have to be able to demonstrate that communities have been involved in both the selection of target areas and the development of programmes, and ministers have referred back several bids that were seen as lacking sufficient local input. The insistence that 'many of the pathfinders will be run by bodies who have not traditionally led regeneration programmes' (SEU 1998: 54) does seem to be having an impact locally. Phase 2 of the New Deal for Communities has involved unprecedented levels of consultation through outreach workers, public meetings and household surveys. Some delivery plans include proposals for community based research and much greater formative evaluation than in the past. There have also been greater opportunities for networking between activists in the different target areas and a widespread feeling on the ground that 'there is permission to do things differently'. (Foley and Martin 2000: 483–4)

Labour appeared to be hitting all the right buttons, but as its crime reduction agenda fully unfolded these early promises of local freedom gave way to a much more authoritarian and enforced 'steering' from the centre. Foley and Martin praised the 1999 Local Government Act for ensuring that local authorities were made more accountable to their service users, that they publish performance plans and consult more widely. Foley and Martin saw the Best Value regimes as 'enabling local people to hold councils to account, and ensure that they are using their funds more efficiently' but they also recommended caution. For this early promise to be realised, they argued, local authorities, and indeed the central government departments, would have to give up some of their powers to communities and local residents would have to accept much greater responsibilities onto their shoulders – perhaps more than they were able or willing to take on. In addition neighbourhood strategies could never really counter wider structural causes of poverty, unemployment, discrimination and exclusion yet the government continued to demand quick-fix solutions and demonstrable change. The government was wedded to an agenda of change and improvement which placed heavy burdens on communities within local partnerships and which demanded wide-scale changes which local initiatives, however vibrant, simply could not bring about on their own. However, underperformance was treated as lack of interest and commitment at the local level, with the result that more targets were set and more 'guidelines' published.

## From community ownership to centralised management

Time has shown that the government could not in the end relinquish its old, top-down management style. As Lawless reflects: 'in its first five years, NDC has evolved from a model based loosely on "decentralisation, local negotiation, and introversion" to one more clearly rooted in "centrally imposed, locally effected, performance management"' (2004: 396). The government started with a vision of cross-cutting and decentralised services, many based in and developed by the local communities which they were to serve. Listening to and learning from the very communities which had been affected by years of social and political exclusion, services would be 'joined up' to present solutions to complex, inter-linked and interdependent problems faced by individuals and neighbourhoods. Paradoxically however, the government considered that to get all local authorities and public services working within their conceptual framework required a degree of coercion and control which stifled the communities' very freedom to innovate and to become directly involved in decision-making, which according to the government's own rhetoric, was supposed to be the very basis of their strength and legitimation (2001). This paradox lay at the heart of much of New Labour intervention in local decision-making – how to give neighbourhoods and local people the power to choose exactly what the government wanted them to!

## Concluding comments

The government's commitment to community-driven policy formation did not unfold as a progressive and inclusive programme of change and can be criticised in a number of ways. While constantly restating the importance of community to the success of the government's agenda to regenerate and strengthen local neighbourhoods, government documents never actually outlined what was meant by the term 'community'. The term can refer not only to local communities of place, but also to where individuals are attached to particular sets of values or interests and can be used to exclude as well as to include (Wilmott 1986). In the government's appeal to community, however, was no sense that different interest groups may have competing or mutually exclusive demands. Communities were instead considered as positive and cohesive units whose members would fundamentally agree on a way forward, and that this way forward would chime with the government aspirations. This approach was flawed in two fundamental ways.

First, it should be recognised that the community safety rather than more mainstream crime reduction agendas has always acknowledged that minority and marginalised groups exist within communities and that their particular experiences and values may be lost to mainstream agendas. The young, the elderly, black and minority ethnic (BME) groups, LGBT communities[3] and women have all at various times been ignored or threatened by existing normative frameworks which have routinely discriminated and excluded them from full participation in community life. Neighbourhoods can also be riven with intra-community conflicts which make common working fraught with difficulties and divisions. All this suggests that 'communities' do not always speak with one voice, that any mechanisms to 'speak to' or 'listen' to local residents must give different voices an opportunity to be heard and that competing perspectives can and should be incorporated into local plans. This refusal to engage with the realities of community life was an obvious and dangerous omission with profound implications for the success of government directives (Crawford 1998, Walklate and Evans 1999).

Second, the government's expressed commitment to strengthening and building communities fit for the twenty-first century foundered on a more fundamental contradiction. The government appeared simply unable to relinquish its power to local or community sources. New Labour's communitarianism was built on a strong sense of moral authority which was driven from the centre. The 'Third Way' demands a loosening of the state's hold on policy agendas but New Labour politicians were keen to drive forward their agendas, their initiatives and their policies as rapidly as possible. In order to make a mark in their first term of office, to prove New Labour as a departure from old ways of thinking, they did not allow a thorough, considered consultation and response to concerns on the ground. Furthermore, while the government was ideologically inclined to pull back from the state-driven welfare policies of old and to replace these with a new layer of civic organisation they shackled the emerging bodies with required outcomes and objectives. Success was measured, not by locally-driven goals but by the need to be seen to deliver on centrally-imposed directives. As this approach was rolled out the contradictions within it became clearer – the government did not trust 'enabled' communities to deliver what each community partnership was required to do. The response was therefore to closely direct change from above. While this approach was problematic from the beginning the establishment of the state as director and enforcer of change became even more problematic as the New Labour government faced more difficult and unforeseen challenges in subsequent years.

━━━━━━━━━━━━━━━━━━━━━━━━ FURTHER READING ━━━━━━━━━━━━━━━━━━━━━━━━

Crawford, A. (1997) *The Local Governance of Crime: Appeals to Community and Partnerships.* Oxford: Clarendon Press.

Hughes, G. (1996) 'Communitarianism and law and order', *Critical Social Policy*, 16: 17–41.

━━━━━━━━━━━━━━━━━━━━━━━━━ NOTES ━━━━━━━━━━━━━━━━━━━━━━━━━

1 Lawless also highlights the problems of time, commitment, burnout and the fact that some community members show interest in partnership repeatedly while others never do so.
2 According to Lawless 'Twenty-nine of the thirty-nine NDC areas would fall within the 10% most deprived wards in England and all but two within the most deprived 20%' (2004: 388).
3 For an exploration of issues surrounding the Lesbian, Gay, Bisexual and Transgender (LGBT) community's experiences of community safety see McGhee (2006).

# 4

# Shifting the control culture

As we have seen in the previous chapters, as New Labour's approach to the prevention of crime rolled out it became increasingly top-down and managerial in its emphasis. The early promises to combat the effects of social exclusion using community expertise and commitment coexisted with a clear agenda to enforce a particular way of reading and dealing with the problem of crime. The criminal justice net was widened, its mesh thinned and, to stretch Cohen's anology to breaking point, the boat was steered towards previously unfished waters adding the 'new problem' (Hughes 2007) of anti-social behaviour to the governmental lexicon.[1] As their second term of office from June 2001 began to unfold the government's fervour in this area only increased. New Labour appeared to be less concerned with exclusion and to become more fixated on problems of the 'anti-social' individual and neighbourhood.

As ever there was more than one string to the government's interventionist bow. On the one hand they were to look for ever more inventive ways to re-engage lost communities (see Chapters 3 and 8), while on the other they were increasingly involved in law-making to manage and order the behaviour of individuals on the ground. While these two approaches might appear dissimilar at first glance, further exploration shows that they both emanated from the government's desire to closely manage 'problem' neighbourhoods and 'problem' individuals and to mould them more closely to the New Labour design. The result, in their perception, would be to create order out of chaos, to cut people off from the criminogenic individuals and communities blighting their lives and to create their communitarian dream of neighbourhoods built on trust and mutuality, politically engaged and imbued with a sense of shared values, collective understanding and social justice. To enforce this eventual social compliance, however, New Labour turned to some extremely authoritarian means, placing firm conditions on attaining the eventual prize of inclusion (Hughes 1996).

Some of the key aspects of the punitive measures adopted by the government to address these 'new' problems are discussed in some detail below and the distinctive approach adopted by New Labour is further examined and explored.

## The anti-social behaviour order

According to Burney (2002: 469) anti-social behaviour orders ('asbos') were introduced into legislation partly as a result of pressure from Labour-controlled local authorities which found themselves using inadequate civil powers to deal with 'problem tenants' in council housing causing tensions and difficulties between themselves and their neighbours. They were not intended to deal with any behaviour that was criminal in intent and practice but were to capture behaviour which was nevertheless a nuisance to others and when persistent in nature could clearly disrupt the victim's quality of life. Burney characterises the 'asbo' as 'a right idea that went wrong from the start' (2005: vii). When Labour was the party of opposition, she argues, their rightful concern to protect individuals and communities from the intimidating behaviour of a few individuals became, when in office, a 'punitive line in rhetoric and legislation' (2005: 10). 'Asbos' were a right idea, she posits because there were clearly documented cases of individuals creating havoc in their neighbourhoods and in such a way that it was sometimes difficult, although not impossible, to find a solution using existing laws. However, the rhetorical and legislative onslaught on this sub-criminal behaviour, she continues, served only to increase a generalised sense of disquiet and a widely-held feeling that the moral and social fabric of British society was in danger of collapsing into utter disorder and anarchy.

As we have seen the 'asbo' was brought into existence through one of the first key pieces of legislation which the Labour government brought into effect, the Crime and Disorder Act 1998. So keen was the government to act on the problem that this highly significant and far-reaching legislative measure became operational in April 1999 before the Social Exclusion Unit's Policy Action Team (PAT 8) on anti-social behaviour had even reported. As a consequence PAT 8's message that enforcement would not work on its own and its emphasis on prevention and resettlement was not reflected in the legislation. Once on the statute books the 'asbo' became more far-reaching than was its original intention and was strengthened little by little at each stage of its enforcement. First, government guidance was altered to gradually lower the age at which 'asbos' should be considered; from initially suggesting they should be used only against adults (and children working alongside them) to accepting their routine use for children of twelve years and upwards. Subsequently, some councils and police began to use 'asbos' to curb the behaviour of young people whom they suspected of crimes but where this could not be proven in the criminal courts. Courts began to impose 'asbos' for behaviour which they were not initially designed to tackle, for example issuing 'asbos' to street sex workers in order to remove prostitution from certain areas. In addition precedents were set which allowed for the use of hearsay evidence and the testimony of professional witnesses in magistrate's courts hearing cases for 'asbos'. This general 'creep' of the legislation into unintended areas meant the 'asbo' was in danger of becoming a very different creature than was first intended. Subsequent legislation began to confirm its changing nature and endorse this in legal terms.

After PAT 8 reported in 2000 the Home Office was given primary responsibility for co-ordinating action against anti-social behaviour, and each local authority district was *required* to appoint a named person to take forward action locally. These measures ensured that 'asbos' stayed firmly within the government's field of view and political agenda and also that local authorities could not ignore them as a possible remedy for too long. In addition the Criminal Justice and Police Act 2001 introduced the idea of 'on the spot' fines for disorderly or nuisance behaviour by adults. The background to this was a reported 8 per cent rise in violent crime which was blamed on misuse of alcohol and a general 'yob culture'. Penalty Notices were introduced which, much like a speeding or parking ticket, could be issued immediately by the police and which imposed fines for a number of behaviours such as being drunk and disorderly, or throwing fireworks. Blair initially suggested that offenders should be marched to cash-points to pay their fines straight away but this suggestion was widely ridiculed and quietly dropped. Nevertheless, refusal to pay the fines meant an appearance at court. The legislation also extended local child curfew schemes to those under 16 years of age and allowed that these could be applied for by a senior police officer.

The Police Reform Act 2002 was also used to strengthen the 'asbo' and widen its use. Henceforth an individual's behaviour could be curbed anywhere in the whole of England and Wales, not only within the local authority area in which the behaviour took place. This Act also allowed any criminal conviction or county court judgment to be accompanied by an 'asbo' (the so-called 'crasbo'). The Act also allowed for interim restraining orders to be made before a court was able to meet to discuss an 'asbo' and added housing associations and other social landlords to the list of those who could apply to the court for such an order to be placed on their tenants. Once the Police Reform Act relaxed the conditions which had to be met before the authorities could apply to the courts for an order to be issued, the police were instrumental in driving up the number of 'asbos' issued (Burney 2005). They were then routinely used, Burney argues, to extend control over persistent offenders and 'crasbos' were often added on to sentences awarded in the criminal courts to further curtail offenders' freedom of movement and action once their sentence for the criminal offence had expired.

Burney's research showed that the 'asbo' and child curfews were actually little used by local authorities or the police in their first three years. Both Jack Straw and David Blunkett[2] when in the role of Home Secretary urged a greater recourse to the use of these legal powers and began to build the 'asbo edifice' (Gilling 2007: 133–40) to greater heights. Hughes suggests that the fact that they were championed by only a minority of councils and that the majority of local authorities limited their use demonstrated a classic adaptive response – predicted by Garland (2001) – to an increase in punitive sanctions which most practitioners actually wished to quietly resist (Hughes 2007: 123–4). However, from 2003 the number of 'asbos' issued started to rise incrementally. At the end of their first two years from April 1999 only 317 had been issued but by the end of December 2006 this had increased to over 12,600.[3] There is no definitive explanation for this more ready recourse to use of the 'asbo'. Campbell's review of 'asbos' for the Home Office in 2002 suggested that a major problem which held some councils back from using the order was the time and money which it took to issue an 'asbo', while Burney's research in the same year found that most councils were happy to use already available, tried and trusted, civil remedies such as housing legislation. The Housing Act of 1996 already allowed for introductory tenancies – which give social landlords the protection of a probation-ary period before full tenant's rights were awarded – and they always had recourse to eviction of any difficult tenants. In addition local government powers awarded from 1972 allowed civil proceedings to be taken out against problem tenants. Furthermore, environmental health legislation already allowed action to be taken against noisy neighbours and it appears that local authorities preferred to use these alternative remedies. Burney further argued that the legal requirement that police and local authorities consult with other agencies before issuing an 'asbo' had the unintended consequence of reducing their use. When agencies got together to dis-cuss the behaviour of particular individuals they were able to identify possible reasons for their troublesome behaviour and were thereby able to find solutions which meant that recourse to the law was often unnecessary. In some cases a solu-tion was found in better health-care and support packages involving psychiatric intervention or treatment for addiction to drugs and alcohol. Nevertheless, the anti-crime agenda was placed ahead of those of health and social support and the gov-ernment continued to issue further advice and legislative reforms continued to 'steer', or more accurately 'push', local authorities towards use of 'asbos' (Burney 2005), leading Hughes to conclude that:

> At both the national and sub-national levels of governance ... the exponential rise of governmental anti-social behaviour agendas would not seem to be about finding 'evidence-based' measures which can be shown to 'work'. Instead they may serve more complex and less easily measurable political ends. (2007: 125)

In January 2003 the government established an Anti-Social Behaviour Unit within the Home Office. The express intention of this Unit was to encourage the use of 'asbos' by publicising 'best practice' in their use. In September that year a national day count of recorded instances of anti-social behaviour was conducted and in October an Anti-Social Behaviour Action Plan was published which offered additional funding and support to initiatives set up to tackle such behav-iour. The government also developed the *Taking a Stand* award to recognise com-munities and individuals involved in exceptional action against anti-social behaviour. Local authorities finally began to get 'on message' and develop their own units to tackle anti-social behaviour – perhaps attracted by the promise of additional funds.

## The Anti-Social Behaviour Act 2003

Soon after the Anti-Social Behaviour Unit came on stream the government published a white paper *Respect and Responsibility – Taking a Stand Against Anti-Social Behaviour* (Home Office 2003) followed closely by the Anti-Social Behaviour Act 2003 which added further to the anti-social behaviour edifice – extending it way beyond its initial intended audience. First, the government used the 2003 Act to extend existing remedies – the Housing Act 1996 was amended to require all social landlords to put in place and to publish policy and procedures to tackle anti-social behaviour. In addition the 2003 Act made exclusion or eviction of tenants for anti-social behaviour easier and quicker to achieve adding 'anti-social behaviour injunctions' to the list of measures which could be used. In addition some of the sections of the 1998 Crime and Disorder Act were made more far-reaching. Parenting orders, for example, were extended so that the courts could now require parents to attend counselling or guidance programmes, sometimes as a residential course. The 2003 Act widened the range of authorities which could use Crime and Disorder Act measures as a legislative tool. Parents could now be made to enter into a parenting contract with their child's school which might stipulate that the parent ensured their child's full attendance and schools could now also apply for parenting orders if this was felt to be in the interests of the pupil. In addition failure to enter into a parenting contract with the school could be taken into account by the courts if they were considering issuing a parenting order. Parenting contracts could also now be employed where a child had been referred to a youth offending team (YOT) and YOTs could also apply for parenting orders if it was thought this would prevent the child from engaging in further acts of criminal or anti-social behaviour. Again failure to enter into a parenting contract with a YOT could be taken into account by the courts when considering an application for a parenting order.

In addition the 2003 Act placed in legislation a range of new powers. Dispersal orders were introduced so that in any area where anti-social behaviour was considered a persistent problem, the local authority could give the local police dispersal powers in an area for a period of up to six months (this authorisation could then be renewed). It was stipulated that any authorisation given must be advertised locally after which groups of two or more young people under 16 could be ordered to disperse if it was thought they may be causing anyone to be intimidated, harassed, alarmed or distressed. Furthermore, if the dispersed young people were not from the area they could be prohibited from returning to it for up to 24 hours and be removed by the police to their usual place of residence. It was not made necessary that orders to disperse be given in writing, a verbal order would suffice, however any breach could be punished by a fine or up to three months in prison. Further powers came into existence after 9pm at night when anyone under the age of 16 'not under the effective control of a parent or guardian' could be stopped by the police and taken back to wherever they lived. All these powers were extended to include possible authorisation to community support officers as well as the British Transport Police whereas previously such orders could only be issued by police constables. Furthermore, the police, on application to a magistrate's court, were given the power to close any premises for up to three months where it was suspected that illegal Class A drugs were being used or if the premises were associated with disorder or nuisance to neighbours. These closure powers applied to residential as well as commercial premises and were commonly seen to relate to the use of properties for the selling and using of crack cocaine.

The 2003 Act further extended the use of fixed penalty notices. These could now be issued to those of 16 and 17 years of age and, with attendant fixed fines, to parents of persistent truants and those caught daubing graffiti or fly-posting. Again the range of personnel who could use these legislative powers was widened to any head teachers, employees of the education authority, or member of the school or college staff authorised so to do. This move to use fixed penalty notices to mete out 'justice' was particularly controversial and was specifically heralded as a means by which the court system could be circumvented (Burney 2005: 36). This was quick and dirty law enforcement which brought with it much criticism but which was nevertheless pushed through into law with much fanfare and publicity. Also incorporated in the 2003 Act was a mish-mash of additional measures such as adding the power of arrest to injunctions to prevent nuisance or annoyance, extending powers of police civilians to stop cyclists committing offences under the Highways Act 1835, giving local authorities further powers to close noisy premises and to deal with graffiti, fly-tipping, litter – and high hedges!

In drafting and pushing through the 2003 Act the government had clearly signalled its intention to continue along its initial punitive vein despite much criticism which cautioned restraint and raised concerns about the human rights' implications of the drive against this ill-defined and poorly researched 'problem' of anti-social behaviour. Signalled too was the government's intention to extend the practice of disorder prevention deeper into the work of public authorities and away from being the sole responsibility of local police forces.

## Creating the 'cultural shift'

This rolling out and down of the anti-social behaviour agenda and the creation of new tiers of crime control meant that the government had to find ways to push its agenda on anti-social behaviour further down to the local level. Coercion was tried[4] but could only go so far and as Hughes and others have demonstrated it met some resistance (Creaton 2003, Edwards and Hughes 2008, Nash and Ryan

2003). It was thought better to 'engender a cultural shift' (Home Office 2003: 16) and win over the hearts and minds of the different partner organisations apparent at each tier of governance and crime reduction activity. The *Together Action Plan* and subsequent Together campaign were designed to do just this. The 2003 Together campaign was heralded as 'a national campaign that takes a stand against anti-social behaviour and puts the needs of the community first' (Home Office 2003: 3).

The government's enforcement agenda was clearly set out in the *Together Action Plan*. 'All local authorities, police forces and other key agencies', it stated, 'will be expected to enforce clear standards of behaviour and will be given the tools to do so' (Home Office 2003: 5). Its main thrust was to put in place a new infrastructure of support to public professionals working within Crime and Disorder Reduction Partnerships (CDRPs). The Together campaign was to have its own website and call centre entitled ActionLine for practitioners throughout England and Wales to gain access to the latest information on methods used to tackle anti-social behaviour and to allow better networking opportunities. A roaming Together Academy would further extend the possibilities for practitioners to meet with each other, access training and work together to find solutions and share best practice. Additional funds were to be made available to CDRPs and in turn each would have to demonstrate that they were tackling anti-social behaviour effectively and strategically.

At the neighbourhood level Together Action Areas were established and Nuisance Neighbour Panels were set up consisting of representatives from local agencies, the police, local authority and relevant voluntary sector organisations which could each 'nominate' households to come before them. Four local authority areas were to become 'trailblazers' in tackling nuisance neighbours (Home Office 2003: 16) and each had to work with a minimum number of households. These families would be subject to intensive interventions and programmes of behaviour modification. Operations Scrub-it (graffiti), Scrap-it (abandoned cars) and Gate-it (alleyways) were initiated to improve the quality of the local environmental, with an obvious reference to Wilson and Kelling's (1982) contested theory of 'Broken Windows' which suggested that small signs of disorder would lead to greater problems if left unchecked.

Alongside the usual concerns with nuisance neighbours, graffiti, abandoned cars, environmental clean-ups and witness protection the Action Plan included the promise of firm action against begging, thus placing this activity carried out by the poorest in society, most often as a last recourse to obtain much needed funds, as firmly within the anti-social canon and as something which should not be tolerated; and this by a Unit whose director had previously worked alongside the homeless for many years. This crackdown on begging would affect the most vulnerable in society – the asylum seekers forbidden by government legislation to seek work and given reduced welfare benefit payments, refugees who had failed in their attempts to gain asylum status and with no entitlement to benefits but who were nevertheless loathe to return to their country of origin, the homeless itinerant individual moving to new areas to seek work and without access to emergency benefits and people with emotional, psychological and learning difficulties who had dropped through the welfare net.[5] In the Action Plan, however, begging was closely associated, not with poverty and desperation, but with drug-taking and criminality and targets for its reduction were clearly set, again using 'trailblazing areas'. Begging was cast as a 'problem street culture' (Home Office 2003: 25) and made a recordable offence and a range of penalties introduced for persistent offenders.

The *Together Action Plan* also signalled the government's intention to require the police to follow a National Policing Plan within which tackling anti-social behaviour would be identified as a policing priority and performance to this end would be monitored. Furthermore, a National Reassurance Project would be piloted in 16 areas where 'signal crimes' and disorder incidents, that is those which tend through their visibility to increase fear of crime in an area, would be prioritised. The legal system would not be untouched either. The government set up a team of anti-social behaviour prosecutors within the Crown Prosecution Service to specialise in these prosecutions and to issue guidance and protocols to the rest of the service and sentencing guidelines for breaches of 'asbos' were introduced for the first time.

Through all these measures incorporated within the *Together Action Plan* the government widened the scope of its definition of anti-social behaviour, driving this down to all partner organisations and insisting that its agenda was taken up throughout the criminal justice system, police service and both central and local government departments. At the same time the scope of different organisations, neighbourhoods and authorities to come to their own definitions, outline their own concerns and proffer their own solutions was severely curtailed. The 'Together' in this Action Plan was an injunction to all to work within the government's guidelines and to their specified agenda. The story of the introduction of legislation to combat anti-social behaviour in the UK certainly seems to follow Cohen's seminal analysis published in 1985 of the changing social control agenda, which suggested that the *management* of groups considered deviant or potentially so, has overtaken rule-breaking as the prime reason for intervention (Brown 2004).

## Restructuring from the centre: command and control

Another technique used to ensure the 'cultural shift' deemed necessary by the government was the use of managerial controls through the requirement and exercise of audits. As Stenson and Edwards (2003) discovered, by 2003 it was clear that, 'the New Labour administration has been anxious to realize its modernization programme through reinforcing centralized control, placing faith in the managerialist procedures of performance management, target setting and auditing' (2003: 214). Paradoxically New Labour's turn to a local governance of crime meant pushing a centralised agenda much harder than their predecessors had been able to. Pushing its crime control agenda down to lower levels meant losing a degree of centralised control over the design and delivery of services. The central state apparatus could no longer be completely sure that the necessary and vital work it was funding was being carried out to an acceptable standard. It was therefore felt necessary to more closely and regularly monitor, audit and measure the work of those organisations to which the central government's previous roles and functions had been devolved (Nash and Ryan 2003). This monitoring role returned a great deal of power back to the centre which had the authority to remove funding from those partnerships and organisations which, in their eyes, did not come up to standard or were not working in the way the centre intended. This process was so successful that Stenson and Edwards concluded that 'Ironically, local partnerships had greater discretion under former Conservative administrations to define the scope and content of community governance' (2003: 214).

## The new youth justice

In pursuing its agenda of 'cultural shift' the government restructured a whole array of statutory services to meet its revised needs. Youth services were some of the first to feel the 'modernising' hand of New Labour. The Crime and Disorder Act 1998 transformed the underlying basis of the youth justice system for the whole of England and Wales.[6] This Act ensured that the 'principal aim' of the youth justice system would be to prevent offending by children and young persons. Previous to this legislation the prevention of offending was only one of the aims of the youth justice system. The care of young people in trouble, together with their resettlement and support were also seen as equally underpinning all its work. As Bottoms and Dignan (2004) outlined, the approach of the youth justice system was previously characterised as one of 'minimum intervention' but New Labour wanted swift and efficient administration of justice, the adoption of punitive sanctions and the respon-sibilisation of young children and their parents to be the new hallmarks of quality in the youth justice system. In order to ensure this outcome a wholesale reorganisation of the youth justice system was proposed and the new organs of criminal justice for young people were designed to incorporate the New Labour vision.

The Crime and Disorder Act of 1998 required all local authorities to establish Youth Offending Teams which by statute were compelled to include officers from the local authority social services department, the probation service and the police as well as from the local health and education authorities. Each of these organisa-tions was driven by the delivery of particular services and had developed markedly different ways of working, organisational practices and philosophy but were required to work together with the common aim of preventing the offending of young people (Paylor and Simmill-Binning 2004). As Pitts observed in 2001 this multi-disciplinary amalgamation of service-providers could have had beneficial effects and acted as a catalyst for positive change but the resulting partnerships were allowed to work only within very narrow confines. Many of these were set by annual Youth Justice Plans which the 1998 Act required local authorities to draft, in consultation with other relevant agencies in order to set out (a) how youth justice services in their area would be provided and funded and (b) how the youth offending team in the area would operate and what functions they would carry out.

In addition the 1998 Act established a central body to oversee the implementation of youth justice in England and Wales – the Youth Justice Board. Although not technically a department within the government its members were to be appointed by the Home Secretary to monitor the operation of the youth justice system and the provision of youth justice services; to suggest how the principal aim of the service should be pursued; to set national standards for the provision of youth justice services; put forward examples of good practice and monitor the work of YOTs locally.[7]

According to Bottoms and Dignan:

> The changes that have been made to the youth justice system in England and Wales have not been confined to institutional reforms and responsibilities but also extend to the youth justice process itself. Indeed, the system as a whole has been so significantly altered since 1998 that it is often referred to as the 'New Youth Justice'. (2004: 78)

The 'New Youth Justice' was not built on the philosophical foundations of the old but was constructed around New Labour's very different agenda which left all agencies involved with a much tighter and closely prescribed room in which to function. Pitts (2001: 174) describes how the net-widening effect of the 1998 legislation, together with its drive to cut the time spent in taking young people through the court process, so increased the workload of the youth justice system that the time available for care and rehabilitation of young offenders was severely jeopardised. YOTs became places for the processing of Court Orders which were so closely prescribed that they took away all discretion and professional judgement from the YOT worker. Bottoms and Dignan's research further demonstrates how the available options for dealing with young offenders were tightly restricted after 1998. Previously the police could, and often did, issue young people with a number of reprimands and formal cautions before taking the much more serious step of charging and referring them to the courts. After 1998 reprimands could only be given for first offences, young people were more likely to be given 'final warnings' (which were actually their first warning too) and referred to their YOT for further assessment. Any subsequent offence would be dealt with through the courts.

## The 'new' probation service

The Probation Service for England and Wales was also changed immeasurably as a result of government intervention after 1998. While the government continued to pay lip-service to the extension of community control in the fight against crime, local control and autonomy were gradually removed from this service (McKnight 2009). The Probation Service had previously come under a great deal of criticism in government circles. It was considered to be part of the 'excuse culture' which Jack Straw had seemingly detected back in the late 1990s wherein offending behaviour had been inadequately addressed through the criminal justice system and in which young offenders in particular were repeatedly warned and cautioned rather than dealt with more severely or brought before the courts. The Probation Service had developed an approach which was closer to the welfare than the punishment model and had knowingly and strategically distanced itself from the more punitive end of the penal establishment although working closely with and within prisons and correctional institutions (Nash and Ryan 2003: 158). This was no longer acceptable to New Labour and its new 'tough on crime' stance. Through its Prisons and Probation Review of 1997 and subsequent report *Joining Forces to Protect the Public* (Home Office 1998) it began to take steps to transform the ways in which the probation service worked, to join the service up to the correctional establishment and to drag it closer towards punishment and away from care and resettlement (Nellis 1999).

Initially the review of prisons and probation suggested that the Prison and Probation Services should be combined. This proposal received such forceful opposition that it had to be dropped. Nevertheless, the Criminal Justice and Court Services Act 2000, with the intention of bringing the different elements of the criminal justice system together, restructured the probations service into 42 areas which were coterminous with those covered by the different local police forces and the Crown Prosecution Service (Nash and Ryan 2003). Each area was assigned a local probation board, appointed in the main part and wholly directed by the Home Secretary who was also given the power to disband and replace any which were deemed to be failing. In addition a national director was appointed to lead the probation service and to represent it more closely in government circles. For Nash and Ryan these changes brought about under the slogan of 'strong centre, strong local' were in actuality a smokescreen for the imposition of increasingly restrictive national guidelines which permitted very little deviation or discretion. In 2004 the Carter Report revisited the controversial proposal to join prison and probation services together proposing the National Offender Management Service (NOMS) to bring prisons and probation 'under a common umbrella' (McKnight 2009: 333). The resultant structures were designed to bring 'contestability' or competition between public and private providers into both arms of the service. There then followed a period of some instability as from 2004 to 2008, according to McKnight, no less than seven possible restructuring proposals for the Probation Service were placed on the table, the final accepted structure resulting in the Probation Service becoming, according to McKnight, no more than 'just the small community wing of the Prison Service' (2009: 337).

The government also intervened in the methods which the Probation Service could use to achieve its goals. In 1998 a report, *Strategies for Effective Offender*

*Supervision*, commissioned by the Chief Inspector of Probation during the previous Conservative administration, was published. The then Chief Inspector of Probation hailed it as 'one of the most important reports it [HMIP] has ever produced'. This report argued that intervention to reduce offending should follow guidelines of *Effective Practice* which were becoming internationally recognised as successful in reducing offending. Following the doubling of crime which had occurred in Britain across the years of Conservative administration, this report was picked up as finally uncovering 'what works' in probation practice and heralding a new era in which crimes committed by known offenders might be reduced by 15–20 per cent. It was picked up by the Home Office as fitting with the Government's modernisation programme, and through its Effective Practice Initiative (EPI) launched in June 1998, it set the framework for probation practice for years to come 'requiring local probation services to draw up implementation plans aimed at transforming every aspect of practice to conform with the "what works" principles' (Furniss and Nutley 2000: 23).

Under the EPI each individual offender was to be assessed for their risk of re-offending and depending on the outcome of the assessment would be placed under an appropriate level of supervision. The OASys assessment tool was developed for the UK and relied on the scoring of both static (i.e. known and indisputable data on the offender such as numbers of convictions and age) and dynamic (i.e. less tangible or quantifiable information such as the offender's skills and abilities) to assess both the individual's likelihood of offending further and which of their needs should be addressed within which available supervision programmes. Both prison and probation services were required to adopt this new way of working, the results of which would be closely monitored and evaluated over ensuing years to keep abreast of which intervention packages were the most effective. In order to ensure this evaluation was meaningful, prison and probation services were required to use only accredited programmes of intervention with offenders and to ensure that the guidelines and training for each were followed to the letter (Furniss and Nutley 2000: 25). To this end the Home Office developed and accredited a 'core curriculum' of programmes for use by the Probation Service, some addressing the nature of particular types of offending, for example those geared towards motoring offences or racially motivated crimes and others which aimed to build up the skills-base of the offender. Cognitive behaviour therapy developing the individual's capacity to reflect on and learn from their experiences and pro-social behaviour modelling, based on reinforcement of positive behaviour towards others, featured heavily in the accredited programmes (Chapman and Hough 1998). As Furniss and Nutley (2000) recognised the move to evidence-based, nationally accredited programmes of work with offenders did not just add to or redesign the available programmes from which probation officers could choose but instead signalled a wholesale change in working practices, service objectives and the entire ethos of probation interventions, affecting 'every aspect of the supervising organization and its supporting environment' (2000: 23–4).

Furniss and Nutley outlined the significant cultural changes engendered by the requirement to adopt this wholesale approach. Henceforth the social harm and victimisation resulting from crime had to be foremost in the probation officer's mind rather than a consideration of the offender's own distress and the social and individual troubles which may have led to their offending. The Probation Service was required to consider the protection of the public and their demands for a safe environment as a key objective, shifting their initial focus away from the offender's needs and towards a harm minimisation model in which the probation service had to be seen to be taking effective action to reduce the risk of further victimisation – accountable to the public first and responding to public fears before the individual offender's needs. This approach took probation away from the values of befriending, building up trusting relationships between offender and probation officer and moved the service further towards a monitoring and enforcement role in which the offender must be seen to be taking up proffered solutions to their offending rather than working alongside the probation officer to problem-solve and design programmes tailored to their particular requirements. What the EPI approach also achieved was a loss of professional autonomy and a deskilling (Fitzgibbon 2008) of the probation officer who henceforth must work to a pre-scribed model of intervention. It also moved the focus away from the local social circumstances in which offending takes place and substituted a national framework for action which all local services had to apply. Perhaps most importantly the EPI approach took the probation service far away from a consideration of the structural elements which lie behind offending behaviour and away from a body of knowledge built up over the preceding decades which recognised the links between economic and social deprivation and offending. It marked instead the ascendancy of an individualised and psychologised approach to offending which suggested that if only the offender was helped to understand and reflect on their own responses to their environment and make better decisions that they would be able to alter their own behaviour and that crime rates in an area would be reduced as a consequence.

The National Offender Management Service was placed within the newly created Ministry of Justice[8] and proposed a new slogan for Probation of 'Punish, Help, Change and Control' which clearly placed the provision of services to offenders closer to the corrective side of the punishment–welfare continuum (Guilfoyle 2008). Nash and Ryan have been so concerned at these moves that they have concluded:

> The probation service 'as was' is being squeezed in all directions. Its training has been fundamentally changed, its management structure has been heavily centralized and its local base, at least at present, is open to question. Daily professional practice is guided heavily by national standards and the professional discretion of probation officers is becoming outdated. Probation policy is almost exclusively led by a range of cross-departmental committees operating at the heart of government. Certainly, now, strong centre appears to be winning out

over strong local. Although not yet formally a part of a unified corrections service, the probation service is certainly a very long way towards it. This revolution has been remarkably swift and is clever enough to have muted almost all opposition. (2003: 167)

## Partnerships and the 'new' privatisation

New Labour's crime control agenda required the inclusion of organisations and individuals working at the level of neighbourhood and community whether within the private, public or voluntary sector. These organisations were targeted through the local CDRPs in order to tap into local expertise and knowledge, to instil communitarian values and improve 'collective efficacy' (Morenoff et al. 2001). They were also useful in embedding a desired culture of crime control right the way through society to its grass-roots. New professional personnel such as community safety officers based with local authorities, anti-social behaviour officers employed within the social housing sector, community support officers working alongside the local police, neighbourhood wardens and private security personnel were all introduced into the mix. Alongside this growth in the number and range of public professionals engaged in community safety work the last decades have seen a sharp increase in the number of private security firms which have developed to cater for a rising demand for private security personnel. Public shopping malls have become semi-private spaces as security guards are paid to monitor who can enter them and for what purposes (Taylor et al. 1996), the massive growth in CCTV cameras on public streets and private spaces has necessitated a growth in the number of camera-watchers (Coleman 2004), more spaces in the night-time economy employ private security personnel and 'bouncers' and some more wealthy neighbourhoods have employed private security firms to patrol the streets to provide a visible deterrence to would-be offenders. Outside the ranks of the paid professional lie the volunteers working with organisations such as Victim Support and engaged and active citizens playing their part in police/community consultation groups, CDRPs, urban regeneration projects, setting up and running local campaigns, working with vulnerable youth and generally being good neighbours and watching out for the community. So running together with, and certainly not replacing, centralised state provision there was also achieved a micro-management of crime and as Burney has put it 'grass-roots social control' (Burney 2005: 31).

As the net of social control agents widened organisations developed to offer different public services have been brought into the realms of crime control. In April 2006, for example, the then Education Secretary Ruth Kelly suggested that schools become routinely involved in the testing of their pupils for illegal drug use after this had been piloted in a Kent school (*Guardian* 2006a). There were further suggestions in April 2008 that schools should keep records of their student's teenage pregnancy rates, drug problems, criminal records and obesity levels (*Guardian* 2008). This call, which emanated from the Department for Children, Schools and Families, obscures and elides the differences between concern for the welfare of pupils and their inclusion within an increasingly harsh and judgemental system of social control. It disingenuously suggests that the care and support of school students is commensurate with their surveillance, assessment and placement within categories of risk for the purposes of possible intervention to maintain the social order. These are not the same or even similar approaches although they have grown almost indistinguishable.

## Concluding comments

In the mid-twentieth century, from the 1960s and onwards, some organisations delivering social services began to develop as an important counter-measure to the hegemony of the state in constructing social order and control. A more radical viewpoint developed which considered issues of oppression and structural inequalities, as 'the public causes, which lay behind so many private troubles' (Lavalette and Ferguson 2007: 3). New theories of social control were developed by these more radical voices which began to see society as dominated by powerful and dominant social forces in the face of which many marginal groups and individuals were unable to make their voices heard or their life experiences understood. In the face of these dominant and overwhelmingly conservative social forces, the more radical social work traditions have struggled to ensure that alternative choices, lifestyles and behaviours be equally valued. Taking diversity into consideration, they further argued, could serve to open up state institutions to more progressive social forces, to challenge existing orthodoxies and to proffer more inclusive solutions to poverty, unemployment and fractured communities. These voices pushed forward the agenda of black and ethnic minority populations and presented minority and marginal lifestyles as valid accommodations to structural realities and inequalities. This alternative perspective was never popular with the state and its institutions and had to be carved out and maintained in the face of vehement opposition. These ideas were never universally accepted and normalised but they did manage, for a period of time, to influence mainstream social work and probation practices even in the face of much vilification and ridicule emanating from government circles and media campaigns during the right-wing backlash of the 1980s in Britain. Sensing a loss of public confidence in these measures the Labour governments of 1997 and beyond positioned themselves so as to be able to remove these hard won alternative perspectives at least from the repertoires of state-funded organisations and institutions. Following the lead of the previous Conservative administrations, New Labour continued to attack and to silence critical voices from within.

## FURTHER READING

Burney, E. (2002) 'Talking tough, acting coy: what happened to the anti-social behaviour order?', *Howard Journal*, 41: 469–84.

Nellis, M. (1999) 'Towards "the field of corrections": modernizing the probation service in the late 1990s', *Social Policy & Administration*, 33(3): 302–23.

## NOTES

1 Gilling suggests this is a new label for an old problem (2007: 131).

2 Blunkett was appointed Home Secretary in a Cabinet reshuffle after the June 2001 election.

3 Statistics available on http://www.crimereduction.homeoffice.gov.uk/asbos/asbos2.htm. These were the latest figures published on the website for England and Wales although the page was updated on 8 May 2008 and accessed on 11 August 2008.

4 Burney (2005: 38) reports that Blunkett threatened local government officials and police officers with losing their jobs if they did not push his agenda on anti-social behaviour further.

5 In Manchester in 2004 boxes incorporating slots for depositing money started appearing on the walls of city centre buildings with the slogan 'Give to the Box, not to the Beggar'. The idea behind this was that designated city centre workers would empty the boxes and distribute the money to homeless people living on the streets – presumably considered the most 'deserving'. It was thought this would stop all begging within the city centre area although still allowing a philanthropic gesture by the concerned passer-by. I am pleased to report that this anti-begging campaign had little effect.

6 For an extremely comprehensive account of the changes in the youth justice system across Great Britain since 1997 see Bottoms and Dignam (2004).

7 Since April 2000 the Board has been given the responsibility for commissioning secure facilities for those under 18 (Bottoms and Dignam 2004: 78).

8 The Ministry of Justice was created in May 2007 to oversee the work of the courts, probation and prison services which were previously part of the remit of the Home Office.

# 5

# The focus on children and youth

New Labour developed both a welfare and a justice agenda for young people. Labour began its first term of office in 1997 with a pledge to halve child poverty in ten years and to eradicate it in twenty but at the same time it promised to deal with persistent young offenders through a new process of fast-track punishment and to cut by half the time between arrest and sentencing (Home Office 1997c). As Muncie (1999) has outlined the political expedience of 'dealing with' young offenders as quickly as possible sat uncomfortably with the government's duty to protect the welfare of all young people. Where the young person was categorised as a young offender these new speedy mechanisms did not always ensure that the young offender's best interests prevailed. Indeed, 'justice' was all too often maintained at the expense of the child (Newbury 2008) and as we shall see the government moved ever more steadily towards a stereotyping of the incorrigible and troublesome youth who played a part in maintaining their own exclusion, as distinct from the troubled young person who might be 'reached' and supported to ensure more positive life outcomes.

## Recognising child poverty: the welfare agenda

The Social Exclusion Unit's Policy Action Team on Young People (PAT 12) reported in 2000. It began by acknowledging that over the past 20 years more young people in Britain than ever before had become socially excluded and were coping with many problems ranging from illiteracy, through drug use and serial offending. It acknowledged that British youngsters were growing up in worse conditions than their counterparts in many other economically developed nations. Furthermore, annually one in six young people from England and Wales between the ages of 16 and 24 were recorded as being the victim of a violent offence, more than in any other industrialised country, apart from the Netherlands. Poverty was seen as a decisive factor in this equation with one in five children growing up in households where no one was in work. Also contributing were difficult family lives, poor education and low aspirations. PAT 12 linked these environmental conditions with some young people's involvement in crime, stating that 'The impact of these problems falls most heavily on the individuals and families concerned' before adding 'But it also impacts on all members of society as taxpayers or as victims of crime' (SEU 2000: 8).

The SEU report then went on to identify broader social and economic changes as leading to the terrible conditions some young people faced together with a gap in support services and the truth that some of the most deprived areas had missed out on centrally and locally provided funds which could have improved many young people's lives. Their solutions, building on the government's existing policies for youth, were to ensure a greater coherence in government policies (the joined-up thinking so beloved by the SEU), a Ministerial Group for Young People and a Youth Unit within government together with a range of preventive programmes to support young people and to help them to deal with problems before they got out of hand and became acute and entrenched. The PAT report, although linking the social exclusion of youth to crime, was therefore framed in welfare terms and in a broadly social democratic framework.

## After Victoria: intervening in the life of the child

Some of the first interventions which New Labour made into improving the welfare of young children recognised the general nature of deprivation and disadvantage within particular areas and set out to turn back the damage previously wreaked in marginalised areas. Sure Start programmes, for example, were set up between 1999 and 2003 within some of the poorest neighbourhoods in England. These were established for all children under four and their families. They were designed to integrate all local services for children and their parents and were targeted at neighbourhoods rather than individuals, thereby avoided stigmatising particular families as a result (DCSF 2008: 2).[1]

Childcare Services received more attention after February 2004 when the appalling murder of an eight-year-old girl, Victoria Climbié, by her great-aunt and partner, revealed the extent of the service's shortcomings. Lord Laming, who chaired the inquiry into Victoria's death concluded that 'Not one of the agencies empowered by Parliament to protect children in positions similar to Victoria's – funded from the public purse – emerge from this Inquiry with much credit' (Laming 2003: 4). If the murder of toddler James Bulger in 1993 by two local children could be said to have shaped the correctional and criminal justice agenda for young people in the ensuing years (Scraton 1997), then the death of Victoria Climbié hastened a full-scale shake up of services for children and their redevelopment during Labour's term of office. Lord Laming's inquiry into Victoria's death reported in 2003 and was followed by the Green Paper *Every Child Matters* and the Children's Act 2004 which put many of Laming's recommendations into action.

The Children's Act 2004 gave legal force to five outcomes for children and young people which had been laid down in *Every Child Matters;* these were that every child should be enabled to be healthy, stay safe, enjoy and achieve, make a positive contribution and achieve economic well-being. In order to ensure these outcomes the Children's Act:

- established a Children's Commissioner to champion the views and interests of children and young people;
- placed a statutory duty on Local Authorities to make arrangements to promote co-operation between agencies and other appropriate bodies (such as voluntary and community organisations) in order to improve children's well-being and placed a duty on key partners to take part in the co-operation arrangements;
- placed a duty on key agencies to safeguard and promote the welfare of children;
- placed a duty on Local Authorities to set up Local Safeguarding Children Boards and on key partners to take part in these boards;
- made provision for setting up indexes or databases containing basic information about children and young people to enable better sharing of information;
- required a single Children and Young People's Plan to be drawn up by each Local Authority;
- required all Local Authorities to appoint a Director of Children's Services and designate a lead member within this;
- created an integrated inspection framework and Joint Area Reviews to assess local areas' progress in improving outcomes;
- set up 20 Pathfinder Children's Trusts to pilot different ways of ensuring joint working remained as effective as possible.

(Adapted from *Every Child Matters: Change for Children* www.everychildmatters.gov.uk)

These reforms rested on the assumption that young children are 'at risk' from society. (James and James 2001: 212) and in need of our particular protection.

The protection of children, vulnerable by virtue of their age, immaturity and dependence upon adults, would seem to be an uncontroversial matter but it is far from such. Under the banner of protection children's lives can become confined and limited in many ways. As we have seen from the provisions of the Crime and Disorder Act, limits on a child's activities can stray into the practice of subjecting young people to increased social control – a perception of children more at risk to society than from society (James and James 2001). The imposition of measures such as child curfews and parenting orders could be read as both protection of unsupervised children or control and surveillance of a risky population. Recent years have seen particular fears emerge of 'feral children', 'ratboys', 'anti-social youth', gang cultures and intimidating 'hoodies' which fuelled the drop in the age of criminal responsibility in England and Wales and which also contributed to a wider perception of a crisis in childhood (Scraton 1997).

# Does every youth matter?

When we consider government policy towards youth – especially teenagers growing out of childhood and into young adulthood – this bifurcation of policy becomes more acute. On the one hand the changes brought about by the Children's Act emphasising the importance of integrating and 'joining up' the whole range of services for children from birth onwards, ensuring more effective communication between services and giving a leadership role to local authorities to ensure that effective practice was pushed through and maintained, continued the welfare arm of New Labour's focus on youth. On the other hand the social control of young people continued to deepen and attitudes to young people not seen to be conforming to normative standards of behaviour, continued to harden. Even within the welfare approach to young people, however, there could be detected a drive to mould youth to a particular communitarian vision of the deserving and respectable individual, taking responsibility for their own personal outcomes, engaging in community and voluntary activities and becoming a full participant in the country's economy and waged work. In 1999 the government established a National Advisory Group on Education for Citizenship and the Teaching of Democracy in Schools (DoH 1999: para. 9.12.1) which clearly laid out the requirement for young people to learn about their 'duties, responsibilities and rights as citizens' (DoH 1999: para. 9.12.7) (James and James 2001: 218) but as James and James point out children and young people cannot be fully engaged as citizens or as community members while they are in the process of learning what it means to be an individual first and foremost. 'By definition of their youth', James and James argue, 'they do not, as yet, have a fully shared history and therefore cannot be assumed to be acquiescent to the values of the community' (2001: 214). Yet much of the government discourse around young people emphasises their need to conform to adult norms and values from an early age.

In 2001 47 Connexions Partnerships were set up to offer support to all young people aged 13 to 19. These projects brought together the work of a number of agencies, together with a dedicated website Connexions Direct in order to ensure that young people had ready access to advice on learning, training, careers and special needs education. The setting up of these partnerships reflects concern that 'changes in the labour market have made young people's transitions from school to work much more uncertain, protracted, insecure and unstable than was the case 30 years ago' (Yates 2008: 13). This work with young people was followed in 2005 with another Green Paper *Youth Matters* (and in 2006 *Youth Matters: Next Steps*) which was designed to include the improvements made to children's services into provision for teenagers and which integrated Connexions into local authority provision.

*Youth Matters* and *Youth Matters: Next Steps*, although ostensibly following on from work to ensure the safety and well-being of younger children, took a somewhat different tone. The same expected positive outcomes were identified for young people as had been produced for children (to be healthy, stay safe, enjoy and achieve, make a positive contribution and achieve economic well-being) yet there was included in the Paper a distinct undertone of New Labour's communitarian, 'rights and responsibilities' agenda. Ruth Kelly, the then Secretary of State for Education and Skills, provided the foreword for *Youth Matters* in which she began to identify distinct groups of young people, notably: those who take full advantage of the abundant opportunities available to them as teenagers; those who cannot because 'they come from disadvantaged backgrounds'; and those who *choose* [my emphasis] not to and as a result 'can get into a downward spiral of anti-social behaviour, crime and drug-taking'. Kelly went on to introduce the idea of punitive sanctions for this latter group. 'It is wrong', she wrote, 'that young people who do not respect the opportunities they are given, by committing crimes or behaving anti-socially, should benefit from the same opportunities as the law-abiding majority. So we will put appropriate measures in place to ensure they do not.'

*Youth Matters* laid out a series of funding opportunities which would be made available to young people, the Youth Opportunities Fund, Youth Capital Fund and a pilot of Youth Opportunity Cards: £115 million was to be distributed between all local authorities ring-fenced for work with young people. The funds were to be administered by the young people themselves with the aim of improving the provision of positive activities for youth and giving them the power to decide how this funding should be spent in their area (Golden et al. 2008). Youth Opportunity Cards were available in some areas to reward good behaviour with credits which might be used to help buy music or other leisure services. All these opportunities, however, would be withdrawn from those who persisted in anti-social or criminal behaviour. As well as providing more and universal leisure opportunities, sport, information and guidance to the young person making the transition from childhood to adulthood, this report suggested targeting young people who were especially in need and with very few chances in life to provide them with a nominated person to help them find their way through the support on offer. At the press launch of *Youth Matters: Next Steps* there was much made of the need to empower and to trust young people but these reforms were also closely linked to the perceived need to be tough on anti-social behaviour (detailed in Chapter 4) and were also closely tied to the somewhat less beneficent *Respect Action Plan* (*DCSF Press Notice 8 March 2006*) which will be discussed in more detail in Chapter 9.

Not all the responsibility was placed on the young person's shoulders. A great deal of the *Youth Matters* agenda considered the part which parenting plays in a young person's life and, as a consequence parenting programmes and support for parents in the difficult job of raising children were heavily promoted. However New Labour's welfare agenda merged with their attempts to control crime so that these became almost one and the same and used to justify a 'cultural shift in the way child rearing is conceptualized and targeted by policy makers' (Gillies 2008:

95). During this period intervention in family life reached new limits (at least in troubled neighbourhoods) and was considered legitimate and appropriate in order to protect the well-intentioned and law-abiding majority from harm and to safeguard the 'innocent' child. Gone, therefore, is the perception of the parenting–child interaction as a private and personal affair which should be negotiated within the family circle to be replaced by an interventionist and directive agenda to address the 'parenting deficit' which teaches parenting as a skill to be passed on by professionals and learned by parents. The policy focus, Gillies explains, has switched to the '"deeply excluded" who are viewed as transmitting their disadvantage through an intergenerational "cycle of deprivation"' despite the fact, she argues, that the evidence-base for this theory of the cultural transmission of crime and anti-social behaviour is somewhat lacking (Gillies 2008: 96). Blair's message, according to Gillies was that 'For the sake of their children's future, and for the stability and security of society as a whole, working-class parents must be taught how to raise children capable of becoming middle-class citizens' (2008: 99).

Reform into children's and youth services has continued apace. In 2007 the Department for Education and Skills (DfES) was split into the Department for Children, Families and Schools (DCFS) and the Department for Innovation, Universities and Skills (DIUS)[2] and in December 2007 the DCFS published *The Children's Plan: Building Brighter Futures* with the somewhat ambitious aim 'to make England the best place in the world for children and young people to grow up'. Alongside the aspirational nature of these goals the plan also recognised that to achieve its objectives the government would have to set aside additional funding and provide support for parents and better nursery, play and educational facilities in order to ensure a happy outcome for as many children as possible.

As James and James observe this more communitarian agenda to solve the crisis of youth conceives young people as 'an *entire* [emphasis in original] social category' (2001: 222) which is troubled in its entirety suggesting that there is a common solution to young people's problems. However, contradicting this stance, many of the policy interventions designed to lift young people out of poverty, to improve their lives and to steer them into education, training or employment were based on the assumption that individual agency and taking personal responsibility are sufficient to improve a person's outcomes in life and given the right information and guidance that the individual has the capacity to act on that advice to take a more positive path. It is a strongly individualising perspective which sees skilful parenting and professional guidance as capable of surmounting widespread socio-economic difficulties. Research on youth transitions conducted by Douglas Smith in 2007, however, suggests that barriers to social and economic inclusion can remain insurmountable for some as a result of structural factors which lie beyond the individual's control. The poor social and physical environments which many young people endure can harm and damage them in ways which severely limit their capacity to take up any opportunities which may come their way.

## Troubled transitions to adulthood

Yates' (2008) review of the literature concerning the career aspirations of young people confirms that most young people who fail to achieve employment and/or complete training do not do so for lack of trying. They face, he argues, futures full of uncertainty in an ever-changing world of work. The transitory and changing nature of employment prospects means that young people do not have steady goals to aspire to which remain in place for the duration of their training period. As the world changes around them they may abandon one career trajectory and move on to another which appears to be more promising. In addition, Yates argues, young people and indeed their advisers, are often ill-informed about possible career paths and ways to attain their employment aspirations. In a changing world, lacking the certainties of the past when career choices were more stable and information on work could be passed down from generation to generation, families today, he found, feel of little help in guiding their children towards stable careers. Young people find they have to rely on imperfect advice and fall back on their own hunches to carve a path towards employment and while they do not lack aspiration they do not know how to get where they want to be. Furthermore, those from poorer backgrounds face the greatest uncertainty and risk in their transition to employment. Young people from these backgrounds, Yates found, are much more likely to drift in and out of unstable employment or to give up on employment and training altogether and become alienated and disengaged as a result. Since labour market disruptions mean that family and friends can no longer provide sufficient information this support must be professionalised. Hence, Connexions youth programmes were intended to help young people overcome some of these difficulties and were set up on the basis that young people need more information and guidance concerning the changing opportunities available to them throughout their period of secondary education and beyond at a time when they are choosing their educational and career paths. In the meantime, however, young people from more middle-class and professional families have less need of such professional intervention. In this social milieu, career paths have remained much more stable, parents are better able to cultivate their children's aspirations and have recourse to bodies of knowledge and to people which they can call on to help their children make informed choices about their futures. Douglas Smith's research suggests that a likely outcome for many young people in the most deprived neighbourhoods is 'the persistence of life-time and intergenerational immobility among those currently excluded' (2007: 6). For Smith structural factors which limit and restrict opportunity leave young people in these areas with little possibility of making a positive change in their lives and without the capacity to make the fundamental shift out of poverty which would be necessary for improvement in their life to occur. In these circumstances young people and their immediate families can become extremely disillusioned and resistant to change through any kind of policy intervention and may appear from the outside to lack the individual motivation to change.

While the government continues to hold on to the idea that individual agency is enough to turn lives around this cannot provide a solution to those who remain marginalised, poor or without employment. For this group the government developed a particular emphasis and vocabulary which served to single them out as needing special attention. These 'hard-to-reach' groups were considered to be beyond the usual level of intervention and ever more authoritarian measures and punitive sanctions were developed to 'persuade' individuals into what they considered to be more pro-social and community-minded lifestyles. At the same time, however, young people, at least those from the less privileged backgrounds, continued to be characterised as generally anti-social, disrespectful of others and socially harmful. Research revealed a Britain ill-at-ease with its youth and in 2006 researchers at the Institute for Public Policy Research (IPPR 2006) coined the term 'paedophobia' to describe the general antipathy felt towards the nation's young people. According to the IPPR many Britons were simply avoiding contact with any young people to whom they were not already acquainted and many adults expressed their reluctance to intervene in any situation where they felt such young people were acting inappropriately.

## Young people and offending

Recorded crime statistics cannot actually reveal much about the extent of offending by young people. Hine and Williams explain some of the drawbacks of Home Office data:

> There is no indication of how many … offences are committed by young people, but NACRO (2006) estimated that in 2004 under 18s were responsible for 112,900 indictable offences. Unfortunately they did not estimate this as a proportion of all offences, and it is not clear from Home Office statistics how many of the 5.6 million crimes recorded that year are indictable. Statistics do show how many young people are found guilty or cautioned for indictable offences, revealing that in 2005 offenders aged 10–17 accounted for 14% of all indictable offences and offenders aged 18–20 for 12% of them. In total young offenders under 21 were responsible for just over a quarter of detected indictable crime. Figures for 21–25 year olds are not available separately. (Hine and Williams 2007: 3)

Hine and Williams concluded that these figures 'belie the image often portrayed by the media and by politicians that young people are responsible for most crime' (2007: 3). Due to the shortcomings of official crime statistics it has been deemed propitious to supplement existing data using self-report surveys to measure the extent of young people's offending behaviour. From 2003 to 2006 the Home Office carried out their own self-report research, the Offending, Crime and

Justice Survey (OCJS). The findings from Roe and Ashe (2006) suggested that the majority of young people were law-abiding. It found that:

- Over three-quarters (78 per cent) of young people aged from 10 to 25 had not committed any of the 20 core offences covered by the survey in the last 12 months.
- Amongst those that did break the law, many did so only occasionally or committed relatively trivial offences.

Of those reporting involvement in offending it was most likely that this offending was minor and not a regular occurrence, although a minority of young people were involved in more serious crime and more frequently. Roe and Ashe reported:

- Just over a fifth (22 per cent) of young people aged from 10 to 25 reported that they had committed at least one of the 20 core offences in the previous 12 months.
- Six per cent of 10- to 25-year-olds had committed an offence six or more times in the past 12 months and were classified as frequent offenders.
- Ten per cent of 10- to 25-year-olds had committed at least one of the serious offences measured in the survey. These groups of serious and frequent offenders overlapped so that 4 per cent of 10- to 25-year-olds were both frequent and serious offenders while 1 per cent had committed serious offences frequently.

Roe and Ashe concluded that much of young people's offending was interpersonal in nature. The 2006 survey revealed that the most commonly reported offence categories were assault (committed by 12 per cent overall within which assault with injury and without injury were each committed by 8 per cent). Other offending involved thefts (10 per cent), criminal damage (4 per cent), drug selling offences (3 per cent) and vehicle-related thefts (2 per cent). Only 1 per cent or less had committed burglary or robbery in the last 12 months. In addition Roe and Ashe (2006) reported no change in levels of offending (including serious and frequent offending) since the survey started in 2003.

As far as anti-social behaviour is concerned the survey revealed:

- Just over a fifth (22 per cent) of young people aged from 10 to 25 had committed at least one of the four anti-social behaviours measured in the OCJS in the last 12 months.
- Those who offended were also likely to commit anti-social behaviour.
- Being noisy or rude in public (13 per cent) and behaving in a way that caused a neighbour to complain (11 per cent) were the most common anti-social behaviours committed. Graffiti and racial/religious motivated abuse were relatively rare (4 per cent and 2 per cent respectively).
- The peak age of offending was 14 to 17 and the peak age for committing anti-social behaviour was 14 to 15.

So there is, to put it mildly, some disparity between the dominant characterisation that all youth are a risk to the social order and the data which reveals that it is a minority who become involved in 'anti-social behaviour' and offending and that the majority of these grow out of it before they reach the age of 18.

## Violent youth? Moral panics and 'knife crime'

The message persists that young people as an 'entire social group' are prone to socially-damaging behaviour. During Labour's third term of office, which commenced in May 2005, the issue of violent youth took on an added significance with the issue of 'knife crime' coming to the fore. It is difficult to trace the origin of the increased attention to 'knife crime' as recorded crime statistics show a year on year decrease in violent crime from 1997, yet in 2005 the Youth Justice Board's annual Youth Surveys included for the first time a question specifically related to the carrying of knives by young people. These surveys, conducted by the market research group MORI, relied on the self-reporting of offending and victimisation by young people themselves and canvassed the experiences of a sample from the ages of 10 to 25. The findings showed that 32 per cent of all young people reported that they had carried a knife in the preceding year and the report further concluded that there had been a significant increase in the carrying of knives by young people from the first year of the survey in 1999. As would be expected, the media picked up on this data and began to run more stories relating to the use of knives by young people. However, a subsequent review of data concerning the use of knives by young people, published in 2006, suggested considerable caution should be exercised in the use of the MORI survey. According to Eades et al. (2006) the MORI analysis was flawed and relied on the direct comparison of data arising from differently worded questions which did not measure the same variables. Furthermore, the survey did not distinguish between legally carried penknives and more lethal knives specifically carried as a potential weapon. However, the subtleties of this critique seem to have been lost on the media and indeed the Youth Justice Board and government analyses, which have continued to uncritically quote the MORI analysis in subsequent years. A more valid measure of recent trends in the carrying of knives can probably be gained from the Offending, Crime and Justice Survey (OCJS) which began in 2003 and was conducted annually for four years (Roe and Ashe 2008). The 2006 OCJS recorded 3 per cent of respondents who said that they had carried a knife with them in the last 12 months. The most common reason given, by 85 per cent of respondents, was for their own protection and 8 per cent said they carried knives in case they got into a fight. Knife-carrying was not a regular occurrence. Just over half (54 per cent) of the respondents said that they had only carried a knife once or twice in the last year and the most commonly carried knife was a penknife (46 per cent), followed by a flick knife (20 per cent) and then a kitchen knife (12 per cent). Of those who did carry knives, a very small minority reported using the knife to threaten or injure someone (4 per cent and 1 per cent respectively).

Whatever the facts of the matter, political opinion decided that something had to be done about an increased propensity of young people to carry and use knives and in May 2006 the police ran a national knife amnesty. At the end of the same year the Violent Crime Reduction Act 2006 raised the age at which a person could legally buy a knife from 16 to 18 years of age and also allowed authorised school and college staff to search any student on the premises who it was considered might be carrying a weapon. This opened the way to the use of metal detectors at school and college entrances and use of handheld Wand Metal Detectors by staff. This legislation also extended the maximum term of imprisonment for those found to be carrying a knife in a public place or school to four years and for anyone carrying or using a knife in the commission of a crime. The thrust of this legislation was aimed at young people strongly suggesting that the 'problem' of knife crime should be laid at their feet and once again an increase in legislative powers and in sentences available to the court was seen as the appropriate response to a perceived shift in crime patterns. Again this move was not without its critics. Indeed, Ann Oakes-Odger mother of Westley Odger a young man attacked and mortally wounded with a knife wrote on her website knifecrimes.org that:

> Having given a great deal of thought to the extended school powers contained in this legislation, I'm glad to note that the decision to use 'search powers' rests with Head Teachers, who would be expected to first consult with School Governors, Parents and Community Leaders, before deciding what is right for their school. Personally, I'm of the opinion that as the 'School' is a place of learning … it should initially be tackled on the basis of educating young people in the form of 'life skills' to enable the 'pupil' to become a responsible member of Society, who does not feel the need to carry a 'knife'.

She continued:

> Ideally, in the first year of Senior School the pupils be given 'Weapon Awareness' … Be Safe 'Knife Talks' to inform and educate. If then a problem arises, then a 'tough' search and punish strategy could be adopted. Whilst I whole-heartedly support a tough clear message that knives will not be tolerated in schools … I cannot help but feel that parents and teachers should endeavour to solve the problem first through education. (Knife-crimes.org, accessed 01.09.08)

So what is the reality of knife crime in Britain and is it on the increase? Again this is difficult to assess, given the paucity of longitudinal data about this behaviour. As a result of the increased concern around the nature of knife-use a new collection of additional recorded crime statistics was started in 2007/8 measuring the use of a knife or a sharp instrument in a subset of violent offences – attempted murder, grievous bodily harm and robbery where it appears that nearly one in five (19 per cent) of such offences in 2007/8 involved the use of knives or sharp instruments (Kershaw et al. 2008:5).[3] It will nevertheless be some years before trends in the use of knives for the commission of these violent crimes will be known.

The use of British Crime Survey (BCS) data is limited for this analysis in that it does not include the experiences of anyone under 16 years of age. Nevertheless, in its 2007/8 analysis the BCS reported that weapons were used in a quarter (24 per cent) of violent crimes. What it terms 'hitting implements' were used in 7 per cent of violent crimes and knives were used in 6 per cent (Kershaw et al. 2008: 5). The BCS also pointed out that the percentage figure for use of a knife in the commission of violent crimes had remained stable for the past decade. Furthermore, the BCS also reported that violent crime appeared to be on the wane. The report stated that:

> Longer-term trends in violence from the BCS show that the number of violent crimes increased since the first BCS results in 1981: gradually through the 1980s and then sharply after 1991 to reach a peak in the mid-1990s. Substantial declines have been noted subsequently (although levels in recent years have appeared more stable) and the number of violent incidents is now at a similar level to 1981. Incidents of violent crime reported to the BCS have fallen by half (48%) since 1995, representing an estimated two million fewer incidents and around three-quarters of a million fewer victims. (Kershaw et al. 2008: 62)

Even police statistics on the use of knives, where this data was kept, showed a decrease in the use of knives in the commission of crimes. In 2007/8 figures collected by the Metropolitan Police, for example, recorded 10,220 knife-enabled crimes, 16 per cent fewer than in the previous year which in turn was 4 per cent fewer than in 2005/6 (Kershaw et al. 2008: 76).

The concern around knife crime and young people in the early years of the twenty-first century bears all the hallmarks of a moral panic (Goode and Ben-Yehuda 1994, Young 1971). A rising fear has been generated in the public sphere around the, admittedly awful, crime of using a knife to maim or kill another person at a time when all indications show that the amount of violent crime is actually falling. Indeed, the evidence for the purported increase in the use of a knife in crime is largely anecdotal. There have been numerous and often salacious media reports of young people involved in violence using knives, as victims and as perpetrators, but the evidence for an increase in this behaviour is slight.

## What is 'knife crime'?

The definition of 'knife crime' used in media reports is particularly ambiguous. What, for example, is recorded as a 'knife crime'? Is it the carrying of knives, and if so which types? Is it the carrying of knives with intent to carry out some unlawful activity at the same time? Is it the using of knives in that unlawful activity? Does using a knife to pick a lock to gain access to a building in order to burgle the premises constitute knife crime? Is it using the knife to threaten, to wound or to kill another person? All these actions could come into the definition of knife crime but they are very different in their form and in their potential consequences. In the media much attention has been paid to murder where a knife is used but while these incidences too can take place under very different circumstances they are 'lumped together' as one category. The murder of the special police constable Nisha Patel-Nasri in 2006 by her husband has been written about in the same column inches as woundings by teenagers, and should the murder of a young man by organised racists be categorised alongside the stabbing of another outside a pub after a drunken altercation? Is violence between young people in a playground where a knife is used a similar incident to the stabbing of an adult man outside his home when he confronts a group of young people vandalising cars? Of course each culminates in the terrible fact of the taking of another's life but to elide the differences between each serves, as do all the classic moral panics of the past, to prolong an event's newsworthiness, to suggest a wave of crime which is out of control. It suggests too that all young people are in equal danger of such violence or that we are all in equal danger of being victimised by young people. Yet the idea of a 'knife culture' among young people persists, a significant minority of young people are perceived as acting in dangerous ways, carrying of knives as a way of earning respect, as protection from other more dangerous youth, or as a way of life. However, as we have seen, the evidence for the existence of such a culture is shaky at best.

In truth Britain remains a country where homicide – both murder and manslaughter – is a fairly rare occurrence. Recorded crime statistics for England and Wales show that the rate of homicide stayed fairly steady throughout the 1970s, 1980s and 1990s at approximately 10 homicides annually per million in the population. In the years between 2000 and 2007 this average has increased to around 15 homicides per million in the population. This could be portrayed as a 50 per cent increase in this category of crime but these years have included the doctor Harold Shipman's victims, which in one year accounted for over 100 homicides, another year includes the 23 cockle-pickers drowned in Morecambe Bay, another year includes the 52 victims of the 7 July 2005 bombings in London and another year includes 58 migrants suffocated in a lorry which was smuggling them into Britain, so the rise in deaths due to homicides in recent years includes all sorts of tragedies which are the result of many different circumstances. There *is* some, mainly anecdotal, evidence that young people are more afraid for their personal safety than ever before and this needs to be taken very seriously but it still remains the case that it is young babies below the age of one year old who are most at risk of being the victims of murder or manslaughter. If we are to take the protection of young people seriously then we must understand what the data is actually telling us, rather than get involved in a media frenzy of speculation around what is in the minds and actions of 'dangerous youth'.

## Young people as the victims of crime

It is now universally acknowledged, and confirmed by more than 20 years of data from the British Crime Survey, that it is young men between 16 and 24 years of age who are the group most at risk of becoming victims of crime in any one year. Recorded crime statistics, however, do not collect information on younger victims of crime.[4] It is possible that children are in fact heavily victimised and for the youngest children threats of and actual violence are most likely to come from their parents and carers. One study which collected data from 29 Accident and Emergency departments in hospitals across England between 2000 and 2006 suggested that, although violent incidents appeared to be reducing across all age groups violence against those under ten years of age appeared to have increased markedly (Sivarajasingam et al. 2007: 5). However, this research could not shed light on who the perpetrators of violence against children might be. According to the OCJS survey in 2006 referenced earlier, 10–15-year-olds were more likely to have been a victim of a personal crime in the past 12 months than 16–25-year-olds. The most common place for this victimisation to occur was in the young person's school or college. For the under 16s their place of education, which they are legally bound to attend, appeared to be a place where they were at some risk. Additionally the survey demonstrated that the perpetrators of the offence were likely to be known to the young victim and were commonly other pupils or friends. For 16–25-year-olds, victimisation was most likely to take place at a pub, bar or nightclub or in the street. For this age group the most common perpetrators were 'someone who the respondent had seen around or friends' (Roe and Ashe 2008: 6–7). Offenders were also more likely to be victims. Half (50 per cent) of those who had committed any offence in the previous 12 months had also been victim of a personal crime in the same time period compared to about a fifth (19 per cent) of those who had not committed any offence. Although all recorded crime statistics and self-report studies can only give a partial picture of crime, as much crime will never be reported or recorded, these figures do tend to show that young people are the social group most at risk of criminal victimisation, that they regularly inhabit spaces where crime occurs and that they are caught up in it as either victims, offenders or indeed as both.

If we know very little about the extent to which young people and children are subject to victimisation we know even less about the ways in which this impacts on their lives. There is a tendency to see bullying in the playground, the theft of dinner money at school or personal insults and threats among children as somehow less serious than the crimes which we experience as adults; certainly there is little official research into the impact of crime on young people's feelings of self-worth and their ontological security yet it takes very little imagination to consider the potential for serious impact which such victimisation may have on children and young people whose ability to avoid such incidents is severely restricted – after all it is a legal requirement that they must continue in education and they must live with their carers. Furthermore, their levels of maturity may not allow them to shrug off these incidents as temporary setbacks which will come to an end.

Children and young people can make few real choices in their lives so may not feel able to carve out a different space for themselves where they can resist peer pressure and feel secure in themselves. The data we do have demonstrates that victimisation is concentrated in the most marginalised and impoverished of areas. It would hardly be surprising then if victimisation was a way of life for some young people in these neighbourhoods, both in accepting that they are likely to be victims and for some that they should protect themselves from this victimisation by using what strength they have against others. What is more surprising is that so many young people do find the resilience to counter these pressures. However this is not how the debate is framed in the media and in political discourse, which has vilified young people as an entire social group which is to be suspected of wrongdoing and feared. Those studies which do further delve into the lives of young people in troubled areas with high rates of victimisation reveal the limitations of young people's choices and the confusion and dilemmas which they face daily in environments where crime and its consequences are very apparent to them (Jamieson 2005, Yates 2008). Unfortunately such studies have recently been far less in evidence than those which quantify and cost the problem of crime committed by young people and which fail to see them as engaged in making sense of difficult and troubled lives.

## Children at risk

Labour began its term of office in 1997 with a pledge to lift young people out of poverty and exclusion. By its second term of office it delivered programmes in schools and the wider community which aimed to ensure that every child and every young person was to be given the best life chances and opportunities. Behind this positive and inclusive policy discourse lay a framework for action which targeted individual young people and their parents, suggesting that the key to combating exclusion was 'personal empowerment' rather than changes in the structures of society. After ten years in office, this approach had narrowed considerably. The Social Exclusion Unit was disbanded in 2007 and its replacement, the smaller Social Exclusion Taskforce (SETF) was set up to '[try] to persuade Whitehall departments to focus on the most severely excluded' (National Literacy Trust 2009). The Taskforce increasingly narrowed its attention to the targeting of resources and prioritising of services for a smaller number of children and families 'at risk' from multiple factors contributing to their deprivation and disadvantage. Yet research has demonstrated that poverty and worklessness are strongly identified with risk factors such as debt, heavy drinking, poor health and overcrowding and that social mobility in Britain – the chances that a young person will exceed the economic and social status of their parents – has persistently fallen since the late 1950s (Blanden et al. 2005). Indeed, a Social Exclusion Matrix developed at Bristol University for the SETF has estimated that 45 per cent of families are multiply deprived in that they experience two or more significant risk factors. Nevertheless the SETF now concentrates its attention on the most severely deprived – in the Bristol research this is the 5 per cent of families which experience nine or more significant risk factors. By 2007 the government was considering plans to assess every child on a range of risk factors in order to pinpoint resources and improve the efficiency of social interventions (*Guardian* 2007b: 6) and even to intervene before birth assigning 1,000 expectant mothers a personal health visitor after 16 weeks of pregnancy (*Guardian* 2007a: 1–2).

## Persistent and prolific offenders

While the 1998 Crime and Disorder Act aimed to deal with the 'problem' of young people's behaviour in general – and not just with those involved in offending (Muncie 1999: 147) – many of the subsequent reforms of the youth justice system were designed to address what was seen to be a hard core of offenders who appeared to be beyond the reach of existing judicial and social measures. A shift towards the management of persistent young offenders was noticeable within the policy of former Conservative administrations and reached new heights under New Labour. This shift was exemplified by the previous Conservative Prime Minister John Major's enjoinder to 'condemn a little more and understand a little less' in February 1993 after the killing of James Bulger by two ten-year-old boys, and accompanied a move away from consideration of the social causes of offending and towards a profiling of the individual offender.

Various 'risk factors' have been identified with offending, notably poor parental supervision, a lack of discipline within the family and lack of suitable role models (and father figures) for young people. Thus, offending has been construed as the result of inadequate parenting and poor socialisation – to be cured through training and education – rather than as emanating from harsh and unequal social conditions – a position favoured by more welfare-oriented youth justice bodies. In 2000 the government set up its Youth Inclusion Programme which, despite its name, was actually designed to identify and then offer positive programmes such as involvement in sport and leisure pursuits, to only the 50 young people at the greatest risk of offending in each of the highest crime areas in England and Wales (Hine and Williams 2007: 11). In 2003 the Persistent Offender Scheme (POS) was set up to focus resources on those over 18 who had been convicted of six or more recordable offences in the previous 12 months. This was closely followed by the Persistent and Other Priority Offender Strategy (PPO) in March 2004. The PPO included a key strand 'Prevent and Deter' to closely monitor and intervene in the lives of the most active young offenders and to prevent them 'from escalating into future prolific offenders, through youth justice interventions and post-sentence support' (Home Office 2007e). Four thousand young people were identified by 179 'Prevent and Deter' schemes across the country, around 20 per scheme, and were subject to close scrutiny and intensive support, some while in custody and others while living in the community.

# Concluding comments

The policy of 'early intervention' to divert young people from offending lay behind many of the government's ostensible welfare programmes for young people and children which have been presented in this chapter. It was also apparent in many clauses of the 1998 Crime and Disorder Act and its emphasis on making parents responsible for the actions of their children. It continued through the emphasis on correcting anti-social behaviour and in its reforms to systems of education and training designed to inculcate certain normative values in young people at an early age. It has been used, as Muncie argues, 'to legitimate interventions ranging from drugs education to containment in a secure environment' (1999: 169). This approach has brought more and more young people within the formal criminal justice environment and has been used additionally 'to provide preventive interventions to young people who have never been charged with an offence but are deemed to be "at risk" of offending' (Hine and Williams 2007: 5).

This ever-tightening agenda of social control has led to a more intrusive style of policing and an unprecedented amount of intervention into family and private lives together with a widening of the range and number of institutions which can exercise control over young people (Muncie 1999). Not only has young people's behaviour become increasingly criminalised but actions previously only considered a nuisance have been brought under the remit of crime reduction authorities and are 'policed' in more robust ways which impact on young people's freedom and sense of self. This has, Jamieson argues, 'helped engender a lack of respect for the criminal justice system and a further withdrawal of trust in the authorities which utilise New Labour's rhetoric and methods' (2005: 190). Labour considered its duty as that of 'remoralising' the nation's youth and its feckless underclass (Muncie 1999) but failed to address the barriers which lay in the way of young people taking a full, positive and purposeful part in everyday life. Indeed, as Muncie powerfully observes, Labour's answer to offending:

> Lies in enforcing the cultural mores of one section of society, onto a population that has become increasingly diverse, through an institutionalization of intolerance. The absence of any acknowledgement of the effect of structures of power, racialized inequalities and gendered social divisions is deafening. The social and material contexts in which offending behaviour arises remain untouched. (1999:170)

---

**FURTHER READING**

Hine, J. and Williams, B. (2007) *DfES Youth Strategy Review. Youth Crime and Offending.* Leicester: Youth Affairs Unit, De Montfort University.
Sanders, B. (2005) *Youth Crime and Youth Culture in the Inner City.* London: Routledge.

1 Sure Start Local Programmes were established in areas with between 400 and 800 children under four. In total, 524 programmes were commissioned in six stages or 'rounds'. They developed into Children's Centres by 2006, run by local authorities.

2 In 2009 this was disbanded and absorbed into the new Department of Business, Innovation and Skills.

3 The 2007/8 data shows that urban forces recorded higher proportions of violent crimes involving knives than the more rural ones. At 18 per cent the proportion recorded by the Metropolitan Police was slightly below the England and Wales average. Wounding with intent to do GBH accounted for the largest number of recorded offences involving knives in 2007/8, at 37 per cent of all incidents. Knives accounted for 15 per cent of all incidents of wounding or inflicting GBH without intent. 37 per cent of all attempted murders involved knives or sharp instruments and 35 per cent of all homicides. Knives were used in 26 per cent of robberies of business property and in 15 per cent of the robberies of personal property.

4 Although there are currently plans to extend the British Crime Survey to children under 16 for a trial period.

# 6

# Confronting racist Britain?

The nine Black and Asian Labour MPs who gained seats in the Labour landslide in 1997 immediately mobilised to put pressure on the government to address a number of issues of concern to black and minority ethnic (BME) communities in the UK which had lain unaddressed for many years. By October 1997 and the first party conference of their term in power, Prime Minister Blair had acknowledged that negative discrimination had held the UK BME population back and he expressed his concern that 'all the talents of the people [should] shine through' while referring in his conference speech to the dearth of BME representation in the top echelons of UK society. The then chair of the Commission for Racial Equality, Sir Herman Ouseley, nevertheless expressed his concern that the Labour Cabinet did not reflect the numbers of BME MPs which had been voted into office. The then Home Secretary Jack Straw pledged his commitment to stamp out racial injustice and to look at positive discrimination and employment policies within the Home Office and Robin Cook, then Foreign Secretary, held an open day at the Foreign Office, where 800 BME children were invited in. 'If I'm going to represent Britain', he told them, 'I need a Foreign Office that is representative of the whole of modern Britain'. Labour also promised to present a more inclusive and less xenophobic face to the rest of the world. Cook further promised to follow an ethical foreign policy agenda and Britain agreed to take its turn in 2005 as President of the European Union (*Guardian* 1997d).

## New Labour: new promises

Perhaps the most high profile and well received indicator of a change in government attitude towards its BME population was signalled by New Labour's announcement in July 1997 that it would hold an inquiry into the death of Stephen Lawrence which had occurred in April 1993. Stephen, at 18 years old, had been murdered by a group of white youths in Eltham, South-East London in what was commonly acknowledged as an attack by five known white racists who were prominent in the area. Stephen's murder took on a particular significance within the black community which stretched beyond the personal tragedy of his death and his family's grief. Britain's anti-racist left joined BME communities in condemnation of the act and two weeks after his death a march was called in protest and further demonstrations and events planned.

No one was ever convicted of Stephen's murder. In 1993 the Crown Prosecution Service abandoned proceedings against two of the five men commonly believed to have taken part ruling that there was insufficient evidence against them to continue with proceedings in the court. In 1996 a private prosecution of three men, taken out by Stephen's parents and financed through donations, was halted on the grounds that the judge believed that the evidence of the main witness, Dwayne Brooks, who was with Stephen at the time of his death, was unreliable. The inquest into Stephen's death which took place early in 1997 unveiled a litany of police inaction, from failure to give first aid to Stephen at the scene, through to incomplete investigation of available leads as well as a misrepresentation of the facts and progress of their enquiries. Complaints into the police handling of the investigation were subsequently made and the Police Complaints Authority agreed to investigate. The day after the inquest ended the *Daily Mail* newspaper printed the photographs and names of the five suspected murderers prominently on their front page daring each to sue the paper if they were innocent. Not one of the photographed ever did.

Stephen's murder took place against a backdrop of increased activity by organised racists in London. In 1992 the far right British National Party (BNP) had their first councillor elected in Tower Hamlets and only approximately one mile down the road from where Stephen met his death the BNP had set up a bookshop and party office in Welling which had attracted calls for its closure. It was reported that there had been a 140 per cent increase in racist incidents in the area and nearby localities since the BNP headquarters had appeared. In the July previous to Stephen's murder Rohit Duggal, a 16-year-old Asian schoolboy, had been the victim of another deadly racist attack only 200 yards away from where Stephen met his death and in the previous year, 1991, both Rolan Adams and Orville Blair had been murdered in separate incidents by groups of white youths in the nearby area of Thamesmead. The Reverend Al Sharpton, a prominent black activist from the United States had led a protest march in the Thamesmead area shortly afterwards but the racist attacks continued and the Black and Asian communities within the area were rightly concerned for their safety and security and were highly critical of the inability of the police to protect them. In a highly symbolic gesture Nelson Mandela, who was visiting London in the weeks after Stephen's death, asked to meet the Lawrence family to offer his condolences and support. Then, in September 1993 Quddus Ali was beaten into a coma in a racist attack, in January of the following year Mukhtar Ahmed was beaten close to death and in May of that same year Shah Alam was badly beaten and stabbed. All were attacked by groups of white males who hurled racist abuse with their punches. After the magistrates' court dismissed the case against those identified and accused of attacking Shah Alam, a campaigning group, the Movement for Justice was set up locally to take up the issue of racist attacks in the area and to highlight the community's 'complete lack of confidence that the police and courts would act against racial violence' (Movement for Justice 1999). The group later gave evidence to the Macpherson Inquiry into Stephen's death – detailing in their submission a litany of attacks against Asian youth in South London and incidents of police discrimination against black and Asian residents.

## Whatever happened to institutional racism?

In London the Metropolitan Police had long earned a reputation for discriminatory behaviour towards black and Asian residents of the capital (Lea and Young 1984) and distrust of police attitudes towards the BME population of Britain extended into the surrounding regions. While Lord Scarman had resisted labelling the police as institutionally racist after riots in Brixton in 1981, instead preferring the 'bad apple' analogy to explain incidents of police racism, a number of organisations representing the black and Asian population of London continued to criticise police attitudes towards the city's BME residents and to argue that there was something rotten in the capital's police service which extended far beyond the racist attitudes and behaviour of a few individual officers. Barely two months after Stephen's death four young men of Bengali heritage from Camden were acquitted of the charge of grievous bodily harm and violent disorder when their trial heard that the behaviour for which they had been accused arose as they were defending their community against an attack by a group of white men armed with knuckledusters and hammers. The jury heard that the police had taken 40 minutes to arrive on the scene and that local Bengali residents had had to protect themselves in the meantime. None of the white youths were ever charged and this fact was hailed as one more instance of discriminatory policing. According to newspaper reporting of the trial such racist attacks were far from rare and many victims claimed that the police were often slow to react (*Guardian* 1993a).

It was not only in the area of policing that the BME community were given cause for concern during the years previous to Labour's return to office. The policing of migration to Britain was another area in which the BME community could feel threatened by state interventions into their lives. Policies to curb migration into Britain had become more draconian and invasive since the early 1970s and generated much popular distrust of the police and immigration authorities within BME communities (Miles 1982). Matters came to a particular, tense, head when in August 1993 a specialist Metropolitan Police Unit, SO1(3), known within the police as 'the extradition squad' was suspended after an inquiry into the death of Joy Gardner, who died as a result of being forcibly deported. Her treatment at the hands of the unit involved her being restrained in her home by the use of a body belt and handcuffs and gagged with a 13 foot length of sticky tape around her head. As a result, Joy died of brain damage caused by asphyxiation. In 1995, three police officers stood trial for her manslaughter but were acquitted (Fekete 2003). Father Olu Abiola of the British Council of Churches raised concerns about other recent forced deportations in which similar restraining methods were used and injuries suffered but no one knew the full extent of the use of this restraining practice, which was later banned. The then Metropolitan Police Commissioner, Paul Condon, revealed that the SO1(3) unit was the only police unit given the power to use these techniques, raising the question of why such a method was considered appropriate for a non-British population and undermining the force's claims to be an anti-racist organisation (*Guardian* 1993b).

As Solomos outlines (1999: 1.2), a 'tragic litany of racist murders and "deaths in custody"' dominated public debates about race relations in the 1980s and early 1990s. When the Blair government took office in 1997 it seemed that the experiences of black and Asian minorities in Britain and the discrimination which they encountered as a matter of course, might begin to be recognised and challenged. Indeed Solomos opined, 'From a symbolic perspective it is clear that New Labour is committed to giving questions about race and social justice a higher profile' (1999: 3.3). The Labour Party Manifesto of 1997 had acknowledged Britain as a multi-racial and multi-cultural society and had pledged that all citizens would be equally protected through the law. It signalled too the government's intention to create a new offence of racial harassment and a new crime of racially motivated violence to protect ethnic minorities. This pledge was delivered in the Crime and Disorder Act of 1998. Where the previous Conservative administration had strengthened the criminal law against persistent harassment as a general offence it would not go so far as to name racism as a specific and particularly damaging form of harassment whereas the Crime and Disorder Act did. In addition the Labour government had pledged to abolish the Primary Purpose rule, a piece of anti-immigration legislation which required foreign nationals married to British citizens to prove that the primary purpose of their marriage was not to obtain British residency, a rule which had long been a source of antagonism between the state and many minority ethnic groups.

Only weeks after gaining the office of Home Secretary Jack Straw, who had visited the scene of Stephen's murder during the general election campaign, announced his intention to meet Stephen's mother Doreen Lawrence and consider taking up calls for an official inquiry into Stephen's death. An Inquiry was finally ordered in July 1997, to be headed by Sir William Macpherson, it began in earnest in March 1998 and the findings were finally published in 1999.

## The Macpherson Inquiry's recommendations

Macpherson's report went beyond the original remit of the Inquiry in highlighting that ethnic minorities in Britain held a general lack of confidence and trust in the workings of the police service. This, Macpherson argued, had to be addressed at the highest level. Macpherson put much of the responsibility on the police themselves who were enjoined to carry out a thorough examination of all aspects of their policies and practices towards ethnic minority peoples. Macpherson acknowledged that ethnic minorities' perceptions of discrimination were largely justified and needed to be taken seriously if relations between the police and all policed communities were to be placed on a more positive footing. He further reiterated that 'distrust and loss of confidence is particularly evident in the widely held view that junior officers discriminate in practice at operational level, and that they support each other in such discrimination' (1999: 46.31). At the same time, Macpherson argued, '"Colour-blind" policing ... must be outlawed' (para. 45.24), the persistence of discriminatory policing of ethnic minorities must be acknowledged and their real experiences of discrimination at the hands of the police must be recognised and addressed.

## On institutional racism

Perhaps the most widely discussed aspect of the Macpherson Inquiry was its new definition of the term 'institutional racism' in which Macpherson rejected the idea that racism had to be consciously applied in order for it to be said to exist. The wording outlined in his report which has since been taken up as the generally accepted working definition accepts that institutional racism occurs as a result of:

> The collective failure of an organisation to provide an appropriate and professional service to people because of their colour, culture, or ethnic origin. It can be seen or detected in processes, attitudes and behaviour which amount to discrimination through unwitting prejudice, ignorance, thoughtlessness and racist stereotyping which disadvantage minority ethnic people. (Macpherson 1999: p. 28)

Macpherson laid the charge of institutional racism firmly at the door of the Metropolitan Police, so reigniting a debate about the meaning and significance of this concept in policy discourses and policing practices which had begun after Scarman's rejection of the term in his 1981 report. Paul Condon, the Metropolitan Police Commissioner in charge when Macpherson reported, was initially loathe to accept the accusation for his force, seemingly misunderstanding the definition given and insisting that not all his officers held racist views while at the same time acknowledging that officers routinely stereotype groups in the course of their policing work. Other Police Chief Constables, most notably David Wilmott of Greater Manchester Police, more readily accepted that institutional racism existed within the organisation which he led (Agozino 2000). Furthermore, the Black Police Association, formed in 1994 by a number of black and Asian police officers within the Metropolitan Police, accepted Macpherson's definition highlighting problems within the occupational culture of the police as a primary source of institutional racism and agreeing that there was indeed a differential treatment of black people by the police.

### Stops and searches

Like Scarman before him, Macpherson singled out the role of police 'stop and search' powers in underlining the widely-held perception that the police routinely discriminate against ethnic minorities. He commented that police use of such powers was universally criticised by community groups throughout the course of the Inquiry. It is clear, Macpherson argued 'that the perception and experience of the minority communities that discrimination is a major element in the stop and search problem is correct' (1999: 45.8). Again, as Scarman had done nearly twenty years before, while strongly resisting calls for these powers to be repealed he recommended that they should instead be much more closely monitored. Macpherson added that all 'stops, no matter under what legal powers they were made, or indeed if they were so-called "voluntary" stops', should be recorded.[1] He added that self-defined 'ethnic data' collected on who the police 'stop' should also be recorded as a matter of routine whenever the police use stop and search powers. At the time of the Macpherson report the statistics available for 1998 showed that those people categorised as 'black' were, on average, five times more likely to be stopped and searched by the police than those categorised as 'white' but use of stop and search powers against Asians and other ethnic groups varied widely. It was clear that Macpherson wanted this 'disproportionality' to be acknowledged and addressed. In 2005, however, the publication Statewatch reported that black people were nearly seven times more likely to be searched and that Asians were twice as likely to be stopped and searched than white people. By this time 'stops' could also be instigated under anti-terrorism legislation which was not in place when Macpherson reported (Statewatch 2005). Indeed, such was the continued concern over disproportional use of police stop and search powers that a Stop and Search Action Team (SSAT) was launched in July 2004 in order to consider once again how such discriminatory use of police powers could be addressed and the 'disproportionality' reduced. However, yet again in 2007 a report of the House of Commons Home Affairs Committee *Young Black People and the Criminal Justice System* found black people were still over six times more likely to be stopped than whites.

### On dealing with racial 'incidents'

Macpherson's report also led to an altered definition of what constitutes a 'racist incident'. Prior to his investigation the working definition stood as 'any incident in which it appears to the reporting or investigating officer that involves an element of racial motivation; or any incident which includes an allegation of racial motivation made by any person' (ACPO 1985 in Holdaway 1999). However, as Holdaway has revealed, individual forces and officers took very different approaches to the recording of such incidents and their prosecution, many simply not taking allegations of racially-motivated crimes and intimidation seriously:

> The inconsistent translation of policy, including definitions of racial attack and harassment, into the routine, operational practice of the ranks has persistently dogged policing ... For many different reasons – wanting to avoid 'paper work', a lack of interest, the effects of negative ideas about ethnic minorities, racial prejudice and discrimination, a failure to realise how a racial motive can enter into an offence – an officer might fail to record an incident as racially motivated.
> (Holdaway 1999: 5.3)

Macpherson recommended that the serious nature of racism and its impact on ethnic minorities within Britain should be fully acknowledged and that more universally understood standards for dealing with racist incidents should be adopted leading to better recording of allegations of racist incidents and crimes, the sharing of information between agencies and local communities, more thorough investigations and a recognition that it is generally in the public interest to prosecute offenders.

In order to focus attention on the harms to individuals and to society generally caused by racism, the Macpherson inquiry altered the definition of a racist incident to give more credence to the experiences of its victims, replacing the existing emphasis on the general and indefinable accusation of 'racial motivation' with the clearer and more easily interpreted definition that '[a] racist incident is any incident which is perceived to be racist by the victim or any other person' (Macpherson 1999). Prior to this, as Holdaway acknowledged, the police or 'other person' involved might have found it difficult to assess the individual *motivation* behind any action, but after Macpherson any behaviour *perceived* as racist should be treated as such. It was envisaged that this would also hold whether or not the police agreed with that perception. As Holdaway explains, in the case of Stephen Lawrence the police at the scene were blind to a racialised understanding of the events of that night, preferring to treat the murder as most probably 'gang-related' and at the same time ignoring the anguished testimony of Stephen's friend Dwayne Brooks, witness to the murder, that the attackers used racist language to abuse them before the fatal blow was struck. After Macpherson, it was hoped, any allegation of racism would be taken seriously from the outset.

Through simplifying the definition of a 'racial' incident and foregrounding the feelings of the victim and witnesses, Macpherson no doubt hoped that the experiences and memories of discrimination and racism long held by ethnic minority populations in Britain would be more readily addressed. As a consequence this might help alleviate to some degree the harm which these had undoubtedly caused and the fear and mistrust which they had generated. However, as Chahal

(1999) argued, Macpherson's definition too was fatally flawed in that he did not link it to a consideration of the structural roots of racism and its disproportionate impact on particular social groups. Macpherson left a situation whereby anyone can cry 'racism' even if they do not belong to a group which has been systematically discriminated against or disadvantaged as a result of their perceived racial origin. By ignoring the structural embeddedness of racism and racialised disadvantage and reducing racism to an interpersonal experience the true nature of racism in society is thereby negated. Bowling has cogently argued:

> The experience of violent racism is not reducible to an isolated incident, or even a collection of incidents. Victimisation and racialisation ... are cumulative ... Some of these experiences are subtle and amount to no more than becoming aware that someone is annoyed or disgusted by the presence of black people ... At the other end of this continuum are the more easily remembered instances when racism is coupled with physical aggression or violence. (Bowling 1999: 230)

In reality the majority population in the UK who are categorised as white, the people of no colour, are not routinely discriminated against because of their skin tones and perceived ethnic origin. Some may experience discrimination for other reasons and may feel excluded and marginalised from mainstream society as a result but the constant reference to race, and the manner in which this separates, divides and limits opportunities, with which the BME population must daily contend plays no part in the experience of the majority population. As Chahal explains, an 'inter-racial incident' is not necessarily racist. For an incident to be motivated by racism it is also necessary that the perpetrator is able to use the power available to them as a member of the dominant group in society to carry out an act which discriminates against an individual or group who, by the nature of their racialised status, is denied that power themselves. As Chahal goes on to argue:

> It is difficult, given the overwhelming weight of evidence of who experiences racism, to continue to define racist incidents or harassment as a two-way process and ignore unequal power relations and the general climate in which minority groups are perceived and represented as different. Although firmly locating the victim as the key decision maker, the Macpherson definition fails to take into account the reality of who has power in the investigating process. It is naïve to develop definitions of what a racist incident is which is based on singular events and ignores the inter-connectedness of black and minority ethnic people's experiences of multiple victimisation and ultimately of having their experiences denied as part of a general social phenomenon. (Chahal 1999: 2.7)

A 'racist incident' can invoke, for some victims, the accumulated experiences of a lifetime of living with racism. This understanding of racial violence and its impact on the victim, however, has not been incorporated into policing practices or understandings. Instead such attacks and insults continue to be decontextualised and processed as discrete incidents.

After Macpherson, then, the new definition of a racist incident, rather than act as a step forward for Britain's BME population, which was surely what was intended by placing the definition in the hands of the victim rather than the police, has been misinterpreted by the enforcers of law so that the anomalous situation whereby the majority, in Chahal's words, 'superordinate' population can use the charge of 'racism' against the 'subordinate' BME population and can use the provisions of the Crime and Disorder Act 1998 in order to ensure that any accusation of racist behaviour is taken seriously. Indeed, in the immediate period after it was enacted the relevant section of the 1998 Act was used to charge minority ethnic people more than it was used against the violence of the white population (Bridges 2002). This proved to be a particularly salient issue only two years later when three of England's northern towns erupted in what was generally reported at the time as 'race riots'.

## 'Race' relations after Macpherson

In the year after the publication of the Macpherson Report the government passed the Race Relations (Amendment) Act 2000. This required all local authorities to promote race equality, imposing on them a duty to have 'due regard to' the impact on race relations of every policy which they implement. They were charged with the requirement to tackle racial discrimination, promote equality of opportunity for all and to work to improve relations between different 'racial' groups in all aspects of their duties. However, in late spring and early summer of 2001 'riots' were reported in the towns of Oldham and Burnley and later the city of Bradford. In each case predominantly young men of Pakistani and Bangladeshi heritage took to the streets in response to what they perceived as a rise in racist attacks on their communities and the lack of protection offered to them by the police.

At the time the British National Party, led by the known racist and fascist-sympathiser Nick Griffin, was actively recruiting in the north of England and campaigning for seats on local councils and in the European Parliament. It is generally believed that the British National Party, together with their close allies the National Front and Combat 18 (who take their name from the position of their hero Adolf Hitler's initials in the alphabet) were working together to foment inter-community tensions in order to raise the profile of their 'race politics', whip up racial tensions and garner support from the region's white communities. In all three towns these racist extremists used the local media to spread rumours and lies which aimed to place their Asian communities in a poor light and to divide them from the rest of the town's population. In each case the criminality of Asian men was a prominent allegation. In Bradford for example there were stories that Asian men groomed young white women for prostitution and in Oldham that there had been an increase in racist attacks on white people and that no-go areas for whites were being patrolled by young Asian men (Ray and Smith 2001). As Burnett (2004a) has outlined, however, the poorly constructed recommendations of the Macpherson Report and the emphasis on prosecuting racially-motivated crime which was a feature of the 1998 Crime and Disorder Act, led to more ethnic minorities being charged and given custodial sentences than whites.

In all three places the BNP fomented spurious claims that their local authorities were giving preference to areas seen as Asian in the delivery of services and crucially in their use of funds for economic regeneration. Days after the disturbances the BNP produced a leaflet which clearly stated who they thought was to blame and once more perpetrated the myth that Asian areas disproportionately benefited from government money. It included the following passage:

> Surprise, surprise! Mobs of Muslim rioters have caused millions of pounds worth of damage in our town, but the only thing the Labour Party plans to do about it is to reward them, by throwing millions more of taxpayers' money into the riot areas 'to end the deprivation caused by the riots'. (BNP leaflet in Oldham 2001, author's copy)

The far right attempted to play on the fears of each town's white population. In the poorer neighbourhoods they appealed to those who felt abandoned, marginalised and excluded from economic and social opportunities claiming that 'Asians' were receiving preferential treatment. In the more wealthy areas of the towns their propaganda was designed to play on the middle-class fear of falling, on the precarious nature of middle England's wealth and its imminent collapse in the face of global forces which were fuelling both wide-scale immigration and economic instability.[2] At the same time, national newspapers, such as the *Sun* and *Daily Mirror* joined in to blame 'Asian' communities for the disturbances and to scapegoat them as isolationist, protective of their own, and as bigoted and intolerant towards those who did not share their religion and culture (Burnett 2004a).

In truth there were many long-standing and complex issues involved in the disturbances that year and many local grievances which the far right were happy to exploit. The old mill towns of the north-west have similar economic histories and current socio-economic profiles. These towns expanded on the back of the British Empire's domination of the cotton and wool industries in Victorian times, with parallel development in engineering and coal mining. In the nineteenth and early twentieth centuries these were boom towns which depended on a skilled labour force. They were centres of capital and also of a strong labour tradition. Towards the middle of the twentieth century, however, the economic base of the region began to shift. In the first instance, increased mechanisation in textile production meant many of the jobs in this sector became semi-skilled or manual. They proved less attractive to the indigenous population who could find better wages working in other industries. Migration from the Caribbean and then South-East Asia, mainly from Pakistan and later Bangladesh, helped to plug a growing shortage of labour. The 1970s, however, saw a collapse of the textile industry in

Britain, factories closed and many of the newly arrived population found themselves out of work. This was closely followed in the 1980s by a similar slump in engineering and after the defeat of the miners' strike in 1985 the remaining pits soon disappeared. Towns in the north-west, became renowned for their high rates of unemployment and deteriorating local economies. However, unemployment did not affect their populations evenly. Throughout the region the industries which attracted migrant workers lost jobs first, followed by retrenchment in the better paid and more white-dominated engineering workplaces and mines. In this declining economic climate, no other industry stepped in to mop up the excess workforce and unemployment remained persistently high. To this day it is the families of the Asian migrant workers which experience higher unemployment than their white neighbours. Across Oldham, for example, unemployment stood at 4.2 per cent in 2001 but among the Pakistani and Bangladeshi population it stood at 25 per cent (Ritchie 2001: 32). The economic demographics of Oldham show it to be low wage economy with almost six out of every ten jobs in low-paying industries and average wage-levels 14 per cent below national scales (Ritchie 2001: 32, 33).

Across the north-west of England the population of Asian heritage finds itself in some of the poorest areas and housing in the city. The children of 'Asian' parents generally attend struggling schools with low rates of academic achievement. Family income levels are low and many rely on self-employment in taxi work, small retail businesses or restaurants. The areas where 'Asians' live have been dubbed 'ghettos', reflecting their social and economic marginalisation. Far from benefiting from government largesse the lack of work opportunities has been countered through generating local, 'Asian' owned, sources of employment and business. People worship in their local areas, in mosques, temples and gurdwaras which they have struggled to build out of money provided by their own communities. These neighbourhoods have some of the worst housing in the region. Schools are often largely segregated along ethnic lines with one school in Oldham in 2001 with 98 per cent of its pupils being of Bangladeshi heritage. Historically, many businesses in these areas simply had not recruited Asian workers and some mill owners had even segregated shifts, giving the less popular night work or less skilled jobs to Asian workers.[3] Black and Asian people in the town have always found their employment opportunities severely restricted. Given these patterns of discrimination it might have been expected that local councils would step in to set a good example to local employers, yet in 2001 less than 2 per cent of Oldham council's workforce was classed as 'Asian'.

It might be countered that the segregation of populations in a town like Oldham has resulted from historical patterns of discrimination which were exposed in the 1970s but which have since been eroded by anti-discrimination policies and equal opportunities legislation – but this does not reflect actual experience. There has been systematic discrimination in Oldham's housing for decades, in both the public and private sectors. As late as 1990 an internal report into the housing allocations of Oldham council revealed that discrimination against those of Asian origin was still wide-scale. This report was leaked to the Commission for Racial Equality (CRE) which investigated further and ruled that Oldham was unlawfully discriminating against this population, denying them access to decent public housing, keeping them on waiting lists for longer than was necessary and out of particular housing estates altogether (CRE 1993). The CRE worked with Oldham to develop a five-year plan to put things right. The plan has since been lost and in 2001 Oldham council refused to provide up-to-date figures on the ethnic spread of its tenancies (Bodi 2001). In 1990 the CRE exposed a number of Oldham estate agents who were 'redlining' or limiting the number of areas to which they would offer housing to those of Asian origin. As a result, the 'Asian' population could be said to have developed a self-sufficient way of life, providing accommodation, finance and employment for itself. In 2001 the anger and frustration felt within these communities exploded onto the streets, goaded by taunts of the far right and the inaction of police and other responsible authorities in the face of this provocation.

## Riot or community self-defence?

The term 'riot' is generally used to denote any civil disturbances enacted by a crowd which involves violence of some kind. However, there is a long history of 'riot' in Britain from the late eighteenth century to the present and this term hides a great deal of variation in size, intensity of activity and motivation of those involved from one 'riot' to another. Indeed, the last 30 years have seen 'riots' develop in many urban and suburban neighbourhoods and also following various political protests, most notably against the imposition of the poll tax in England and Wales in 1990. 'Riots' have been variously explained as 'anti-police' (Farrell 1992: 122), protests against rising unemployment (TUC 1981 in Cowell et al. 1982: 2) a response to relative deprivation (Lea and Young 1984), the cry of a desperate people denied their voice within the local state (Jan-Khan 2003: 35) and a reaction to insensitive and over-policing of certain communities (Lea and Young 1984). Other more conservative thinkers contend that they are fomented by criminal elements within a locality or are a result of 'alien' cultures clashing with the wider society (see Gilroy 1987: 236, Lea and Young 1984: 5–7).

From the 1950s to the 1970s 'riot' was associated with the African-Caribbean diaspora in Britain, resulting either from the reaction of the indigenous population – schooled in notions of imperial power and race – to the presence of this migrant population within their midst or later associated with second generation African-Caribbeans born in Britain but denied opportunities available to the white population.[4] The early Thatcher years saw disturbances in communities across England and Wales which were triggered by the heavy-handed policing of minority groups most notably in 1981 and then at Broadwater Farm, London in 1985. The insertion of 'race' as a factor in the history of riot has led to a shift in emphasis to the discussion of riot more as a cultural than a politically inspired event. This shift has taken place on both the political right and the left. Lea and Young, for example, discuss the 'street culture of black youth' (1984: 8) which, although born out of 'adversity and oppression' (1984: 9) results, they argue, in anti-social and criminal behaviours which come to the attention of the state authorities triggering a focused intervention which, underpinned as it is by racist assumptions and stereotypes, can only fuel conflict and animosity on both sides. Asian culture, on the other hand, they posit, being more insular and self-protecting was as a result less likely to come under the gaze and therefore condemnation of the state. Communities of Asian heritage were considered less troublesome and were therefore less troubled by the authorities (Lea and Young 1984: 8). Such explanations emanate from a shift in thinking around race and ethnicity which eventually came to dominate in Britain in the late 1980s in what Malik has recently bemoaned as 'a shift from the political to the cultural arena' (2005: 56). The riots of 2001 have been cast in such cultural terms – as resulting from a clash between two populations, living close to each other yet separated by distinct cultures, religions and ways of life.

Yet such interpretations of riot based in cultural explanations suffer from a very short-term memory. They cannot, for example, explain the growth of the Asian Youth Movement in Britain in the 1970s,[5] nor the active involvement of many young and older 'Asians' in civil disturbances such as the defence of Southall in 1987 and the riots of 1981 (Gilroy 1987). The slogan 'self-defence is no offence' became part of the anti-racist movement in Britain as a result of campaigns such as that to free the Newham 8[6] and the Bradford 12[7] both groups of 'Asian' men charged with violent offences after acting in defence of members of their community who were being racially assaulted. In the latter part of the 1970s and early 1980s Asian communities across the country underwent a number of attacks from various quarters and responded to these. This was the period which saw the incursion of the extreme right into British politics in England and Wales in the form of the National Front. At the same time immigration laws were enacted which were particularly targeted at migration from the Indian sub-continent and which insisted on intrusive and humiliating procedures such as virginity tests for brides from Asia. People hoping to bring family and friends from that region of the world to Britain were particularly affected. Under these conditions communities marched, protested and sometimes 'rioted' together in demonstrations of black and white unity against these attacks specifically and more generally against a political system which was marginalising more and more working class people and youth in particular. These were cross-cultural protests and, as Sivanandan (1990) has argued, flowed from a system in which class and race are inextricably linked. In the media, however, 'riots' appear as spontaneous outbursts, their provenance unexplored, or explained only in terms of immediately preceding events.

## Segregated communities and alien cultures

The civil unrest of May 2001 was inspired by events which took place at a political, not at a cultural level, and yet the argument that the unrest was the result of a clash of cultures persisted. In the official reports which followed the 2001 disturbances, chaired by Ritchie in Oldham, Clarke in Burnley and Ousely in Bradford, however, the region's 'Asian' populations were described as 'separate' and even 'segregated' and in many ways were blamed for their own fate. '[T]o "be" Asian' Burnett argues was always to be stereotyped as 'communal, protective, secretive, private' (2004a: 4), but to this stereotype was now added the 'problem' of separate religious faith and identity. 'Asian' communities became characterised as different, as 'alien', as culturally separated from the indigenous majority, as fundamentalist and anti-western. It was these cultural beliefs which were said to be behind the increased criminality of 'Asians' but also their increased victimisation as their separate identity fuelled antagonisms from the white indigenous populations. And this was before 11 September 2001 and the emergence of Al Qaeda as a political force and 'enemy of the west' generated a further degree of anti-Muslim and anti 'Asian' feeling which was unprecedented in the UK.

## The new racism

Yuval-Davies and others have written very cogently about the changing face of racism in the Britain of the late twentieth and early twenty-first centuries. Anti-black racism, it is argued, was fuelled by the imperialist ambitions of the emerging capitalist nations which raided the lands of others to feed their own growing populations and to meet the increasingly insatiable demands of their industrialising economies for raw materials (Whyte 2008). The ideology of white racial supremacy was used to justify this theft and later to underpin the trade in largely African slaves and the setting up of slave plantations in the Caribbean and the Americas. It was used too to justify the continued presence of white westerners in resource-rich continents even after the decline of this initial imperialist phase, as 'civilising' and 'developing' forces. Thus, economic imperatives and the desire to maximise profits through use of the cheapest form of labour shaped the form of racism which emerged at the time and which has persisted for many centuries since. It was bolstered by the development of scientific racism which gave an academic respectability to the idea that possession of certain physical characteristics denoted defects in both physicality and mentality.

The latter part of twentieth century, however, saw an increasing sophistication in the form taken by racist ideologies. Crude racial stereotyping was largely abandoned and scientific racism declined as a credible force in academic and policy discourses (even as both have persisted in much popular discourse). It has been replaced with a set of pronouncements on the desirability of certain *cultural* and economic forms and the argument that membership of a global economic system, signing-up to a neo-liberal agenda of market capitalism and acceptance of the economic and cultural dominance of the west brings undreamt of and unanticipated 'freedoms' based on what market mechanisms can bring. As freedom is bought through incorporation into the economic marketplace then earnings potential and wealth is its key and Yuval-Davies has perceived a degree of incorporation of the black middle-class into what she terms the 'British collectivity' and as a result, she argues, overt 'crude racialized behaviour towards [the black middle-class] is considered not justified anymore by large sections of the British population'. (Yuval-Davies 1999: 3.10). However, she concludes that far from Britain becoming less racist, the targets of the new 'cultural racism' or 'xeno-racism' (Fekete 2002) have widened to include refugees, asylum seekers and economic migrants. The targets of cultural racism are all those who the majority culture deems cannot or will not assimilate and they are, in the main, poor. While the old forms of racism have not disappeared new forms are placed alongside them further extending and complicating racialised discourses. The new cultural racism is not even always recognised as such as it is presented as a 'simple common-sense' and even as a unifying principle. Those who do not accept and adopt the hegemonic culture are consequently blamed for their own isolation, for perpetuating differences and for bringing on the condemnation of others and the racism which they experience as a consequence.

Yuval-Davies' observations marry well with the changing face of western imperialism which now dresses up its military invasions of other countries as necessary to maintain global democracy and freedom and, all too often, 'the American way'. The west has maintained its economic dominance through control of global finance and the use of conditions linked to the financing of loans and the allocation of aid packages to struggling regions of the world, to impose its particular agenda. Today capitalism needs a global workforce and this is facilitated through the transnational movement of capital, and to a much lesser extent labour. As international markets in capital and labour have opened up so visual embodied differences such as skin tone, which marked previous forms of racism, are now joined by cultural signifiers of difference (after all the opening up of the European employment market – the Single European Market has brought many white-skinned 'foreigners' to the UK). The war on terror, and the subsequent invasions of Afghanistan and Iraq which Bush, back in 2001 openly referred to as a crusade (*Daily Telegraph* 2001b), has fitted perfectly with this new ideology of cultural supremacy. The ensuing demonisation of Islam has served to drive a wedge between populations across the globe and within nation-states as Muslims become 'the enemy within'. As Bosworth and Guild have articulated, in the current climate:

> Cultural or social difference is routinely presented as a cause for concern, to be homogenized through assimilation, integration and citizenship. Similarly, and notwithstanding official support for certain expressions of cultural diversity, great

effort has been expended over the past decade in erecting external and internal barriers to differentiate decisively between foreigners and citizens and to catego-rize the various groups of non-citizens in the United Kingdom. (2008: 704)

At the same time then that the British government has been at pains to demon-strate its political credibility with its indigenous BME populations through the championing of the cause of the Lawrence family and its initial promise in undo-ing some of the worst excesses of the anti-immigration policies of the previous 17 years of Conservative administrations, ultimately it fell in behind the 'harsh rhetoric against foreigners' (Bosworth 2008) which featured within national state discourse across Europe and Northern America and which, Bosworth argues, ulti-mately also destabilised 'race' relations within these nation-states. In Britain 'Asian' communities were portrayed as failing communities rather than those which had been failed.

## The 'new' assimilation

The key to establishing peaceful and co-operative relations between BME and indigenous communities was cast as the task of inculcating common social values. This approach was dangerous in a number of respects. First of course, it suggested that the values of the BME peoples of Britain were not shared with the rest of the population – as though British-born or newly-arrived people were not workers, trade unionists, parents, students or pensioners along with the rest of the popula-tion. The government's community cohesion agenda also in effect meant an emphasis on the values of the super-ordinate, white and indigenous people of Britain and suggested that those who were not fully British would have to com-promise their own moral, religious and family agendas in some way in order to 'fit in'. This agenda was not too far away from Norman Tebbitt's infamous 'cricket test' in which, when Chair of the Conservative Party in 1990, he questioned the loyalty of Britain's BME population asking whether they cheered for national cricket teams of England, the West Indies or Pakistan.

## Building safer communities for all?

The regeneration and social exclusion agenda espoused by New Labour has claimed as a goal the building of neighbourhoods which would prove to be safe and secure places for *all* citizens (SEU 2001: 58). As a consequence crime preven-tion policies began to address the experience of those populations considered particularly vulnerable to crime such as the elderly, women and ethnic minorities. Indeed, the needs of Britain's ethnic minority communities could not be totally sidelined as BME people made up a high percentage of the population in New Deal for Communities (NDC) areas. According to the NDC evaluators:

> Race becomes an issue for NDCs in a way which has probably not been true for any previous ABI [area-based initiative]. In response, many partnerships have placed a considerable stress on engaging with local BME groups. To give just two examples, Hackney has developed outreach programmes for Turkish and Kurdish groups, and Sandwell has instigated capacity-building and capital projects for Yemeni, Sikh, and Bangladeshi groups. (Lawless 2004: 388)

Indeed, national statistics indicate that Black African and Caribbean groups make up approximately two and a half times as high a proportion of the population in the most deprived areas of the country as for England as a whole and 80 per cent of Black African and Black Caribbean communities live in Neighbourhood Renewal Fund areas which are those which have been identified as England's most deprived (House of Commons Home Affairs Committee 2007: 30). The Social Exclusion Unit also flagged up this problem with its information that 70 per cent of all people from ethnic minorities live in the 88 most deprived local authority districts (SEU 2001: 14). By 2002, according to Lawless, race equality was being mainstreamed across neighbourhood renewal as a whole (ODPM 2002) after having been championed by the NDC two years earlier (DETR, 2000b in Lawless 2004: 386). However, its area-based approach to regeneration was criticised by Cantle in his response to the events in Oldham as being possibly destructive of 'community cohesion'. Nevertheless, the government was locked into this method of delivering regeneration and renewal agendas and continued with area-based initiatives despite concerns that they were ultimately divisive and allowed one community to be pitted against another.

The government's 'community cohesion' agenda moved steadily from an early emphasis on unlawful discrimination against minority groups and seeking to put in place a raft of measures from policing to prison officer training to address its negative consequences, to become a call for minority groups to embrace British citizenship and a British way of life.

## Protecting the white working class

The defence of multi-culturalism began to wane in the face of the criticism that the acceptance of a multitude of cultures divided neighbourhoods rather than bringing them together. Behind this stance lay an attack on so-called 'political correctness', an attack which claimed that the feelings and experiences of ethnic minorities were routinely and crudely placed before those of the indigenous white population. In reality the previous 20 years had seen a slide in the fortunes of the working class in general, yet some framed the decline in employment, housing and educational opportunities in terms of a competition for resources between major-ity indigenous and minority ethnic communities – whether recently arrived or long established in which the white majority were losing out (Sveinsson 2009: 3).

These sentiments were clearly expressed by Ruth Kelly, then Secretary of State for Communities and Local Government in August 2006 when launching the government's Commission on Integration and Cohesion. While paying lip-service to the benefits of a rich and diverse British cultural life, Kelly spent much of her launch speech outlining what she saw as the dangers which immigration brings. She highlighted the 'problem' of new migrants bringing their own (questionable) national and ethnic 'loyalties' to mainland Britain, developing tensions within neighbourhoods and 'white Britons who do not feel comfortable with change' and who remained '[d]etached from the benefits of those changes' (Communities and Local Government 2006). Rather than dispel the myths that BME or faith com-munities receive 'special treatment' and attention, she pandered to these views. During the course of her speech Muslim populations were specifically highlighted as problematic and while much migration to Britain originates from developed countries and their predominantly 'white' populations, Kelly singled out a list of non-white, African and Asian countries as posing particular concerns. Her message was clear – these are alien countries with alien cultures whose populations, in moving to the UK, are unbalancing 'our' hitherto settled and stable communities. There is much to question in Kelly's assumptions but her speech was clearly intended to placate a 'white' fear and to put a responsibility on migrants them-selves to integrate, contribute and to find a way to fit into a British way of life.

## Concluding comments

New Labour has found itself as ready to use the 'race' card to gain popularity and support as any other government which preceded it. Its initial promise to address decades of discrimination against the country's BME population was clearly sur-passed quite early on by its pandering to the growing right-wing and racist forces across Britain. From Labour's second term of office onwards the BNP began to gain a few seats on local councils and by 2009 it had gained one elected mayor and two seats on the European Parliament. Their vote had risen from around 3–4 per cent of the votes in whichever area in which they stood to come closer to 10–15 per cent, sometimes more, and actually beating Labour in a number of constituencies. In 2006 a report published by the Joseph Rowntree Charitable Trust suggested that between 18 and 24 per cent of the electorate might consider voting for the BNP. Arun Kundnani of the Institute of Race Relations summed up the situation thus:

Over the last few years, much of liberal England has given up on the idea that racism is a significant social problem. Instead the real problem is taken to be social fragmentation exacerbated by multiculturalism. For every mention of institutional racism, we have heard a thousand references to the 'crisis of multi-culturalism', 'Muslim self-segregation' and the need for 'integration'. Hence the official bodies established to tackle racism, however ineffectually, have been dismantled: the Commission for Racial Equality has been subsumed into a more nebulous Equality and Human Rights Commission, local racial equality councils have been pressured into reinventing themselves as promoters of assimilation and community-based anti-racist organisations have had their funding removed on the grounds that they cater exclusively to the needs of minority groups. Defending these trends, figures such as Trevor Phillips have argued that the real issue is not racism but 'separatism' and the solution is the imposition of a cohesive British national identity. (Kundnani 2009)

This chapter has begun to outline some of the events which led to New Labour taking this turn in its perspective on race relations; the next chapter will explore this more fully.

## FURTHER READING

Hall. S, Critcher, C., Jefferson, T., Clarke, J. and Roberts, B. (1978) *Policing the Crisis: Mugging, the State and Law and Order.* London: Macmillan.
Spalek, B. (2008) *Ethnicity and Crime: A Reader.* Milton Keynes: Open University Press.

## NOTES

1 Previously the police were only required to record searches conducted under their statutory powers laid out in sections 1 to 7 of the Police and Criminal Evidence (PACE) Act 1984. Following Macpherson's report Police and Community Support Officers in all force areas were required to record all stops by 1 April 2005.
2 Author's own research files.
3 The Shiloh Mill in Oldham, for example, recruited 100 out of 450 men for their night shift who were of Asian origin, whilst day-time shifts were mainly for white employees (Ritchie 2001: 33).
4 For example, see Sivanandan (1990: 83) on the Notting Hill riots of 1958, Brockwell Park 1973, the Carib Club 1974, Chapeltown 1975 and Notting Hill Carnival 1976.
5 See www.tandana.org for a digital archive of material from this period.
6 See the Newham Monitor August 1982 at http://www.tandana.org/pg/search.php?Ref= MH89&No=1 (accessed 12.09.05).
7 See http://www.tandana.org/pg/PDF/MH/MH67.PDF (acessed 12.09.05).

# 7

# War and securitisation

The Home Office in London in 2009 has wrapped itself within an unprecedented level of security which is even designed into its built environment. This heightened level of 'security', which could be said to border on paranoia, is encountered from the moment a visitor steps through the main door into the initial entrance lobby of the Home Office building. Authorised visitors and staff are required to go through airport-style security barriers and baggage x-rays and can only be finally admitted to the building through a number of glass 'pods' in which the entrance door must be securely closed and locked before the exit door will open. Once through the security barriers a light and airy atria opens up with stairs leading to office spaces and meeting rooms on the floors above. On the available white spaces encircling the stairs and adjoining corridors are permanently painted, in colourful letters of commanding heights, slogans such as 'Securing Our Borders: Controlling Migration for the Benefit of our Citizens'. The very fabric of the building is utilised as a propaganda space reminiscent of an Orwellian fiction. This built environment in which the Home Office conducts its business could not more amply reflect its ideological stance towards visitors to Britain, which has been shaped in the last decades by an increasingly suspicious stance towards 'foreigners', a spiralling agenda of security and the ascendancy of exclusionary discourses.

## Securing the borders: deterring immigration

As early as 1998 the New Labour Government introduced its first policies concerning immigration and the tone was set for subsequent Home Secretaries to follow. Jack Straw's White Paper *Fairer, Faster and Firmer: A Modern Approach to Immigration and Asylum* invoked the government's modernisation agenda to streamline 'immigration control', to expedite applications for political asylum while removing a long backlog bequeathed by the previous government and to reduce many avenues of appeal against Home Office decisions to one single right of appeal. The background to this policy, Straw wrote in the preface to the White Paper, was the unprecedented rise in the number of travellers to the UK. In particular he singled out the increase in claims for asylum which had gone from 4,000 to 32,000 each year since 1988. Rather than attribute this to increased political instability and wars across the globe fuelling asylum claims, the 'blame' was firmly placed, without any evidence being presented, at the door of the economic migrant 'abusing the system' by falsely claiming refugee status and unscrupulous 'advisers who exploit the vulnerable and profit from delays'. This emphasis on weeding out the illegal and illegitimate was couched in terms of ensuring a fair approach to the 'genuine asylum seeker'.

## Cutting the costs of immigration

Contained within Straw's Preface to the bill was a commitment to cut costs, both in the processing of claims and in maintaining the 'non-genuine' seeker of asylum. The cutting of costs was achieved through the restriction of benefits to those awaiting decisions and their complete removal from those whose claims were turned down but who could not be forced to leave the country, leaving them completely destitute. Those who do not return to their place of origin – which many will not do because they are fearful of the consequences and the continuation of the persecution from which they originally fled – can apply to be accepted by a third country or rely on the beneficence of others and there are many examples of religious establishments and concerned individuals who have taken 'failed asylum seekers' into their homes. Failing this, those refused legal status can turn to the illegal employment market where they will be exploited, paid extremely low wages for long working hours and will live in constant fear that their status will become known and that they may be arrested and charged. In another extremely controversial move, those seeking asylum were not even trusted with cash benefit payments but from the autumn of 2000 were given vouchers which they could only use in certain shops (Eagle et al. 2002). These vouchers limited the amount of financial support available to asylum seekers to 70 per cent of the benefit payment which would be given to the permanently resident and British citizens. Asylum seekers were forbidden to seek paid employment and were thereby forced into accepting these reduced payments through the National Asylum Support Service (NASS).

For many the voucher system was both unfair and the ultimate stigma which publicly proclaimed the individual asylum seeker's (lack of) status. Shops which took the vouchers were not even allowed to give the holder any change. It was later made illegal for third parties to buy the vouchers off the holders (this was a tactic which a number of supporters would use to put cash into the hands of those paid benefits in this way). The voucher system was short-lived, being scrapped by 2002 but not until after anti-voucher campaigns were set up across the country. In 2007 the House of Lords and House of Commons Joint Committee on Human Rights declared that in 'refusing permission for asylum seekers to work and operating a system of support which results in widespread destitution' the government met the threshold of inhuman and degrading treatment outlawed by Article 3 of the European Convention of Human Rights (2007: 5). The committee's evidence, which was refuted by the government in their reply to the report, clearly stated:

> Many witnesses have told us that they are convinced that destitution is a deliberate tool in the operation of immigration policy. We have been persuaded by the evidence that the Government has indeed been practising a deliberate policy of destitution of this highly vulnerable group. We believe that the deliberate use of inhumane treatment is unacceptable. We have seen instances in all cases where the Government's treatment of asylum seekers and refused asylum seekers falls below the requirements of the common law of humanity and of international human rights law. (2007: para. 120)

In addition further legislation barred homeless asylum seekers from applying for local authority housing. Instead they were to be provided with accommodation through NASS under a special form of tenure which removed any housing law protection and allowed easy and swift evictions. Fekete (2009: 30–1) has argued that these changes to the welfare system for asylum seekers have taken this group back to the pre-welfare state system of poor relief and the workhouse.

## Monitoring and dispersing

Straw put in place a 'modernisation programme' for the control of immigration which has seen the full force of modern science and technology employed to 'root out' (Home Office 2005ba: 5) illegal immigrants – from the x-raying of freight vehicles to ensure they did not include stowaways, to the fingerprinting of all visitors requesting visas and the insertion of biometric chips in all new passports issued so that an individual's progress through immigration and passport controls can be closely tracked. Straw's immigration bill also began a process of controlling the movement of refugees and asylum seekers within the UK which has continued up until the time of writing in 2009. He introduced a system whereby at the time of arrival those claiming asylum or refugee status were 'dispersed' to various parts of Britain (but not, at that time, Northern Ireland) with no say as to where they might end up. Not only was the personal cost of this scheme high – with individuals unable to settle in their chosen communities or with nearby friends and family – but it gave out another clear message that communities of asylum seekers living together was intolerable, a drain on educational and housing resources and an undesirable state of affairs. A number of asylum seeker support charities argued that the dispersal policy deprived people of their right to live where they choose and took them away from much needed informal support systems; instead individuals were routed through NASS for all their support needs. As a government funded body, however, its support was limited to that offered within government guidelines and procedures only.

## The criminalisation of immigration

Straw was succeeded as Home Secretary by David Blunkett. Blunkett's precursor to the Nationality, Immigration and Asylum Bill of 2002, the White Paper *Secure Borders, Safe Haven: Integration with Diversity in Modern Britain* (Home Office 2002a), rehearsed many of Straw's initial arguments but went even further in condemning what he termed as as an 'international "free for all", the so called "asylum shopping" throughout Europe', suggesting that further abuses of the immigration system were taking place. A recurring theme in Blunkett's pronouncements was the concern that Britain's benefit system and public service ethos was attracting groups of people who wished to take advantage of its welfare system and social safety net. Blunkett questioned the motivations of many of those attempting to visit or to settle in the UK and cast people seeking asylum as 'duplicitous' (Fekete 2009: 8), attracted to Britain for purely selfish reasons, draining the country's resources rather than adding to them. He introduced the idea that those newly accepted as British citizens should be required to pledge their allegiance to Britain and that migrants had a duty 'to facilitate their acceptance and integration' into the host population. Blunkett also signalled his intention to commence a debate concerning 'internal identification procedures' or entitlement cards such as were utilised in countries like Germany, in order that Britain would not look 'out of line' with other European countries. He suggested that the UK, without an identity card system, appeared as a soft touch for those seeking asylum on spurious or false grounds – all this despite the fact that Germany was known to take in more asylum seekers than other European countries.

In a strange twist of logic Blunkett also claimed that the numbers of migrants found trying to get into Britain through often dangerous and illegal means demonstrated the success of the Home Office in closing off legal means to enter the country. His argument might be seen to be based on strange and questionable logic but it perfectly summed up the government's attempts to severely restrict numbers of economic migrants and those seeking political asylum from reaching Britain's shores. As the 2002 Bill went through Parliament in April of that year Blunkett further announced his intention to remove refugee status from anyone committed of a serious crime whilst in Britain. A more insidious nod to the treatment of asylum seekers and refugees as though they were criminals came with his determination to put systems in place to keep a close watch on individual asylum seekers, to monitor not only their progress concerning their asylum claim but also to keep tabs on their movements around the country and their various addresses in the meantime. In addition those seeking asylum were to be tracked and made to report to government offices or police stations on a regular basis, as though under probation or other supervision orders.

Included in Blunkett's proposal 'to set up an end-to-end process of induction, accommodation and removal centres to support and monitor asylum seekers during the process of their claim' (Home Office 2002b) were plans for the incarceration of asylum seekers in specialist accommodation or detention centres, especially when facing removal from the country after a failed claim. These plans applied both to individuals and their families, placing children in prison-style accommodation blocks, isolated from the communities, schools and support groups on which many relied. While residents were technically free to come and go as they pleased from accommodation centres many were in isolated or rural localities without affordable links to larger centres of population. Educational, medical and other services were provided on site further isolating residents from the local community. Furthermore, a refusal to live in such a centre could mean removal of benefits. It was not only the physical buildings and surroundings of the accommodation centres which resembled the prison environment. Many of the centres were run by security companies such as Group 4 who were roundly criticised for treating residents as though they were detainees. Some designated detention centres were specifically designed to house those who had been refused permission to stay in the UK and who were awaiting 'removal' to another country. One such centre Yarl's Wood, opened in 2001, suffered a massive fire in February 2002 after a protest by those detained inside. According to news coverage the protest was triggered by complaints that staff regularly physically manhandled residents. After the fire at Yarl's Wood Blunkett responded that he would not rule out the use of the publicly funded Prison Service running such centres – as though the problem was not the philosophy behind such treatment but merely its insensitive or inappropriate practice in the private sector. There have since been a number of hunger strikes at the centre, a riot in November 2006, continued claims that the needs of children within the centres are neglected and further claims that women residents' need for privacy is not respected.

## Spiralling numbers?

All this attention on deterrence suggested that the numbers seeking asylum and migration to the UK were spiralling upwards and needed to be firmly taken in hand in order that the government could take control of the situation. In fact government statistics demonstrated that, while numbers seeking asylum had indeed risen, from just over 36,000 in 1997 to just over 119,000 in 2001, the majority were never granted asylum or exceptional leave to remain. In 2001 only 9 per cent of applications were fully granted and another 17 per cent allowed to remain, mean-ing 74 per cent were refused – a figure close to the 80 per cent refused in 1997. Furthermore, of those who were allowed to appeal the decision of the Home Office the vast majority (79 per cent in 2001) had their appeal dismissed (Hansard 2002). Far from Britain being a 'soft touch' on asylum, the system was in fact being robustly policed and most applications denied. Numbers seeking asylum in Britain peaked in 2002 but by 2005 applications had fallen by more than three-quarters (Home Office 2005a) while the number of people seeking asylum in other European countries was on the increase (Home Office 2007c).

## The debate around ID cards

Nevertheless, the rhetoric of a country under siege continued and by the end of 2004 Blunkett had introduced the Identity Cards Bill which, in the teeth of some opposition, made provision for a National Identity Register. It was justified in terms of its ability to:

- make the use of false and multiple identities more difficult thereby disrupting the activities of organised criminals and terrorists;
- tackle the abuse of immigration laws and prevent people working illegally without permits;
- ensure that free public services such as the National Health Service could only be used by those entitled to do so;
- allow the subsequent development of biometrics on identity documents.

In reality asylum seekers had been required to carry cards verifying their identity since 2000 and as Liberty, the national campaigning organisation set up to protect civil liberties, pointed out in its literature, ID cards were much more about provid-ing a mechanism for internal immigration control than to prevent fraud or to protect Britain from terrorism (Liberty 2009). Nevertheless, Blunkett continued to claim that the National Identity Card Scheme would strengthen civil liberties by protecting individuals from having their identities stolen (Home Office 2004a). In 2008 all foreign nationals from outside the European Economic Area (EEA) and Switzerland given permission to extend their stay in the United Kingdom were issued with ID cards. The categories of visitors to the UK who must have such a card was gradually extended so that by April 2011 anyone visit-ing the UK for a period of more than six months would be required to carry such a card. In effect this gave the distinct impression that asylum seekers, refugees, migrant workers and visitors to Britain must be policed differently from the rest of the population and that they somehow pose a serious security risk.

In 2007 the House of Lords and House of Commons Joint Committee on Human Rights warned the government that claiming asylum was not a criminal offence and that asylum seekers should not be treated as if they had broken the law but the government responded that they saw detention of those seeking asylum as normal, reasonable and a legitimate element of immigration control. Their anxieties, Bosworth comments:

> have found new resonance in the so-called 'immigration offender'. In turn, this shadowy individual has justified considerable extension in the state's powers of detention, surveillance and deportation, mechanisms that, increasingly, have come to impact on all our lives. (2008: 19)

Frances Webber (2006) concurs with such analysis concluding that the adoption of a penal framework to prevent the arrival of would-be refugees and to aid the departure of failed asylum seekers across Europe undermined the 1952 Geneva Convention which sought to protect those fleeing from persecution and has eroded the maintenance of a human rights discourse which had previously underlain treatment of claims for refugee and asylum status.

## Points-based immigration and responsibilisation

In 2005 a new White Paper *Secure Borders, Safe Haven: Integration with Diversity in Modern Britain* (Home Office: 2005a) set out government strategy on asylum and immigration for the next five years. Charles Clarke had succeeded David Blunkett as Home Secretary but once again the message of firm controls and the removal of illegal visitors and 'over-stayers' predominated – so much so that as Bosworth argues the government had succeeded in 'effectively erasing the distinction between criminal and asylum seeker' (2008: 18). In addition the tone of the White Paper was particularly exclusionary and framed immigration in a poor and negative light. One section entitled 'Who we admit and why', far from describing categories of people who would be admitted to Britain, consisted of a number of reasons and scenarios in which admittance would be denied. As a consequence the landscape of immigration was hardened in various ways. First the definition of the genuine migrant was much more closely prescribed; those wishing to work in Britain were henceforth to be subject to close testing in order that they demonstrate that their presence in Britain would deliver 'economic benefit' and a points system was introduced in order to facilitate such a test. The majority of overseas workers, all but the most highly skilled, were now required to prove that their time in the UK was sponsored – with the threat that loss of sponsorship would mean immediate removal of the right to remain. Financial costs were also to be added for workers in employment wherever, the White Paper suggested 'there has been evidence of abuse' (Home Office 2005a: 10). This would de facto exclude the poorest and in fact, low skilled workers from outside the EU were positively discouraged from applying for work in Britain in the first place. It was made clear that only highly skilled workers would be allowed to remain permanently.

For those seeking permanent residence in Britain there were further hurdles to jump. Clarke made it clear that entry criteria would be tightened and that all would be subject to English language tests. Little consideration was given to the personal circumstances of those who might forge relationships and strong bonds in the UK and instead temporary leave to remain was introduced for all seeking asylum so that if, in the first five years of a stay in the UK, the political situation altered in a refugee's country of origin in such a way that the Home Office considered their return to be safe, they would be required to leave the UK and for those who were already settled in the UK but with family abroad there was to be no immediate or automatic right for them to bring their relatives over to live with them on a permanent basis.

The use of technology to check and monitor migrants to Britain was also expanded. Most of these measures had previously been used only in the context of policing, arrest and punishment. Fingerprinting of *all* visa applicants, further use of detention centres and the electronic tagging of all asylum seekers whose applications had failed were to be introduced. All those arriving without documents were to be prosecuted and employers found to be using workers without the requisite papers and permissions subjected to fixed penalty fines. The White Paper also extended its agenda to minors, pledging to find ways to return unaccompanied child asylum seekers to their country of origin under the assumption that enough children were guilty of taking advantage of leniency within the immigration system that this 'loophole' had also to be tied up. Previously it had been acknowledged that the government had a duty of care towards any unaccompanied children finding their way into the immigration system[1] but this was now seriously diminished. In reality much of the increase in the numbers of people migrating to the UK reflected the success of the British economy in attracting a much needed workforce and an increase in numbers of overseas students (Home Office 2007b: 5). The continued expansion of the area covered by the European Union had also led to an enlargement of the European Economic Area and entitled citizens of numerous member-states to work and live abroad. These were steps seen to be of positive benefit to the British economy yet debates about increased numbers of migrant workers were also often couched in negative terms.

In debating his strategy in Parliament Charles Clarke signalled a key change in the government's approach to the policing of immigration. Henceforth, the responsibility for monitoring individual migrants was to be shared with a number of institutions – in this speech he singled out the university sector – and was no longer to be seen as solely the responsibility of the Border Agency and Home Office. He explained:

> The big issue involves a change of culture that runs right through the whole five-year strategy. We need to understand that responsibility for the migration and asylum system in this country is a matter not only for the Home Office and its agencies but for those who benefit from that migration. (Hansard 5 Jul 2005: Column 197)

These comments closely mirrored the crucial and much reported Home Office Circular 8/1984 which set off the community safety and partnership agendas in the policing of local communities (Crawford 1998: 36) and which culminated in the 'responsibilisation' of a range of public and private institutions in the prevention of crime. The new policy of issuing penalties and fines to businesses found to be employing workers 'knowing that they are not legally entitled to work in the UK' (Hansard 5 Jul 2005: Column 198) similarly 'responsibilised' the private business sector in the prevention of illegal migration.

## Wars and terror

Of course little more than four years after Labour came to power in 1997, the events of 11 September 2001 (9/11) when the New York Twin Towers and the Pentagon were struck by planes with the loss of nearly three thousand lives, dominated world headlines. In July 2005 four bombs placed on the public transport network in London brought a similarly shocked people across Britain eliciting the response from Tony Blair, then Prime Minister, that henceforth Britain was 'at war with terrorism' (*Guardian* 2009a). After 11 September 2001 and then again after the London bombings in 2005 the government updated its legislative powers, however its legislative programme on terrorism had commenced before the attacks on the United States and came with the passing of the Terrorism Act 2000.

## The Terrorism Act 2000

The Terrorism Act 2000 was intended to replace the Prevention of Terrorism Act (PTA) 1974 which had been enacted as a temporary response to violent events in Northern Ireland and which was replaced by the PTA of 1989 which was in turn renewed annually until the year 2000. At this point the threat of terrorist activity emanating from the political situation in Northern Ireland had dramatically receded and the old Act was seen as in need of replacement. However, rather than downsizing the government's response, the 2000 Act widened the definition of terrorism to include the use of 'serious violence' against persons or property by anyone motivated by a 'political, religious or ideological' cause. This move was condemned by civil rights organisations such as Liberty who were concerned that acts of vandalism could be treated in a similar way to violent attacks on people – for example anyone destroying a field of genetically modified crops, or breaking into a building to free captive animals from experimental laboratories, might be treated as involved in terrorist activities. Lord Carlile, chair of an independent review of terrorism legislation in 2007, noted the Act's 'broad definition' of terrorism and cautioned restraint in its implementation (Carlile 2007).

Previous anti-terrorist legislation, acknowledging the extreme nature of much action against terrorism and the removal of taken-for-granted human and civil rights which is often deemed necessary by the state under extreme circumstances, had always been justified on the basis of it being a temporary or emergency measure but the 2000 Act made its definitions and legislative responses a permanent state of affairs. This clashed somewhat with the government's stated pledge to protect human rights which it had enshrined in the passing of the Human Rights Act in 1998 but which could be argued to be incompatible with subsequent terrorism legislation. The 2000 Act allowed for the proscribing (in effect banning membership of but also making positive reference to and flying the flag of) a wider number and range of organisations than ever before. The list of proscribed groups was contentious and spurred claims that organisations such as Nelson Mandela's African National Congress would have been outlawed under the legislation which would have severely hampered the fight against injustice and apartheid in South Africa. A new offence of 'inciting terrorism' was also created, allowing individuals to be detained for seven days before being charged. Police powers were increased, including facilitating their stopping and searching of suspects.

## The Anti-Terrorism, Crime and Security Act 2001

The US response to 9/11 was rapid. Approximately six weeks after the attack the US government had put together a coalition of forces to invade Afghanistan,[2] from where Al Qaeda were said to operate, and rushed through anti-terrorist legislation in what was to be widely known as 'The Patriot Act'.[3] The British government was hot on its heels publishing its own Anti-Terrorism, Crime and Security Act 2001 by mid-November. This Act was controversial in both its scope and in the haste with which it was drafted and set up. Some particularly draconian measures were passed, especially concerning the treatment of foreign nationals on British soil who were suspected of aiding or committing terrorist acts. Henceforth, they could be indefinitely detained, without charge or trial and their rights to appeal against such detention were severely limited, appeals being heard by a closed and specially constituted immigration commission. First published on 13 November 2001 it had entered the statute book by 14 December and the first foreign nationals detained under the Act were interned on 19 December. Three years later on 16 December 2004, the legislation came under severe criticism when a specially-convened committee of nine Law Lords held that detaining foreigners without trial breached the European Convention on Human Rights incorporated into domestic law by the Human Rights Act 1998. This section of the law was also deemed by the Law Lords to be discriminatory as it only applied to foreigners, not to citizens of the UK.

In addition to an increase in powers of detention, the 2001 Act granted the British police and security services the power to ask public bodies to disclose personal records whenever terrorism and criminal investigations were taking place. It extended penalties already in existence for those staging bomb hoaxes to other hoaxes such as false anthrax attacks. The legislation also allowed for freezing the assets of suspected terrorists at the start of an investigation to prevent any funds being moved or used and enabled the Treasury to make such a freezing order if it reasonably believed that any action likely to be of detriment to the United Kingdom's economy was likely to take place. Controversially this part of the anti-terrorist legislation was later used against the country of Iceland after the collapse of that economy threatened to destabilise parts of British industry in 2008. Extending its strategy of 'responsibilisation', all airlines were required to ensure that passengers were genuine; communication service providers were asked to ensure that their data on individual users could be accessed by law agencies investigating terrorism or criminal activities and all financial institutions were obliged to monitor accounts and to contact law agencies if they believed there were 'reasonable grounds' to suspect an account was being used to finance terrorism. It has been argued that this Act 'established firm legislative links between asylum and terrorism by including measures meant to deny prospective or suspected terrorists access to asylum and allowing applicants' fingerprints to be kept for ten years in order to prevent multiple claims by such individuals' (Bosworth and Guild 2008: 703–4). These links were to be further continued in subsequent anti-terror laws passed by the UK parliament.

## The Prevention of Terrorism Act 2005

The 2001 Act was followed by legislation in 2005, again in 2006 and also in 2008.[4] By the end of March 2003 both the United States and the British government were embroiled in the invasion of Iraq despite global opposition to this escalation of military action. In fact the global opposition to the invasion spawned what was almost certainly the largest political movement in social history as millions marched in co-ordinated demonstrations across the world on 15 February 2003. The government response under Blair, however, was to continue its rhetoric of 'war on terror' and to continue the war in Iraq and to legislate against terrorism at home. The Prevention of Terrorism Act 2005, was partially designed to respond to the Law Lords' criticism of the detention of suspects without trial which had been made possible, and swiftly put into practice after the 2001 Act. While repealing those parts of the previous legislation which had allowed for detention without trial, the 2005 Act created a more draconian measure to control suspected terrorists in the form of the 'control order'.[5] Control orders could be used to restrict the movements – even to the point of house arrest and electronic tagging – of those suspected of 'involvement in terrorism-related activity', even if this activity took place abroad. Addressing the Law Lords' concern that detention orders had discriminated against foreign nationals, control orders were made equally applicable to those with British nationality. Similar to the anti-social behaviour order,[6] control orders required a lower standard of proof than in a criminal case but breach of an order was designated a criminal offence punishable by imprisonment. While control orders could only be issued for up to a 12-month period they could be annually renewed and were therefore, in reality, issued for an indefinite period of time. They were later dubbed 'an affront to justice' and a contravention of human rights law (*Guardian* 2006c).

The 2005 Act received royal assent in March of that year yet only a few months later, on 7 July, four suicide bombers in London took the lives of a further 52 people on the London public transport system. Only two weeks later four more men attempted, but failed, to detonate bombs in tube carriages and on a London bus – and a fifth abandoned his attempt. It was reported that both attacks were motivated by anger at the invasion and continuing occupation of Iraq and to bring attention to the treatment of Muslims by western forces, most notably in Palestine and Chechnya (*Scotsman* 2005). Whatever the motivation, London and the wider British population was left in a state of shock. On 22 July a Brazilian man, Jean-Charles de Menezes, was followed from his home and shot dead by London Metropolitan Police officers on a tube train waiting to depart from Stockwell station after being wrongly identified as a terrorist suspect, raising many concerns about the ability of London's police to stay calm and respond in a measured way in such circumstances. This fear was compounded after the police presented a number of misleading accounts of the events to the media (McLaughlin 2007). Nevertheless, neither the police, nor the government were shifted from their existing course and the subsequent Terrorism Act 2006 extended the allowable detention period for terrorist suspects pre-charge from 14 days, following The Criminal Justice Act 2003, to 28 days. The government had wanted a 90 day pre-charge detention period but this proved politically unpopular and had to be dropped from their plans.

## The Terrorism Act 2006

The 2006 Act focused on curtailing the supporters or sympathisers of terrorism. It was written in response to the fact that the people who planted and set off the 7 July bombs in London were 'home-grown'; not only British passport holders but also British-born. The previous clampdown on 'foreigners' entering the UK was obviously no longer seen as able to hit the mark and attention was turned towards those British people and British communities who it was considered might foster terrorists or their sympathisers. In effect this meant a surveillance of Muslims and the communities to which they traditionally belonged. The new legislation included a prohibition on the 'glorification' of terrorism or the 'praising' of terrorist actions in any way which might increase support for the act or its perpetrators, with a maximum penalty of seven years' imprisonment. Expressing anything less than condemnation of terrorist acts, expressing sympathy or understanding of the motives or political ideologies of those engaged in terrorist acts, might be branded as support. The act also introduced penalties for anyone publishing material relating to any proscribed group or those who trained in terrorist techniques. It extended terrorism stop and search powers to cover bays and estuaries and enabled the police to search boats and other vessels, leading to a number of bizarre arrests of those found to be too near certain docksides and seafronts. The Act also turned to the threat of a terrorist 'dirty bomb', making it an offence to make or possess radioactive devices or material. It amended the Serious Organised Crime and Police Act of 2005 to make it a criminal offence to trespass on a nuclear site, the penalty for which – imprisonment for up to 51 weeks – additionally acted as a serious check on the activities of anti-nuclear protestors who had secured a tradition of protesting annually outside, and if possible within, such sites as the Faslane nuclear submarine base in Scotland.

## The Counter-Terrorism Act 2008

While the debates raged around the efficacy and advisability of existing and new legislation to combat the threat of terrorism, the media and government officials reported continued threats to the UK and 'foiled' terrorist attacks. In June 2007 another innocent civilian was shot by the police in London, this time in his own house. The police acting on what turned out to be faulty intelligence that chemical or biological weapons were being made in a house in Forest Gate, London, organised a raid at which one of two brothers arrested was shot in the shoulder, but not fatally. So much damage was meted out to the home in which the brothers lived that the police had to spend over £120,000 in repair costs (*Daily Telegraph* 2009) Later, in June that year, two unexploded car bombs were found outside London Haymarket nightclubs and the following day two men drove a Jeep packed with gas cylinders into the front of Glasgow airport. The resulting fireball burned one of the Jeep's occupants so badly that he later died in hospital while another was arrested at the scene. The survivor, a British-born Muslim, was later sentenced to 32 years in prison.

The following year saw the Counter-Terrorism Act 2008 which further increased the powers of the police investigating terrorist threats. It allowed the fingerprinting and taking of DNA samples from individuals subject to control orders introduced by earlier anti-terrorist legislation and allowed this information to be shared with the national police database. It also gave the police the power to enter, using force, the homes of anyone subject to such a control order. This civil order was thereby moved even closer to a state of penal detention and a fully-fledged 'house arrest'. The Act also allowed for extended sentences to be meted out to those whose offence was connected to terrorism in any way. It also allowed the police to place restrictions on the right to travel abroad for anyone convicted of terrorist offences. In perhaps one of its more controversial clauses it is now a criminal offence to elicit or attempt to elicit any information about a member of the armed forces, the intelligence services or a constable which is likely to be useful to a person committing or preparing an act of terrorism. This section of the legislation was later used to prevent tourists taking pictures of typical London scenes – the photographing of a London bus by one man and his young son was even seen as suspect – but perhaps more importantly journalists and political activists have also been impeded from taking footage of the policing of demonstrations. The 2008 Act also amended the Regulation of Investigatory Powers Act 2000 (RIPA), explored further in Chapter 9, which allowed more types of evidence gathered through intercepted communication to be used in court. Post-charge questioning of terrorist suspects was also extended to allow for an initial charge to be replaced with a more appropriate offence at a later stage.

## The continued erosion of civil liberties

Throughout the passing of the anti-terror legislation from 2000 onwards there were concerns from organisations and individuals concerned with the protection of civil liberties that the legislation was being enacted in haste, that it represented a knee-jerk and ill-considered reaction to the problems of terrorist actions on British soil and that its measures were removing hard-won civil liberties which had protected the rights of British citizens for many centuries and been enshrined in the Magna Carta since the thirteenth century. This 'Charter of Freedom' had curtailed the powers of the monarchy and granted the individual subject of the crown a range of personal freedoms, and protection against unlawful imprisonment. It was generally perceived that the surveillance, monitoring and regulation of individual behaviours by the state had significantly eroded these rights and that state powers over the individual had reached hitherto unanticipated proportions. All this was aided by the introduction of new technologies such as iris scanning, the taking and storing of fingerprints electronically, the use of biometric chips which enabled much personal information to be stored on documents such as passports and improved and extended computer programming which allowed for the sharing of personal data held by the state across a number of different databases.

The 2008 Bill garnered less support both within and outside Parliament. The civil rights organisation Liberty, backed by the Council of Europe's human rights commissioner, pointed out that the UK had the longest period of pre-charge detention for terrorist suspects in the western world,[7] and that at 28 days this was seven times the limit for someone suspected of murder (*Guardian* 2008a). The government first pushed for an increase to 90 days' detention and the idea of indefinite detention was even mooted (*Guardian* 2007c) while settling for 42 days detention in 2008. Although narrowly winning this in the House of Commons the government found in the face of mounting opposition and outright rejection of this clause in the House of Lords that this proposal eventually had to be shelved. Many other severely criticised proposals were placed on the statute books however, leading to warnings from many quarters including senior judges and police officers that the state was abusing its powers.[8] Control orders, for example, have been persistently challenged as inhuman and degrading. Individuals and their families held under such orders are routinely electronically tagged, restricted in who can visit them in their homes, in access to the internet and subject to long curfews when they must not leave their homes. Many who are so 'detained' without trial, will not know what the charge is against them and therefore cannot mount a legal challenge against their imposition although they may be subject to these conditions for many years (*Guardian* 2007d). In November 2007 Britain's highest court backed control orders while ruling that 18-hour curfews were inhuman (but accepting 12 hours) and ruling that suspects must be given access to any evidence held against them. Nevertheless, certain planned provisions of the 2008 Act were subsequently dropped in the face of mounting criticism – as well as the plans for 90 days' pre-charge detention, plans to allow certain inquests to be held in secret for the sake of 'national security' were also shelved

## War-weariness?

On a less severe but no less serious note, anti-terrorist measures have changed many more mundane practices of the British people since 2001. It has become much more usual to see British police armed with guns and rifles at airports, in major city centres and at transport interchanges. Those places considered terrorist targets such as the City of London and Parliament Square have gained an architecture of security (Coaffee and Rogers 2008) with large concrete anti-blast barriers and police road-blocks. Posters urging everyone to look out for and report suspicious objects and persons festoon the London transport services. All air travel has been subject to severe restrictions and anti-terror laws have limited many legal protests and demonstrations. In the background to this changing scenery of British life the media have reported on the inhumane and degrading treatment, together with the torture,[9] of prisoners abroad, most notably in the US facility at Guantanamo Bay and within Iraq at Abu Ghraib prison by American and British military forces and special services alike. These revelations have provoked much outrage. Perhaps reflecting the public's growing distaste with the state's actions, in December 2007 a jury refused to convict Cerie Bullivant, a British Muslim subject to a control order, of any offence after he admitted going on the run after feeling that the restrictions of his control order were leading him close to a nervous breakdown (*Guardian* 2007e).

From 2001 onwards the government has repeatedly warned of a growing terrorist threat in Britain and has constantly sought to justify its increased powers by reference to foiled terrorist acts and plans. However, a number of these warnings have turned out to be unsubstantiated. Well-publicised terrorist 'plots' and arrests have turned up no evidence and some of those charged have been released.[10] By the time the 2008 Act was published opposition to the government's agenda on terrorism was growing, Blair had left the Prime Ministerial leadership role to be replaced by Gordon Brown as Prime Minister, and Blair's leadership and that of his former cabinet was under increasing criticism. As far as anti-terror measures were concerned, there was a growing feeling that the government may have over-stepped the mark in continuing to push for more legislative powers in the face of growing criticism (Bosworth and Guild 2008). In the face of this uneasiness, how-ever, Blair had claimed that Britons would have to accept a reduction in their civil liberties in order that the government had the tools at its disposal to combat ter-rorism (*Guardian* 2007f).

Criticism was growing too of the ways in which the police and other authori-ties were (mis)using terrorist legislation for different ends (Mythen et al. 2009). The granting of extensive stop and search powers under section 44 of the Terrorism Act 2001 had, by 2008, led to year-on-year increases in numbers stopped. According to media reports in the year 2002/3 the number of stops and searches of 'Asians' had increased by 302 per cent, by 230 per cent for 'blacks' and 118 per cent for 'whites' compared to the previous year. And after the Haymarket bombs of 2007 numbers of Asians stopped trebled again. Anti-terror legislation allowed the police to make stops without any grounds for suspicion and it was estimated that only six out of every ten thousand people stopped under these powers were arrested, and even fewer charged or found guilty of an offence. (*Guardian* 2009b: 15).

## Linking crime, terror and immigration

In April 2008 the UK Border Agency was formed, according to its website 'to improve the United Kingdom's security through stronger border protection while welcoming *legitimate* [my emphasis] travellers and trade' (Home Office 2008). It brought together work which had been previously carried out by a number of agencies – the Border and Immigration Agency, Her Majesty's Revenue and Customs and UK Visa Services. The new agency was driven by its 'security' agenda and closely linked 'foreigners', security and immigration rules. It was followed later in the year by the then Home Secretary Jacqui Smith's announcement of increased measures to 'ban foreign-born "preachers of hate" and other violent extremists from Britain' (*Guardian* 2008b). In a speech which reiterated many of the agendas which the government had stressed over previous years, Smith claimed 'Coming to Britain is a privilege and I don't want to extend that privilege to individuals who abuse our standards and values to undermine our way of life'

(*Guardian* 2008b: 10). Migration had become a security issue linked to crime and terror and invoked threats to a mythical public order which was in need of considerable protection by the forces of the state (Yuval-Davis et al. 2005). Green and Grewcock (2002) have gone further in arguing that the UK state was involved in a 'war against immigration' paralleling their stated 'war on terror', linking both in the minds of the public. At the same time Smith's restatement of 'our values' counterposed a preferred 'British way of life' to those 'foreign' values which sullied a pre-existing culture and set of national standards.

## Concluding comments

Throughout the development of the legislation explored above, discourses around migration, whether this had come about through economic hardship or political persecution, and the threat of terrorism have become ever more closely entangled. In the popular media, as well as in government pronouncements, discussion of one too often becomes a proxy for the other (Malloch and Stanley 2005: 53). As Bosworth and Guild explain:

> Post 9/11, the anti-terrorism legislation added a potent master-signifier to the mix of risky non-citizens in the form of the terrorist suspect. Subject to many of the same exclusionary strategies used for asylum seekers, most notably detention, the terrorist suspect has come to represent both the most extreme threat, and inherent danger, posed by all migration not strictly regulated. In other words, just as the 1998 White Paper presented asylum as a possible route for 'bogus' claimants who were in fact seeking economic opportunities in Britain, after 2001, asylum and economic migration in turn became commonly viewed as possible 'routes in' for foreign terrorists. (2008: 703)

A country which already detains and imprisons more asylum seekers than any other European nation (Malloch and Stanley 2005) set about increasingly excluding 'foreigners' both in terms of their actual numbers and from full social participation and citizenship rights. This shift has 'demonstrate[d] a move away from a rehabilitative model of crime control towards a law-and-order approach that emphasizes deterrence and incapacitation [which] is not simply a case of punitive crime control strategies leaching into migration policies' (Bosworth and Guild 2008: 703). Although this leaching has undoubtedly occurred the regulation of those who are termed 'non-citizens' has also served to set up divisions within the nation, between its regions and its communities and has moved government policy dangerously further away from a discourse based on rights and justice. This move has also affected more *local* crime control measures as Fekete (2009: 9) aptly observes once barriers, exclusions and contested practices are set up for one group of people they become more respectable and are easier to extend and implement for other groups. It is to 'the enemy within' that we now turn.

## FURTHER READING

Fekete, L. (2009) *A Suitable Enemy: Racism, Migration and Islamophobia in Europe*. London: Pluto Press.
Kundnani, A. (2007) *The End of Tolerance: Racism in the 21st Century*. London: Pluto Press.

## NOTES

1  In 2006 unaccompanied children accounted for 84 per cent of the total granted Humanitarian Protection and Discretionary Leave to remain in the UK, despite only accounting for 9 per cent of initial decisions (Home Office 2007a: 9).
2  The invasion of Afghanistan was justified by the need to oust the Taliban, who were thought to have links with Al Qaeda the purported instigators of 9/11, from its control of the country.
3  PATRIOT is an acronym for 'Providing Appropriate Tools Required to Intercept and Obstruct Terrorism'. Among its provisions the Act allowed for the searching of telephone, email, and financial records without a court order and expanded the access of law enforcement agencies to many public and privately held information, including library, medical and financial records. It also allowed immigration authorities much discretion in the detention and deportation of foreigners suspected of terrorism-related acts. The legislation was heavily criticised for its curtailment of civil liberties and the haste with which it was enacted.
4  These were the Prevention of Terrorism Act 2005; the Terrorism Act 2006; and the Counter-Terrorism Act 2008.
5  These are enacted under civil rather than criminal law.
6  Indeed, it was dubbed by some 'the anti-terrorist "asbo"' (Macdonald 2007: 601).
7  The Prevention of Terrorism (Temporary Provisions) Act 1989 allowed the police to detain suspected terrorists for 48 hours on their own authority, with the possibility of an extension or extensions of detention for a maximum of a further 5 days authorised by the Secretary of State. The Terrorism Act 2000 allowed for pre-charge detention up to 7 days. This was subsequently amended by the Criminal Justice Act 2003, which increased the maximum period for pre-charge to 14 days. The Terrorism Act 2006 further extended pre-charge detention up to 28 days (though periods of more than 2 days should be approved by a judicial authority).
8  In 2007 the *Guardian* newspaper even reported that police sources suspected that the Home Office was leaking information on possible terror plots in order to divert attention away from the government's own problems (*Guardian* 2007i).
9  It was alleged that the British government was complicit in the torture of both British citizens and foreign nationals abroad. The *Guardian* newspaper complained that the government had 'outsourced' interrogation techniques involving the torture of British nationals in Pakistan, thus in effect handing British nationals over to intelligence services which it knows to use torture and so turning a blind eye to the use of techniques outlawed on British soil. It also claimed that the British government was involved in the

'rendition circuit' wherein prisoners are secretly moved from areas where such techniques are outlawed to those where they are practised (*Guardian* 2008d).

10    In 2004, for example, nine men were arrested in Manchester and were reported as plotting to attack the Trafford Centre and Manchester United football ground but this was later proved to be conjecture. In 2009 the high profile arrest of eleven students supposedly engaged in terrorist planning in the North West resulted in no charges under terrorist legislation although all were subsequently held under threat of deportation.

# 8

# Fighting the enemy within: building cohesive communities

Although the Labour government came to power in 1997 voicing a commitment to involve communities in crime prevention, the actual infrastructure which they put in place for community participation 'was far from solid or robust' (Gilling 2007: 92). The 'local governance of crime' rested upon the formation of Crime and Disorder Reduction Partnerships (CDRPs) which were loose organisational structures which, although they included 'lead' partners from a variety of local and community-based organisations thought to have a stake in the prevention of crime in the neighbourhood, proved to be rather top-down and bureaucratic in their approach. They were led in the main by their local authority partners, together with the police, and directed to a large extent by externally fixed targets for crime reduction. Their particular organisational ethos was based around a target-driven agenda to reduce key crimes and this moved them away from a 'social-needs' model which encompassed a broader definition of the 'safety' agenda. Missing from this agenda were any matters which fell outside the usual, normative crime reduction framework such as safe employment practices, sustainable and environmentally-aware production methods, fraudulent businesses or indeed monitoring of policing practices.

## Setting the agenda for communities

That the community should gaze on the crimes of the locally and nationally powerful, although not explicitly ruled out by Home Office guidance (Whyte 2004: 54) was generally not ruled in either. Indeed, Whyte's research clearly shows that Home Office priorities, most notably on vehicle crime, burglary and youth offending also dominated the lists of priorities set by local crime reduction and community safety partnerships. Furthermore, his research sample of partnerships in the north-west included no organisations, such as the Health and Safety Executive, Trading Standards or indeed local environmental health departments which might have lent the community safety agenda its wider focus, although all included representatives of businesses and other local elites. The community safety agenda was supposed to be more sensitive to the needs of a wider range of community members than the narrow, Home Office generated, crime reduction model of old. The needs of minority ethnic groups and women should have featured strongly in its remit yet even domestic violence and hate crime – issues which had been fought over and achieved recognition as generating serious harm and which had been pushed up the criminological agenda in the preceding decades – found themselves well down the list of these supposedly community-generated priorities.

Crime and Disorder Reduction Partnerships were used to drive the old priorities of administrative criminology down to the level of the community while offering a veneer of community input which helped to obscure this reality. The 'safety' agenda was once again dominated by the priorities of the state and properly constituted community-led prioritisation was marginalised and suffocated from the beginning. The spaces which had previously existed within which community groups could raise their voices were now passed over as the government funding for community safety work was increasingly channelled through narrowly focused CDRPs. Glossy brochures were posted through every door detailing the findings of community safety audits and advertising the priorities for the local neighbourhood. As control over the direction of crime prevention shifted inexorably upwards, some of the real troubles which beset particular neighbourhoods and the vulnerable groups within them were lost and largely forgotten.

## 'Community cohesion'

It was in the north-west, as we have seen in Chapter 6, that the complacency surrounding the new community safety agenda was blown out of the water. The civil disturbances in Bradford, Burnley and Oldham in 2001 demonstrated the fragility of community relations on the ground, at least in these particular areas, while signalling that divisive and dangerous forces might well be at work in other similar neighbourhoods. These street confrontations in the three towns were followed by their own local enquiries which focused on separation and segregation of diverse communities as a key catalyst for these troubles. The then Home Secretary, David Blunkett responded by setting up a Ministerial Group on Public Order and Community Cohesion in order 'to examine and consider how national policies might be used to promote better community cohesion, based upon shared values and a celebration of diversity' (Cantle 2001: 2). Blunkett also established a Review Team, led by Ted Cantle, 'to seek the views of local residents and community leaders in the affected towns and in other parts of England on the issues which need to be addressed to bring about social cohesion and also to identify good practice in the handling of these issues at local level' (Cantle 2001: 2).

The ensuing 'Cantle Report' expressed surprise at the extent to which different religious and ethnic communities in the towns and cities visited by the authors led 'parallel lives'. It reported that:

> Separate educational arrangements, community and voluntary bodies, employment, places of worship, language, social and cultural networks, means that many communities operate on the basis of a series of parallel lives. These lives often do not seem to touch at any point, let alone overlap and promote any meaningful interchanges. (Cantle 2001: 9)

This theme of communities living 'parallel lives' dominated the debate after publication of the report. Cantle criticised the piecemeal and short-term funding initiatives which had hitherto supported community groups and which served to institutionalise ideas of separation and difference. He argued that building 'community cohesion', and bringing disparate communities to the same table to work together on common difficulties, was the answer to the problems of cultures at variance with each other' (Burnett 2004a). In the ensuing debate progressive ideas of multi-culturalism which allowed for diversity and difference to flourish and be celebrated were questioned and posed as problematic. Another discourse gained ascendancy – that building commonalities in culture and values, a common identification with the nation-state and a shared concept of 'Britishness' (which has itself remained poorly defined) were posited as solutions to divided lives. Inherent in this turn away from consideration of difference and towards the seeking of commonality was an implied criticism of cultural systems or sets of beliefs which lay outside this particular framework. Consequently, there emerged a tendency to blame for their isolation those who insisted on a lifestyle which was not deemed 'British' enough.

Cantle's report looked at the perceived 'problem' of immigration into the UK which was raised in consultative meetings across the country. He concluded that henceforth all people wishing to take up British citizenship should take an oath of allegiance to Britain, that there should be a discussion of the rights and responsibilities conferred by 'citizenship' and that what it means to be 'British' should be more clearly delineated. Blunkett took this approach a step further – focusing, not only on new migrants to Britain but also calling for all British people of Asian heritage to integrate, adopt British 'norms of acceptability' and marry other British Asians rather than anyone from their country of origin (Werber 2005: 746). Unsurprisingly Blunkett's comments were met with much outrage. Migrants to Britain and particular minority ethnic communities were singled out for specific attention and their own 'internal cohesiveness and cultural distinctiveness' (Werber 2005: 746) constructed as a problematic rather than as a positive force, while the part played by white separatists and extremists in attempting to divide communities and neighbourhoods was largely passed by.

## A clash of cultures?

Cantle went on to head up the government's new Community Cohesion Review Team as the idea of promoting 'community cohesion' gained major political currency. By 2002 Beverley Hughes, a Home Office Minister, was charged with co-ordinating a ministerial group supported by the Community Cohesion Unit (CCU) based in the Home Office. The Local Government Association (LGA) published guidance 'designed to assist all local authorities ... and their partners in strengthening and building community cohesion' (LGA 2002: 2). This guidance stressed the importance of the mainstreaming of community cohesion in all areas of a local authority's work and the building of 'a common vision' (ibid.: 6) for all communities. Its main message was that the failure of communities to relate positively to one another was the key to understanding the violent disturbances of 2001. As Werber has pointed out, all economic and political explanations were set aside as problems at neighbourhood level were placed firmly at the feet of a clash of cultures:

> Not economic deprivation or racism, or the sense of threat to community provoked by the presence of racist organisation in the towns where the riots took place, but a lack of community cohesiveness and leadership were thus blamed. (Werber 2005: 748)

This foregrounding of an explanation for local troubles rooted in the clash of cultures thesis mirrored developments at a national and international level whereby anti-west terrorism and the prosecution of war in Afghanistan and Iraq after 9/11 were largely understood in the same terms.[1] At the neighbourhood level this culminated in a largely superficial set of solutions to locally-experienced problems which emphasised the importance of dialogue between segregated communities while the material circumstances which had led to segregation were left unaddressed and the role of extremist politics in setting alight underlying tensions remained underplayed. The marriage of local and international concerns with suspect 'cultures' led to a powerful and persuasive focus on the most culturally distinct groups, rather than the more amorphous and unorganised indigenous white population. Yet 'Britishness' was held up as culturally and morally superior to all other ways of being and, as the fundamentals of Islam were questioned and attacked on a global scale, so this translated easily down to the local level.

## Pushing the 'community cohesion' agenda forward

Despite its shortcomings, the community cohesion agenda has become further entrenched in the policy-making of national and local government. The Community Cohesion Unit worked closely with the already established Neighbourhood Renewal Unit and Local Strategic Partnerships (LSPs) (see

Chapter 3) to ensure that regeneration of local areas gave full consideration to the smoothing out of local tensions. 'Community cohesion' was not seen to be something that the government could impose on neighbourhoods, it could merely facilitate its development. However, while one CCU factsheet on Community Cohesion and Neighbourhood Renewal stated 'cohesion is something which people themselves generate' (ODPM undated), it also emphasised the importance of all communities taking on board the government's nationally-generated agenda. This agenda was imposed on local neighbourhoods in various ways. In 2003 the Community Cohesion Pathfinder Programme funded 14 areas for an 18-month period with £6 million of funding committed to develop a range of pilot programmes available to communities desperately in need of financial support and to be used to explore ways of engaging communities within regeneration and cohesion agendas. In addition the LGA's guidance on community cohesion published in 2002, which made reference to 'unity in diversity', 'cultural pluralism', the celebration of difference and building respect between different faith communities (LGA 2002: 13, 22), outlined how numerous service-providers from policing, to education, employment and housing should play a part in developing cohesive communities and pushing the agenda forward. Furthermore, local authorities were charged with mainstreaming community cohesion in their service delivery and developing community cohesion plans delivered through and led by LSPs but evolving strategies for community involvement.

## Local authorities and the corrosion of care

Fears over rising crime have spawned a number of government initiatives which are played out at the local level, extending the local governance of crime into wider areas than before. Some of these initiatives have fundamentally changed the relationship between citizens and their local government forged since the creation of the local authority's duty of care to those which come under its remit. Previously local authorities were given a duty to look after and provide services for all people, especially the vulnerable, living within their geographical locality. However, deep cuts in welfare provision, together with policies which have pushed the privatisation of social provision, have seriously eroded local authorities' ability to provide for its local populace and this has been true for some decades. Additionally, however, the years spanning the turn of the twenty-first century saw a more punitive relationship develop between local government and citizen. As Aas has noted 'one does not need prisons to be, or feel, incarcerated in the locality' (2007: 293). He argues that 'Beyond the detention estate, a web of surveillance and enforcement has been constructed through workplace sanctions, citizen reporting campaigns, ID cards, dispersal policies, destitution tests and a separate system of voucher-based welfare for asylum seekers' (Aas 2007 in Weber and Bowling 2008: 362–3) and local authorities and locally-based organisations have been forced to become complicit in the punitive turn.

## Active communities and the culture of 'respect'

In 2003 the Office of the Deputy Prime Minister (ODPM) launched Sustainable Communities Plans in all regions which set out to strengthen their economic base, to tackle housing shortages, to create pleasant living environments for all and once again to ensure strong communities flourished. Combating crime and signs of social deprivation were key to these strategies but they also took a wider view of the regeneration problem and set out to improve transport links and embed economic growth throughout the UK, not just in the south-west and London, to make the most of a growing national economy. While John Prescott at the ODPM was engaged in the building of local economies, housing and cleaner environments David Blunkett, as the then Home Secretary, launched an initiative to develop 'active citizens'. In many ways the work of these two politicians within and around communities demonstrated the 'old' and 'new' style of Labour politics at work at one and the same time. Prescott's office was concerned with altering the material conditions within which communities could take action while Blunkett's approach was focused around the changing of personal behaviour and attitudes. Prescott was concerned with tackling economic inequality and social polarisation while the New Labour agenda, as epitomised in Blunkett's approach, to a great extent denied the link between inequalities and criminality (Goldson 2002). Blunkett clearly identi-fied manifest problems as emanating at the 'community' level – from a lack of respect, from the attitudes of young people 'who bad mouth and abuse those around them' (Blunkett 2003: 2) and from those who demand their rights without taking up their responsibilities. Blunkett's agenda on 'active citizenship' was respon-sibilisation writ large, encouraging people to solve their own problems, but with the support of government to help them do so. In a clear separation from Prescott's approach 'civil renewal', Blunkett added, 'is not a programme, but an on-going ethos to be applied to the development of active citizenship, strengthened communities, and a partnership approach to delivering public services' (Blunkett 2003: 38).

For Blunkett, communities without active citizens were particularly crime-prone and the strengthening of community ties was key to tackling crime at the local level. Blunkett's office was responsible for the White Paper: *Respect and Responsibility: Taking a Stand Against Anti-Social Behaviour* (Home Office, 2003) which set out the government's approach to the promotion of individual respon-sibility for tackling crime and anti-social behaviour. Blair was later to return to the concept of 'respect' to underpin his own anti-crime agenda. As he considered attitudinal changes as paramount to the engendering of civil renewal, Blunkett's ethos provided little in the way of concrete aid to communities. A pamphlet, *Active Citizens, Strong Communities: Progressing Civil Renewal* authored by

Blunkett himself, set out his agenda. It highlighted many examples of community groups organising action against crime and he devoted a section to descriptions of ongoing reforms to make the police more accountable, a commitment to expanding networks of Neighbourhood Watch, encouraging more people to become Special Constables and to bringing the criminal justice system closer to people with the use of restorative and community justice. Blunkett also pledged to do more for the protection of victims.

In 2004 Blunkett launched the policy paper *Building Communities, Beating Crime*. In the context of falling crime rates (he estimated a 30 per cent reduction in crime since 1997) (Home Office 2004b: 5) he put forward a strategy to greatly extend neighbourhood policing and ensure greater community accessibility to their local police service, making £50 million available for 2,000 new community support officers. This shift to a 'modernised' and more accountable police service reflected what McLaughlin has perceived as:

> An overwhelming public desire, in the context of a full-blown crime panic, for a return to traditional order maintenance policing in the form of uniformed officers on foot patrol, working from local police stations, keeping the streets and neighbourhoods free of petty crime and anti-social/morally offensive behaviour. (2007: 189)

By 2005 Charles Clarke had replaced Blunkett as Home Secretary but the government's perspective of community cohesion and community empowerment remained little altered. Clarke and Hazel Blears, then Minister of State within the Home Office but later to become Secretary of State for Communities and Local Government, launched the *Together We Can Action Plan* which continued in the same vein as Blunkett's earlier work. *Together We Can* pledged to bring communities, the public and voluntary sectors and businesses together in order to build safer communities, reduce reoffending and increase confidence in the criminal justice system. Also following Blunkett's lead the first Community Justice Centre – situated in north Liverpool – was opened in September 2005 and eleven more were later announced. Following a model developed in New York in 2002, Community Justice Centres bring a 'one-stop-shop' approach to criminal justice with courtrooms, other criminal justice agencies and general advice and support for offenders together under one roof.

While many of these policy developments could be seen to invest communities with positive strategies for action the call for communities to be active in their own renewal began to take on an increasingly moral tone. In September 2005 the Respect Task Force was created. Situated within the Home Office, and reporting to Hazel Blears, this was a cross-departmental initiative which strove to create a 'culture of respect' at neighbourhood level. In early 2006 Tony Blair, with much fanfare, launched his *Respect Action Plan* – its language was particularly condemnatory of anti-social behaviour and petty offending and drove a clear line between the law-abiding and the troublesome and at times, with its tag-line 'Give Respect: Get

Respect' it was almost evangelical in tone. In the Foreword to the plan Blair promised 'tough action so that the majority of law-abiding, decent people no longer have to tolerate the behaviour of the few individuals and families that think they do not have to show respect to others' (2006: 3). The Plan's 'new approach' to 'problem families' was described as 'challenging them to accept support to change their behaviour, backed up by enforcement measures' (Blair 2006: 3). What were perceived as the causes of anti-social behaviour? According to the *Respect Action Plan* anti-social behaviour occurs as a result of four major factors: 'Parenting': poor parenting skills or families involved in criminality; 'Schools': truancy and schools letting bad behaviour go unchallenged; 'Community': deprived and neglected communities where peer pressure pushes individuals into troublesome behaviour and 'Individuals': the misuse of drugs or alcohol and getting into trouble at a young age (Blair 2006: 5). For the authors of the plan, the context to a rise in increasingly disrespectful behaviour was a fall in unemployment, 700,000 less children living in poverty and much improved public services which had been put in place since 1997. Poverty, unemployment and poor public services were thereby ruled out as contributory factors and instead the parents, the individual, the school and the community were singled out instead. The fact that more anti-social behaviour was reported in the poorest wards was conveniently sidestepped and instead the plan focused on the four major factors identified above. In truth there was little new in the *Respect Action Plan;* it followed an already established line of reasoning and an existing policy framework but the terms in which the problems of anti-social behaviour and a lack of respect were framed took on a new and worrying tone.

While an initial reading the *Respect Action Plan* can appear quite mundane, as just another canon in the armoury to 'support the government's neighbourhood renewal, anti-social behaviour, alcohol and violent crime strategies; to promote parental/guardian responsibility; and to encourage respect for public servants and services' (Jamieson 2005: 180), in its zeal to take action to protect the 'law-abiding' and the vulnerable majority from a troublesome minority, the *Respect Action Plan* proclaimed the government's intention to move away from existing judicial measures and a centuries' old rule of law. These were to be replaced by a much greater reliance on the use of out-of-court, summary powers to manage and to punish offending behaviour. Rather than relying on the court process to test an individual's innocence or guilt and allowing a right to defend one's actions before magistrates, more out-of-court measures such as Fixed Penalty Notices (FPNs) and Penalty Notices for Disorder (PNDs) were to be administered. The use of civil orders and injunctions to close premises or curtail the activities of those seen to be causing a nuisance were also to be extended. While these measures were lauded as cheaper, speedier and less bureaucratic methods of justice, they also require lower levels of proof, can be more easily misused and rest on the judgement of the initiator of the order, rather than the viewpoint of the accused.

It is telling that in Blair's speech to launch the *Respect Action Plan* he focused his initial remarks, not on the policies and processes of the plan itself but on his intention to engender a new approach to the practice of criminal law and it is worth spending some time exploring his words on this matter. We start, Blair stated, with two propositions with which he believed everyone could find common ground: that 'An innocent person should be protected from wrongful accusation' and that 'The public at large should be protected from crime'. He then continued by arguing that the first of these propositions no longer fit 'in a post-war, modern, culturally and socially diverse, globalised society and economy at the beginning of the 21st century'. Why? Because, he argues, 'The scale, organisation, nature of modern crime makes the traditional processes simply too cumbersome, too remote from reality to be effective.' His solution was to bypass bureaucracy and an outdated legal system born of nineteenth-century values. He went on to iterate his particular philosophy and perspective in some detail:

> The real choice, the choice on the street, is not between a criminal law process that protects the accused and one that doesn't; it is between a criminal law process that puts protection of the accused in all circumstances above and before that of protecting the public.
>
> A few years ago, we began to change this. The Proceeds of Crime Act gave the police the power to seize the cash of suspected drug dealers. ASB law imposed FPN fines, instant on-the-spot (usually down at the police station, in fact). Asbo's came into being where general behaviour not specific individual offences was criminalised.
>
> This has, bluntly reversed the burden of proof. The person who spits at the old lady is given an £80 fine. If they want to challenge it, they have to appeal. The suspected drug dealer loses the cash. He has to come to court and show how he got it lawfully. (Blair 2006)[2]

In this speech Blair sweeps away a centuries-old legal philosophy which has protected the innocent and falsely-accused and which has delivered justice, if slowly and in a complex and no doubt costly manner, and replaces it with swift, summary justice which is meted out by the police (down at the police station). The Respect plan bypasses the professionals involved in the court process with magistrates and judges trained in the complexities of the legal code, and hands it to a police service which has been heavily criticised in the past for holding prejudicial positions against particular social groups (see for example Chapters 6 and 7 of this volume). This monumental shift is nowhere interrogated and questioned in his speech but is instead simply announced and celebrated as Blair signals his clear intention to push this process still further. Everywhere, he concludes, 'traditional thinking will have to be overthrown'. And all this he suggests is done in the name of 'respect' which is 'about the duty I have to respect the rights that *you* hold dear' (ibid. 2006). And Blair pronounces this while removing the rights of the innocent not to be falsely arrested and summarily punished. It is a contradictory and dangerous stance, which informs his thinking – and all this from a trained lawyer – which was enthusiastically taken up by the Cabinet and wider government which accepted the speech and continued to push this agenda forwards.

The Respect Agenda has also been criticised from other perspectives – for its 'penal populism' (Jamieson 2005: 189); its punitive emphasis which may be satisfying in the short term but offers no solution to the social and economic problems which underlies the behaviour of troubled young people and adults (Burney, 2005); its promotion, not of tolerance and understanding but of vilification and negative portrayals of many social groups (Squires and Stephen, 2005); and its emphasis upon and enforcement of individual responsibility which obscures the government's role in perpetuating the conditions in which 'anti-social' and 'criminal' behaviour can take hold (Hudson, 2003). While purporting to build respect within the community, its approach appeared to some to be extremely divisive, setting groups against each other and doing little to engender tolerance, understanding and respect for difference within neighbourhoods or even between citizens and public servants.

## Safer communities, crime prevention and combating extremism

While the Respect Agenda was championed by Blair the Respect Task Force was wound up in December 2007 shortly after Gordon Brown succeeded him as Prime Minister. Nevertheless, the legacy of this 'step-change' in perspective continued to have profound implications on the way in which the future criminal justice system was envisaged and was further embedded in politicians' rhetoric and government policy linking community and crime; after Blair, the Safer Communities agenda carried on unhindered. In the regions Local Area Agreements (LAAs) were piloted in 21 local authority areas to devolve decision-making powers further into the regions and were subsequently rolled out nationally and the Safer and Stronger Communities Fund rationalised the many funding streams responsible for all manner of community crime prevention, community policing and community empowerment initiatives.

Significant changes in the mechanics of policy delivery took place while the agenda on community involvement was moving forward. These were to have serious consequences for future policy developments. In 2006 a Department for Communities and Local Government (DCLG) was created. It took over many of the roles of the former Office of the Deputy Prime Minister (ODPM) but was also given an expanded remit. Alongside housing, regeneration and the improvement of locally-delivered public services, the DCLG was tasked with tackling anti-social behaviour, working towards race equality, taking on the community cohesion portfolio and also given a more recent focus of public policy – that of combating what was termed 'extremism'. DCLG was a hybrid department. While crime and the criminal law remained outside its remit, anti-social behaviour which had previously been the concern of the Home Office was included. This move brought communities and the prevention of crime (at least anti-social behaviour) close together in one office. In addition while the first Secretary of State for Communities and Local Government was Ruth Kelly, formerly a Minister for Education, by July 2007 Hazel Blears, a former Home Office Minister, was appointed in this role, thus further cementing the link between community action and crime reduction. The ODPM's link to community regeneration, and with it Prescott's old Labour credentials and perspective, were lost as Kelly and Blears, both closely allied to Blair and supporters of New Labour's approach to community disorder, eagerly took up the banner.

One of the first policy documents which emanated from the new DCLG was the local government white paper *Strong and Prosperous Communities*. While stressing the government's continued commitment to a devolution of power to local authorities and the empowerment of local communities it also restated many of the divisive elements which characterised the Respect Agenda. In introducing the White Paper on its website and in the White Paper's Executive Summary, the DCLG proclaimed the report to be 'on the side of individuals and families who want to make a difference' (DCLG 2006) suggesting, of course that it was not on the side, or in direct opposition to, those families and individuals who have opted out either of community activism generally or the New Labour ethos driving it. Any consideration of why people find themselves unwilling or unable to take part in community issues is ruled out and a blanket condemnation of their position was placed in the public domain instead.

## Combating extremism: the focus on the local

The DCLG's role in 'tackling extremism' emanated directly from the need to respond to the bombings in London in July 2005. However, once again a complex problem which could have been linked to all manner of government policies, and not least the geo-political positions which the British government was taking internationally, was reconstituted as a problem to be tackled at the level of community. In the immediate aftermath of the bombings the government set up seven different working groups – all with the objective of 'Working Together to Prevent Extremism'. The focus of these groups was almost exclusively on the Muslim community – indeed very few of the working group members were not of the Muslim faith. The working groups were constituted under the following headings:

1  Engaging with Young People
2  Education
3  Engaging with Muslim Women: Supporting Regional and Local Initiatives and Community Actions

4   Imams' Training and Accreditation and the Role of Mosques as a Resource for the Whole
    Community
5   Community Security – Including Addressing Islamophobia
6   Increasing Confidence in Policing
7   Tackling Extremism and Radicalisation.

The working groups were charged with making concrete recommendations and identifying a small number of proposals which could be immediately implemented which would shape Government-led actions to help prevent extremism. Furthermore, they were asked to 'help improve overall partnership working between Government and Muslim communities, through developing shared understanding and dialogue on issues associated with extremism and disaffection' (Home Office 2005c: 107). The groups had only six weeks to report their findings. They participated in this exercise in the context of increasing Islamophobia and what they perceived as:

> The relevance and critical nature of this exercise due to the hostile climate that followed the events of 7th and 21st July, in the form of attacks on the Islamic Faith, the incessant demands for Muslims to repeatedly demonstrate their allegiance to the country, the demonisation of a whole community together with the unprovoked and marked attacks on Islam and Muslims by the media and in other more direct forms of physical attacks on mosques and individuals. (Home Office 2005c: 2)

While working under terms of reference set by the government which foregrounded the responsibility of the Muslim community in finding solutions to extremism, each participant volunteered for the work and took no remuneration. They did not hold back from directing their criticisms outside of the Muslim community where this was appropriate and the report included a statement which placed some responsibility on to government policies. The final report stated:

> From the outset it was recognised that whilst this process was largely looking at Muslim communities, that the responsibility for tackling extremism and radicalisation in all its forms was the responsibility of society as a whole. The Working Groups are united in the view that whilst the remit for various working groups was to tackle extremism and radicalisation, most if not all the strands see that the solutions lie in the medium to longer term issues of tackling inequality, discrimination, deprivation and inconsistent Government policy, and in particular foreign policy. (Home Office 2005c: 3)

The recommendations of the groups largely concentrated on ensuring that the moderation and tolerance of the Islamic faith was represented both within and outside of the Muslim community and that the government set up mechanisms to listen to and involve Muslim youth and Muslim women. The report also included some recommendations which were more difficult to achieve. The report asked for a public inquiry into both the bombings and the response of the government and other public agencies to the events of 7 and 21 July; monitoring and addressing Islamophobia; including Muslim communities in discussions of proposed anti-terrorist measures and a review of the policing of Muslim communities, especially where they are subject to anti-terrorist legislation.

In July 2006 a Commission on Integration and Cohesion was launched by Ruth Kelly. Operating in England only, the new Commission was to work within the context of existing Government policy on managed migration and 'preventing extremism'. Its remit was to examine the issues that raised tensions between different groups in different areas, make suggestions as to how to further push the government's agenda on cohesion and integration, to empower local communities to tackle extremist ideologies and build capacity in communities to recover from any periods of tension. It was a fixed term advisory body which produced its final report *Our Shared Future* in June 2007. While accepting that globe-wide transformations had altered the terrain within which the nation-state operates and that migratory flows of people around the world had led to super-diverse, fluid, multiple and hybrid identities and complex allegiances to nation, religion and family, the report concluded that it is at the level of community where many of these tensions are played out. Perhaps unsurprisingly, for a commission chaired by a local authority Chief Executive – Darra Singh – this report emphasised what can be achieved at a local level: 'it is through millions of small, everyday actions', Singh argues, 'that we can all either improve or harm our local communities' (Commission for Integration and Cohesion 2007: 4). Indeed, the Commission's remit was particularly designed around work in local areas and the authors of the report were specifically asked 'to consider how local areas themselves can play a role in forging cohesive and resilient communities' (Commission for Integration and Cohesion 2007: 18). When, in February 2008, Hazel Blears while Secretary of State for Communities and Local Government, formulated the government's response to the report, once more the emphasis was on improving cohesion at the local level and putting in place 'the national framework within which Local Authorities and their partners can deliver improvements to cohesion' (DCLG 2008).

## The alienation of British Muslims

Since early 2003, the United Kingdom has had a long-term strategy for countering international terrorism (known within Government as CONTEST). Its four principal strands being: Prevent, Pursue, Protect, and Prepare (HM Government 2006). As part of its Prevent strand which is concerned with tackling the radicalisation of individuals, the work of the Preventing Extremism Together working groups was key and had, by mid-2006, culminated in a national grassroots-led campaign targeted at Muslim youth (the Scholars' Roadshow); Muslim Forums on Extremism and Islamophobia and a Mosques and Imams National Advisory Board. The government policy programme on The Prevention of Violent Extremism was cast as a different matter than that of creating community cohesion. It was, in the words of Ruth Kelly 'about the more specific problem of a small minority of young Muslims being attracted to violent groups' (DCLG 2007: 1). In the financial year 2007/8, £5 million was dedicated to helping Muslims in Britain:

- identify themselves as a welcome part of a wider British society;
- gain acceptance as a welcome part of a wider British society by the wider community;
- reject violent extremist ideology and actively condemn violent extremism;
- isolate violent extremist activity;
- support and co-operate with the police and security services;
- develop their own capacity to deal with problems.

(DCLG 2007: 3)

The familiar refrain of community responsibilisation was clearly present here – Muslims were to be encouraged to make themselves appear trusting and moderate to the wider community and to deal with their own internal problems. No reference was made to the responsibility of British government and the part it might play in fostering extreme reactions either in Britain or the rest of the world. Neither was reference made to the extremism of the right within British politics which had sullied the relationship between Muslim and non-Muslim communities in many areas and which the police and government had done little to tackle. Wherever reference was made to those British actions abroad which might have contributed to the growth of radicalisation and anti-government sentiment among those of the Muslim faith these were quietly dismissed. The government's 2006 Counter-Terrorism Strategy, for example, dismissed such reactions to British involvement within predominantly Muslim countries in the following way:

> Specific events – for example, the Coalition action to restore sovereignty in Kuwait, the UN authorised actions in Afghanistan to remove the Al Qa'ida terrorist organisation and the Taliban government sponsoring it and then restore stability there, and US and UK action in Iraq to remove a serious threat to international security and subsequently to promote a democratic and pluralist government – are sometimes portrayed as attacks on Islam itself, regardless of the actual rationale for the action. (HM Government 2006: 10)

At the same time, atrocities committed by western forces in Muslim countries were portrayed as isolated incidents which did not reflect the standards of the forces more generally. This 'bad apples' explanation for unacceptable behaviour within the armed forces exactly mirrored the explanations which used to be given whenever police officers failed to respect the rights of BME communities and individuals. It was an old, tired excuse which was rarely accepted within those communities which experienced discriminatory policing at first hand.

By the time the strategy on Preventing Violent Extremism was announced a number of bungled raids and increases in stops and searches of Muslim people in the UK had already resulted in reports that Muslim communities were losing faith in British policing methods (*Guardian* 2006d) and Tarique Ghaffur, then an assistant commissioner in the Metropolitan Police, stated publicly that the whole Muslim community was being stereotyped, targeted and alienated, by anti-terrorist measures (*Guardian* 2006e). Despite these warnings the government continued to follow a line which painted the 'radical' Muslim as anathema to an open, democratic and tolerant society. In December 2006 Blair set out the government's stall in this regard when he told a group of Muslims invited to Downing Street that they must take up the British values of tolerance and respect for the law, adding 'Conform to it; or don't come here' (*Guardian* 2006f). Just under one year later, with Blair no longer Prime Minister, it was reported that 'counter terrorism officials' were 'rethinking their approach to tackling the radicalisation of Muslim youth' admitting that they had at times 'been offensive and inappropriate' in their language. Henceforth, the term 'war against terror' was to be abandoned and terrorism would not be described as a 'Muslim problem' (*Guardian* 2007g). Nevertheless, Jacqui Smith in her role as Home Secretary continued to place emphasis on tackling violent extremism within Muslim communities and in June 2008 the government announced a 'nationwide "deradicalisation programme" to tackle Islamic extremism in Britain' (*Guardian* 2008c).

The problem of terrorism has been cast as an issue of both domestic and foreign relations (Spalek and Lambert 2008) and the domestic criminal justice system has thereby been charged with responding to problems relating to religious radicalisation and terrorism (Heal 2007). Legislation curbing both immigration and terrorism has been justified as necessary for ensuring co-operative community relations and 'social cohesion' within the UK (Home Office 2002b) and the 2005 White Paper, *Controlling our Borders: Making Migration Work for Britain* (Home Office 2005b) underlined the government's intention that those settling permanently in the UK must work, place as little pressure as possible on the British welfare system and must make all efforts to integrate into local communities and national social mores. Behind this injunction was the fear that migrants were coming to Britain to largely feather their own nests rather than to contribute to British society, that they would remain more loyal to their country of origin than to their country of choice and that they would destabilise UK communities by preferring to stick to their own social conventions rather than accepting those of their indigenous neighbours. Furthermore, the popular media portrayed people from certain national origins as almost naturally criminogenic – with Eastern Europeans, recent additions to the European Community, as particularly prone to criminality (Bosworth and Guild 2008).

These cultural threats to a supposed British way of life were also assumed to be present in Muslim communities, especially after the 'war on terror' was declared by then US president George Bush in 2001. The constant refrain of protection from 'outsiders' was heard throughout the rhetoric aiming to justify anti-terror and anti-immigration legislation – people coming to the UK from abroad had to be 'tested' first to establish their 'true' identity with biometrics and other techno-logical probing and later they were subject to testing as to their commitment and loyalty to the 'new country'. With the adoption of the 2006 Identity Cards Act and the 2007 UK Borders Act British citizenship became contingent on subse-quent adherence to normative frameworks of beliefs and behaviours as it became clear that citizenship could and would be revoked if individuals stepped outside of certain rules and codes of behaviour. Religious and political extremism were particularly frowned upon and the government set out to induce moderation and to persuade Muslim communities to preach and follow 'acceptable' political and religious views.

With this emphasis Muslims in Britain were labelled as more foreign than British. Politicians such as Ann Cryer MP for Keighley and Ilkley in West Yorkshire and Jack Straw MP for Blackburn, Lancashire and former Home Secretary began to decry the strange and un-British behaviour of Muslims in their constituencies, attacking such cultural practices as arranged marriages and the wearing of the veil. As they and other well-respected individuals spoke out publicly, attacks on Muslims and those who could be mistaken by the ignorant for Muslims, increased on the streets and in the tabloids. The government answer was to urge British Muslims to work harder to ensure their acceptability to British society. As Spalek and Lambert point out:

> Legitimate Muslims are perceived to be those who engage with governments on the terms set by those governments. Those Muslims who refuse such an engage-ment (irrespective of their motivations or reasons) are likely to be perceived as 'radical' and hence a potential terrorist threat. This creates an untenable situa-tion for many Muslims. (2008: 262)

## Concluding comments

New Labour's first term of office seemed to present a number of positive oppor-tunities to more fully involve community in the field of crime prevention and problem analysis. However Crime and Disorder Reduction Partnerships proved to be, with few exceptions, top-down policy-making bodies which pushed particular agendas down from above onto the communities and neighbourhoods below (Gilling 2007: 98). While the programme of strengthening communities and building their capacity to deal with social and crime problems appeared to con-tinue apace during the next two terms of Labour government this was offset by numerous policy perspectives which singled out problematic individuals and social groups which posed risks to cohesion and collective efficacy (Carson 2008).

These more negative portrayals of difficult and dangerous citizens, damaging beleaguered communities proved much more powerful and enduring than the message of programmes such as *Together We Can* which set out to promote social solidarity and collective capacities. As Crawford (2006) has argued, the government's over-emphasis on insecurities and problematic, 'risky' groups within neighbourhoods could not promote common understanding and encouraged a focus on criminality, difference and deviance, constructing some groups as those to be avoided rather than understood and included.

Furthermore, the government built its programme of community cohesion from 2001 onwards by abandoning support for multi-culturalism and its tolerance and celebration of diversity, insisting on the contrary that everyone must become more 'British'. Any individuals and groups which fell short of their standards of 'Britishness' were framed as problematic, required to alter their behaviour and to further integrate. On top of this the active citizen's agenda moved away from the idea that social and citizenship benefits are universal and rested instead on the concept of 'relational citizenship identified by Rose (1999) in which rights and responsibilities become conditional upon what an individual citizen can provide for the wider public good as opposed to universal citizenship entitlements based solely on the criteria of nationality' (Raco 2007: 309). The principle that rights must be 'earned', and are thereby not extended to those who do not deserve them, was carried on through the Respect Agenda championed by Blair himself. The division into 'good' and 'bad' citizen was here made complete. Finally, the agenda on combating extremism took all the above elements and wove them into a policy framework which has been widely acknowledged to have exposed the Muslim population of Britain to a great deal of negative attention, from the media, in policing strategies and through border and immigration controls.

Governance through crime (Simon 1997) has been extended into many more elements of governmentality than previously. Long applied within domestic politics to direct funding to struggling neighbourhoods its reach has deepened and widened and more citizens and 'foreigners' are considered suspect and as risks to be managed. Afforded the status of 'outsider' they are portrayed as beyond the pale and unable or unwilling to assimilate into an acceptable 'British' way of life and new 'structures of exclusion are erected' (Fekete 2009: 9).

---

**FURTHER READING**

Bosworth, M. and Guild, M. (2008) 'Governing through migration control security and citizenship in Britain', *British Journal of Criminology*, 48(6): 703–19.

Spalek, B. and Lambert, R. (2008) 'Muslim communities, counter-terrorism and counter-radicalisation: a critically reflective approach to engagement', *International Journal of Law, Crime and Justice*, 36: 257–70.

## NOTES

1  On 20 October 2001, for example, the respected BBC *Panorama* programme joined up with Radio Five Live, BBC World Service Radio and World TV for an international debate. They asked political leaders and the public to discuss the following questions – Is the Muslim community right to regard the US as arrogant and imperialist? Are the two cultures so different that they cannot meet? Have the cultural differences been hijacked by the terrorists to fuel a new world war? (http://news.bbc.co.uk/1/hi/programmes/panorama/1607421.stm) (accessed 01.07.09).

2  All these quotes are taken from the 'PM's *Respect Action Plan* launch speech' of 10 January 2006 available through the direct.gov website www.direct.gov.uk (accessed 20.09.06).

# 9

# Serious and organised? Legislative and mission creep in 'the sick man of Europe'[1]

Despite years of initiatives to prevent and deal with crime and disorder, Britain continues to be categorised as a 'high-crime' country. In 2007 a crime and safety survey published by the European Commission (van Dyk et al. 2007) found Britons and the Irish were more likely than residents of any other European country to fall victim to the ten most widely reported crimes. The same survey designated London as the crime capital of Europe and, while acknowledging that crime rates had fallen across the UK, calculated that they had not fallen as quickly as crime rates across the rest of the European Union. Within Britain it had been widely acknowledged that the rate of recorded crime, as measured by police-recorded crime statistics and the British Crime Survey (BCS), had begun to fall from 1995 onwards and that this trend began under a Conservative-led administration. Seven years into Labour's period in office recorded crime had fallen by a further 30 per cent and the risk of becoming a victim of crime was estimated to be at its lowest level since the BCS was introduced in 1981 (Home Office 2004b: 2). After 2004, however, this fall in crime appeared to bottom out. Despite the fall in recorded and self-reported crime, satisfaction surveys continued to show that only around half of the adult population considered that the police and local authorities were dealing adequately with crime or even with anti-social behaviour and that the majority of adults thought that most crimes were still on the increase (Walker et al. 2009: 9–10). As the New Labour project moved from its first through to its second and third terms it therefore faced the reality of improved statistics on crime and the meeting of a number of crime reduction targets while popular satisfaction with its delivery of crime prevention and criminal justice reforms remained at a low level. Faced with this contradiction, successive Home Office ministers set further targets and sought through other measures to convince the population that inroads were being made. Within this process the tone of the government's crime prevention rhetoric became ever more strident and combative. By 2008 a report for the Cabinet Office, authored by Louise Casey, formerly head of the Home Office Anti-Social Behaviour Unit, boasted:

> The Criminal Justice System has been reformed so that more offenders than ever are brought to justice and punished more severely – partly reflected in a doubling of those now locked up in prison and 93% of offenders being made to pay their fines. (Casey 2008: 2)

Casey's report confidently stated that 'Crime is tackled most effectively when the law-abiding majority stand together against the minority who commit it' (Casey 2008: 4) although there is no evidence cited to demonstrate that this assertion is correct. At the outset the new Labour government had appeared more tentative and circumspect in its approach and analysis of crime. The debate around social exclusion, its causes, impacts and solutions included an input from practitioners and the academic community and the subsequent reports reflected their considered approach. Ten years later the government appeared to rely less on the professional community and more on various appointed 'tsars' and celebrities as its advisers.[2] After pursuing a 'what works' agenda for the previous ten years the government had also become more emphatic in its claims as to which interventions were necessary and effective – more people locked up in prison, harsher punishments, record numbers of policing officers, dedicated Neighbourhood Policing Teams in every local area (Casey 2008: 4). While these remain controversial and contested policies they are presented in government publications as definitive and proven solutions to crime and criminality.

Also presented in Casey's report is a clear narrative on increasing the visibility of punishment and sentencing – which must be more punitive, more restrictive and more public in its deployment. Again there was little evidence to back up her assertion that this is what the public itself wanted and her claims that such punishment was more effective. Indeed, the European Commission report on crime and safety published in 2007 had specifically singled out more punitive strategies for particular consideration and concluded that they were unlikely to have had much effect on a decade of falling crime rates across Europe. In fact the fall in crime rates in Europe was comparable to the decrease in crime recorded in the United States which had taken a much harsher stance on criminalisation and punishment. Nevertheless, Casey's recommendations included 'community payback' proposals which advocated the dressing of offenders in brightly coloured uniforms while on community service, a sight often seen in the United States of America where 'chain-gangs' can be seen working on public projects such as road maintenance but hitherto perceived across Europe as somewhat barbaric, humiliating and counter-productive. Casey claimed:

> While people experience ... signs of crime around them, they do not see enough visible action being taken to challenge, catch and punish criminals. Too much of this work is invisible. In other words, while the public see high profile 'signal crimes' that create fear and mistrust, they do not see any 'signal justice' to counter those concerns. (2008: 7)

Casey argued too that information on convicted criminals should be published by various means and that their photographs should be placed in the local media. At least one police force, the Greater Manchester Police (GMP) produced posters and billboards with the faces of young men found to be guilty of gang-related crimes, digitally altered to show what they might look like after their life sentences were completed. The GMP poster campaign was ostensibly created with the purpose of thanking local people who helped bring the two before the courts but this departure from previous policy and practice which protected the privacy of offenders and their families, demonstrated the government's intention to assuage the public's concerns before those of the criminal justice practitioners who were clear in their condemnation of such proposals. The government's Respect agenda had also voiced concerns that justice was organised for the offender, rather than the victim, and that this should be countered by very public statements on the importance of punishment and the visible presentation of punishment wherever possible.[3] As Blair opined in his speech introducing the Respect Action Plan in 2006:

> Since the self reinforcing bonds of traditional community life do not exist in the same way, we need a radical new approach if we are to restore the liberty of the law-abiding citizen. My view is very clear: their [the public's] freedom to be safe from fear has to come first ... Anything else is the theory, loved by much of the political and legal establishment but utterly useless to the ordinary citizen on the street. (Blair 2006)

## Serious and organised crime

In 2006 the government launched the Serious and Organised Crime Agency (SOCA). This agency brought together the work of various existing organisations in order that their databases and intelligence could be shared and links made between the work which they were already carrying out but in a more piecemeal fashion. The agencies amalgamated into SOCA were the National Crime Squad, a nationally organised police service which had dealt with issues such as major drug trafficking, illegal arms dealing, human trafficking, computer and high tech crimes and the counterfeiting and laundering of money; the National Criminal Intelligence Service, a policing agency set up as to centralise the gathering and distribution of intelligence on serious and organised criminal matters; HM Customs and Excise (now HM Revenue and Customs) investigative and intelligence work on serious drug trafficking and recovering related assets and the Immigration Service's work on organised immigration crime. At its launch then Prime Minister Blair, backed up by a voxpop film, emphasised the impact which such crime has on local communities. The actual crimes seen as belonging to the remit of 'serious and organised' which were identified by the participants in the film were as wide-ranging as rape, identity theft, protection rackets, drugs, trafficked women and the use of guns in the commission of criminal acts. While many of these crimes are indeed both serious in scope and organised in nature, the inclusion of rape as a crime which should be taken up by SOCA demonstrated an ambiguity in the remit of the unit. In his launch speech Blair did little to tighten the definition of 'serious and organised crime' but spoke of the money which is made through the illegal drug trade, drug use and crime linked to immigration, people-trafficking, and computer crime. Always emphasising the costs to people on the street and in local neighbourhoods, he added that communities and individuals are clearly affected by these crimes which are played out on international stages, but which nevertheless can engender fear and blight lives, while financial fraud, he added, pushes up costs for everyone. In a familiar refrain he added 'The victims have to be paramount' (*Guardian* 2006g).

Blair emphasised that serious crime damages people's liberty, and takes away their right to free passage through the streets, to property or even, in the case of trafficked women, to their own bodies, but at the same time he proposed the introduction of an agency whose officers were to be given sweeping new powers to act against crime which also impinged on a suspect's individual rights. Crime, Blair explained, can be broken down into anti-social behaviour and vandalism which needs one kind of policing and to sophisticated, organised crime which requires a new and integrated approach. The old methods used to interrupt serious crime, he added, do not work with highly efficient and organised gangs. He proposed a constant surveillance and monitoring of suspects, wider use of the most modern technology and new ways of prosecuting gangs and dealing with their profits. One thousand organisations, he said, have been put on 'most wanted' lists and would be pursued. Blair outlined four new powers given to SOCA officers. First, the rules on turning Queen's evidence (when somebody who took part in a crime gives evidence to a court usually in exchange for a more lenient sentence) had been placed on a more statutory footing awarding prosecutors statutory powers to offer immunity from prosecution or reduced sentences to anyone testifying against those higher up in the criminal hierarchy of their organisation. Secondly, financial reporting orders were introduced so that convicted criminals could be ordered by the courts to report business affairs and thirdly disclosure notices could require the production of financial and any other documents to the court. Blair openly acknowledged in his speech that these powers limited the offender's right to silence. Lastly, he gave SOCA enforcement officers multiple powers to act as police, immigration and customs officers at one and the same time giving them powers to arrest, charge and also deport if necessary. If any more new powers were seen to be necessary Blair assured the directors of SOCA, then they would be added. Nothing, Blair reiterated, should come before the basic liberties of ordinary people to be freed from the tyrannies and brutality of organised crime. As with the launching of the Respect Action Plan, fighting twenty-first-century crime with new and more appropriate methods meant, for Blair, extending the powers of enforcement officers into new avenues.

The institution of SOCA was first mooted in 2004 by the then Home Secretary David Blunkett. In the Home Office White Paper *One Step Ahead: A 21st Century Strategy to Defeat Organised Crime*, Blunkett had highlighted the impact of crimes organised across international borders such as the drug trade, people-trafficking and immigration crime. He used the case of the Chinese cockle-pickers drowned while working for a gang-master in Morecambe Bay as an example of the tragic outcomes of such crime as well as noting that terrorists were also exploiting lax international border controls to raise funds for their own activities. SOCA reorganised much police detective work and it was first mooted when a wide-scale review of policing was underway culminating in the White Paper *Building Communities, Beating Crime* which aimed to build closer connections between the police and the people for whom their service is delivered. As the Paper set out:

> A successful approach to organised crime is therefore inseparable from our wider effort to improve the overall effectiveness of policing in this country and to make vulnerable communities and law-abiding citizens safer. It requires that our police forces, our prosecutors, our intelligence services and our national enforcement agencies work together still more closely. (Home Office 2004b: 157)

At the same time the Paper set out the government's intention to ensure that SOCA's links with regional police forces continued to function efficiently, sharing intelligence and operations 'to ensure that there is an effective link between its efforts to combat organised crime at national level and the work being done by police forces at local level' (Home Office 2004b: 157).

The 2004 policing review saw the mainstreaming of the National Intelligence Model of policing which all forces were subsequently required to adopt. This aimed to move the policing service away from a reactive model of policing where crimes already committed are recorded and detected, to one where the forces' strategic plans and activities are shaped by research and the building up of intelligence to direct policing operations, anticipating crimes which might be committed rather than solely investigating those already reported. This model was to be applied in all aspects of police work 'from organised crime to road safety' (NCIS 2000: 7) and lent itself to many of the requirements set for Crime Reduction Partnerships, notably the auditing of crime and community safety issues, crime mapping to establish areas to target specific crime prevention measures and the meeting of performance and crime reduction targets. The language of business and business modelling was applied to set the requirements of operational policing and the National Intelligence Model (NIM) literature urged forces to consider that, 'Without such a product [the NIM], business planning cannot have the required focus to permit the accurate judgements that are necessary to set priorities and commit resources' (NCIS 2000: 11). The tools necessary for successful working of the NIM required that the police adopt a more targeted approach to crime than had previously been seen as necessary. Targeting and gathering intelligence on particular crimes also meant the targeting of specific groups seen to be more likely to yield positive results for the police. Yet the NCIS claimed that such targeting would not be carried out in a discriminatory or an over-zealous manner emphasising that:

> Compliance with the European Convention on Human Rights is secured. The target profiling and risk analysis disciplines applied within the model to the selection of targets helps in establishing 'proportionality' and the management of risks and duties of care. (NCIS 2000: 11)

However, a number of complaints to the police in recent years have seemed to suggest that such safeguards were not in fact in place, that these new police powers were used in a disproportionate manner and that their management of risks led to a number of police operations which singled out particular groups for a great deal of attention.

## Investigating from the local to the international

In 2002 the government extended the Regulation of Investigatory Powers Act (RIPA) 2000 to grant public bodies wide-ranging powers to conduct surveillance on British citizens. The 2000 Act had introduced a number of new powers to the police allowing the intercepting of emails, accessing private communications data, and extending the circumstances in which the planting and monitoring of surveillance devices was to be acceptable – with the safeguard that a warrant should be obtained before such activities could be undertaken. In 2002 these new powers which had been extended only to the police were further extended to other public agencies such as local authorities, fire authorities, Jobcentres, the Gaming Board and the Charity Commission.[4] According to the *Guardian* newspaper Jack Straw, Home Secretary in 2000, had hastened the original bill's passage through Parliament so that it became law before the UK was brought into line with the European Convention on Human Rights in order that this did not interfere with powers such as the use of covert surveillance on people who had not been convicted of any involvement in criminal activity. From 2002 the powers granted by RIPA could be, and as we will see later, were used to monitor all sorts of behaviour which fell far short of the criminal, such as fly-tipping or giving a false address to an education authority. Straw claimed that the 2000 bill merely formalised and more closely regulated existing powers. However, RIPA required Internet Service

Providers to ensure that software was in place to allow the police and security services to monitor and intercept all internet traffic and email and to keep phone and internet records for all users for at least a 12-month period. This form of communication had not previously been monitored. The Act was criticised for not putting in place a body which could effectively oversee and monitor the use of these extensive powers or offer redress to individuals who felt that they had been misused, despite the implications this had for the possible infringements of personal liberty. Indeed, the Act was given the nickname the 'snooper's charter' by its critics and it was claimed that with the 2002 extensions, the Home Office had breached a commitment that RIPA would not become a general surveillance tool for the government itself. Shami Chakrabati, director of Liberty even suggested that as a result of the passing of RIPA in 2000 and 2002 the British people were the most spied upon in the world.

## Serious Organised Crime and Police Acts

SOCA was created by the Serious Organised Crime and Police Act 2005 (SOCPA 2005) which additionally put in place a number of legislative changes which increased police powers generally – not only in relation to the detection and prevention of organised crime. The Act made every offence an arrestable offence – formerly only some offences (for example those which carried a penalty of five years' imprisonment) were arrestable. This was a major increase in police powers to detain, and therefore to fingerprint and take the DNA of, individuals arrested for even very minor offences such as flyposting or graffitti. Since the Criminal Justice and Police Act of 2001 had allowed all fingerprints and DNA samples to be retained indefinitely on the National DNA Database, regardless of whether the person arrested was charged or convicted of an offence, this was a considerable inroad into civil liberties. In addition the Act introduced a new offence – that of failing to obey a police direction to leave an exclusion area and also allowed police to take photographs of people away from a police station. This power was also extended to Community Support Officers in certain circumstances. Even people suspected of carrying fireworks could be stopped and searched.

In a further controversial move, SOCPA (2005) also extended the powers of the police to control demonstrations and individuals participating in demonstrations. Any demonstrations – no matter how small – had to be authorised by the police, preferably six days beforehand and exclusion zones could be set up where unauthorised protests were made a criminal offence. A permanent protest exclusion zone was set up around the Houses of Parliament in London and this was vigorously policed. Indeed, in May 2006 a sole demonstrator, Brian Haw, who had been camped in Parliament Square since 2001 in protest at the government's invasion of Afghanistan and Iraq, was surrounded by 78 police officers and arrested under SOCPA 2005 provisions – he appealed against his arrest and was later allowed to return to his protest site but under strictly controlled conditions. The Act contained many other provisions too numerous to mention here, such as lifting the restrictions against reporting on those individuals receiving 'asbos' and creating a new offence of interference with contractual and other relationships with the intention of harming an animal research organisation. The Act was later amended by Section 12 of the Terrorism Act 2006 which made trespass at nuclear sites licensed by the Health and Safety Executive a criminal offence and similar restrictions were announced on a selection of non-military sites including royal palaces and government buildings. While ostensibly put in place to confound the activities of serious and organised criminals, there was little attempt to hide the motivation for this later extension of the Act and according to a report in the *Independent* newspaper the amendment was justified by the Ministry of Defence (MOD) precisely because the sites had been the scene of regular anti-nuclear protests. A spokeswoman for the MOD told reporters that policing such protests 'unnecessarily diverts police resources. ... This legislation is about keeping police focused on the job they are paid to do' (*Independent* 2006).[5]

An Act which had been set up to challenge an organised criminal body committing crimes which had significant social impact had become associated instead with the up-tarriffing of minor crimes, the control and criminalisation of protest, an extension of the criminal justice system into further areas of activity and the erosion of individual rights. The Policing and Miscellaneous Provisions of the Act did not touch upon the prevention and detection of serious and organised crime but furthered a trajectory of change which saw successive governments use legislation to control behaviour considered problematic in some way. This mirrors the 'net-widening' and 'mesh-thinning' already apparent in government policy where more people are captured within the criminal justice system and a wider range of behaviour is considered to be suitable for a criminal justice response. This creeping criminalisation has been openly condemned and critiqued by civil liberties organisations and numerous campaigns have been spawned to resist such moves (see Chapter 10) yet there has been little acknowledgement from government benches that these criticisms have much legitimacy and the creep of criminalising legislation has continued apace.

The impact of this legislative creep has been felt in many quarters. Minor transgressive acts have been conflated with major criminal activity and accordingly 'over-policed'. In the case of the curbing and control of protests the 'transgression' can be merely that of vocally and publicly opposing government policies. The Terrorism Act 2000 was used in 2004 against one elderly man who was stopped by police and questioned because he was wearing a T-shirt with an anti-war message outside a Labour Party conference, and the same legislation was also infamously used to forcibly eject the 81-year-old, Walter Wolfgang from a Labour Party conference in 2005 after he heckled the then Foreign Secretary, Jack Straw during a speech in which Straw tried to justify the invasion of Iraq.

## The social organisation of youth: controversies and contradictions

The Social Exclusion Unit's initial report into the life experiences of young people stressed the acute difficulties faced by a 'significant minority' of young people in Britain living in a changing world which offers them little opportunities or social support (SEU 2000b) and any recourse to offending was placed in this context with disadvantage and inequalities perceived as major contributing factors to some young people's criminal behaviour. From this explanation young people, free floating and without positive models of acceptable behaviour within their lives, were increasingly atomised, alienated and living apart from the social and collective experience which could bind them to a set of social mores and morals. The social disorganisation of their lives was perceived as a significant factor which separated them from their wider community and its values, reducing their resilience and capacities to reject negative influences in their lives. A few years down the line, however, young people were increasingly portrayed as organised in their criminality and offending, acting together in gangs or as part of a pack goading each other on into ever more dangerous and damaging behaviour. Understanding the social conditions which produce damaged children was laid aside in government rhetoric and replaced with condemnation and lack of tolerance towards the disruptive behaviour of troubled young people.

The actual commission of *serious crime* by young people, however, is extremely rare and fewer young people again are involved in serious crime which is also organised. At the turn of the twenty-first century, however, the fear that young people are increasingly drawn to organised criminality and that their involvement in serious crime has increased as a consequence is deeply held. Official police recorded crime figures have contributed to this fear. From the years 1999 to 2005 recorded police statistics demonstrated an increase of 66 per cent in the numbers of people found to be carrying an article with blade or point, the numbers carrying an offensive weapon without reason or authority increased by 30 per cent and the number of people found to have a blade or point on school premises increased by 500 per cent (from a very low base figure). Much of this increase has been attributed to a culture among young people of carrying knives and other weapons to gain 'respect' from their peers or to protect themselves from attack (this is further explored in Chapter 5). The evidence for young people's involvement in such a culture is mainly anecdotal. Furthermore, the data demonstrating the increasing use of weapons may also be an artefact of both a change in police recording practices or the result of a greater targeting by police of this offence (Squires et al. 2008: 19–20).

By 2004 the government had introduced a Tackling Violent Crime Programme (TVCP) which in its first three years was targeted towards Crime and Disorder Reduction Partnerships in 32 areas where violent crime was seen to be particularly problematic. TVCP was focused on alcohol-related violence in and around licenced premises as well as domestic violence as it was claimed that 'domestic violence accounts for 16–25% of all violent crime, and ... approximately half of violent crime incidents are alcohol-related' (Home Office: 2008b). However, another real concern was a perceived growth of youth street gangs and the participation of increasing numbers of young people within them.

## Some facts about gangs and gang-related crime

In the late 1990s those who wrote about gangs acknowledged that the problem of youth street gangs in the UK was in no way comparable to the problems which were encountered in the USA. Across the United States and in many parts of Latin and South America youth street gangs have posed a particular problem for crime control. They were embedded in many neighbourhoods and some research suggested that they could be hundreds or even thousands strong (National Gang Research Center 2004). The annual National Youth Gang Survey, for example, estimated there to be around 788,000 gang members and 27,000 gangs active in more than 3,550 US jurisdictions in 2007 (OJJDP 2009). In the UK, however, youth street gangs had been found in very few cities and in 1996 the reknowned American gang expert Malcolm Klein concluded that American-style gangs 'simply did not exist' in the UK. While Manchester gained a reputation for gang-related crime in the 1990s earning the nickname of 'Gunchester' and nearby Salford was also notorious for its 'Young Firm' (Evans et al. 1996) it was the city of Glasgow in Scotland which had suffered the most and for the longest from youth gang activities (Patrick 1973). From around 2002, however, the problem of youth 'gangs' and 'gang-related' crime in the UK was pushed to the forefront of media coverage and political debates. Research by a gang researcher and anti-gang activist in Manchester (Shropshire and McFarquhar 2002) warned of an unprecedented rise in gang activity which they believed was migrating out of its established areas to other towns and cities which had hitherto remained gang-free. Whether this growing concern was justified or not is difficult to ascertain. Certainly some reports suggest that there has been an inexorable rise in 'gang membership' among young people. The excellent work of Pitts (2008) and Matthews (2009) falls into this category. Both accept that young people's involvement in gangs and gang-related activity has spiralled in recent years, however, the definitions of 'gang', 'gang-related' and 'gang membership' which are used are slippery concepts which remain inadequately defined and 'some police forces have used a very broad definition of gang activities, which ranges from congregating in a group, smoking cannabis, drinking, to anti-social behaviour and criminal activities' (Street Weapons Commission 2008: 23) leading to an 'over-definition' of groups of young people as 'gangs'. In 2007 the Youth Justice Board warned against the indiscriminate use of the term arguing that wrongly labelling young people as gang members 'could exacerbate the extent and seriousness of group-related offending or create problems where none had previously existed' (YJB 2007).

Who can be defined as a gang member? No official lists are kept and membership dues taken. Some people defined as 'gang members' may be highly involved in organised criminal activities, others may join in on occasion while others still may merely associate with 'gang members' in friendship or kinship groups. Pitts (2008) has identified the 'reluctant gangstas', often quite young individuals, who are coerced into association and action alongside other more organised young people and adults who do identify as gang members – but whether such young people bullied and forced into criminality should be similarly defined as the adults who co-opt them is a moot point. Certainly the police targeting of 'gangs' has meant that a wide layer of young people have been defined in the police records as 'gang members'. As the Street Weapons Commission reported, the Metropolitan Police survey in 2007 which found 171 'youth gangs' in London based its count 'upon a fairly loose and all-inclusive conception of gangs which stretched: "from organised and armed crime syndicates to low-level groups of youths"' (2008: 39). This casting of the net so wide does not help us define the nature and extent of the 'gang' problem and indeed considerably muddies the water while at the same time ensuring that a great many young people are targeted by police as though they were seriously involved in criminal and unacceptable lifestyles.

## Operation Trident

Operation Trident is the name of a specialist unit within the London Metropolitan Police Authority's Specialist Crime Directorate. According to its website it is 'an anti-gun crime operation that was set up in 1998 to help bring an end to a spate of shootings and murders among young, black Londoners'. It is staffed by around 350 police officers and works in partnership with a group of black community leaders, formally set up as the Trident Independent Advisory Group (TIAG) in 2000 and prioritises the London boroughs of Brent, Hackney, Haringey, Lambeth and Southwark. The Operation Trident website claims that it was set up in response to pleas from the black community that police should be proactive in specifically targeting the criminals particularly affecting the black community. This claim is mirrored by at least one member of the advisory group, TIAG, who describes Operation Trident as an example of 'affirmative action' put in place in the wake of Macpherson's criticisms of the policing of the black community to 'gain the trust of the community and regain the law and order on the streets' (TIAG: undated). To this end the Operation Trident claims to listen to and accept advice on policing from the TIAG and has also mounted media campaigns as well as distributed posters, leaflets and booklets on dealing with gun crime within the neighbourhoods affected. The unit claims an intelligence-led approach and has linked gun crime among the black community in London to local markets for illegal drugs and the international networks which supply such drugs and has turned its attention to gangs, referred to as 'yardies' which operate from Jamaica, on occasion sending police personnel over to the Caribbean to conduct enquiries there. In a similar vein the police later set up a specialist policing unit, to tackle organised crime within London's South Asian communities. The unit was posited as 'a response to an apparent rise in crimes ranging from kidnapping and gun-use, to drug-running and passport scams with transnational links in human trafficking' (Burnett 2004b).

## The blaming of 'black culture'

Operation Trident is a typical case of a targeted police initiative. It was set up as a response to what was seen as an increase in the carrying and use of guns by one particular social group which was closely defined in terms first of its ethnicity and then by gender, age and locality of residence. In drawing its targets so closely the truth that the different organisations known as youth gangs are clustered within the most deprived boroughs of London (Gangs in London 2009) is obscured and the problem is defined instead as 'cultural' and in particular a product of black culture per se rather than a wider alienation and discontent born out of economic and social hardship. In 2007, a year when numbers of shootings in London appeared to be particularly serious, the debate raged in the media and parliament as to whether black youth culture and the musical genre of 'gangsta rap' in particular was fuelling a vicious, self-serving and violent attitude amongst black youth in Britain. This was underlined by then Prime Minister Blair who stated on a number of occasions that he considered gun crime to be the product of 'a specific problem within a specific criminal culture' which was unrepresentative of 'British young people'(BBC News 2009). Through this statement not only did Blair single out the problem of youth gangs as shaped by cultural norms rather than social and economic conditions, but also that these were cultures which rejected 'British norms' of behaviour. Furthermore, the media attention which the work of Operation Trident generated suggested that black culture and 'gangsterism' were somehow inextricably linked – as a result the violent death of anyone defined as from the black community was initially perceived as gang-related leading the organisation Gangs in London to claim that 'many of the victims who die in Trident shootings are innocent law-abiding citizens yet unfairly become scrutinised by media because of Tridents [sic] reputation and association with black criminals' (Gangs in London 2009). By April of the same year Blair was publicly announcing that murders by both knife and gun were 'not being caused by poverty, but a distinctive *black* culture [my emphasis] and that pretending otherwise, because of political correctness, was not helping' (*Guardian* 2007h).

The location of gang-related crime as a product of deviant cultures flew in the face of decades of research into the 'gang problem' (Mares 2000) but by this time the point had been variously reiterated that black culture was problematic, that this problem was somehow imported from overseas and that it was a result of 'un-British' ways of being and acting. This conclusion was also at odds with much of the advice given to Blair by many of those politically close to him – Lady Scotland, then a Home Office Minister and later that year appointed the first black, female Attorney General, specifically argued against the notion that gun crime was a result of black culture, arguing that the disproportionate number of black youths in the criminal justice system was a function of their disproportionate poverty. Nevertheless, in the last months of his time as Prime Minister Blair spoke many times of the need to locate gun crime within the black community and for a further targeted response by the police against those very communities which harboured such crime and criminals. The response was indeed targeted and tough.

## Investigating the use of street weapons

Early in 2008 and with Gordon Brown now as Prime Minister, the Street Weapons Commission chaired by former Prime Minister Blair's wife, Cherie Booth QC, was appointed to visit various parts of the country and to gather evidence about violent street crimes, listening particularly to community activists and those who were closer to the experience of such behaviour. The data used for the report was collected in a number of cities which were seen to have a higher than usual incidence of 'gang' membership and crime using weapons. The cities chosen were Liverpool, London, Birmingham, Manchester and Glasgow. In these cities the situation was much more complex than the story suggested by Operation Trident and its focus on black culture. In Liverpool, for example, 96 per cent of those 'gang members' who came to the attention of the Tackling Gang Action Programme in 2006/7 were white and within Glasgow 'gang members' were also profiled as predominantly white (although there are no accurate figures). In London, Manchester and Birmingham the Commission reported that 'gang members' were classed as predominantly non-white but numbers of gang members counted were low – 356 in London, 127 in Birmingham and 76 in Manchester – hardly representing a general problem within 'black culture' or indeed youth culture as a whole. In all these cities victims of gun crime were, in the majority, white, from 85 per cent of all victims in Liverpool to 52 per cent of all victims in Birmingham. In Glasgow, where rates of violent crime are the highest within Britain, the victims were again predominantly white (Street Weapons Commission 2008). Although police recorded crime statistics continue to show that young black people fall disproportionately victim to violent and weapon-enabled crime, the Street Weapons Commission concluded that the cultural context in which young people are engaged, their choice of music, games playing and films, cannot be said to shape their involvement in crime as the majority of youth who share the same interests and influences are not so involved (Street Weapons Commission 2008: 79).

The Street Weapons Commission, using the example of a pioneering Violence Reduction Unit set up in Strathclyde, Scotland in 2005, recommended a public health approach to violent behaviour, one in which the stresses, strains and deprivations of youth were as important to address as monitoring, surveillance and enforcement of the policing agenda against gangs. As they advised in the report which accompanied their consultation and advice-gathering exercise:

> The youth violence issue is overwhelmingly constructed as a *criminal justice problem*, as if it were amenable to criminal justice solutions alone, something which more or tougher punishment, stronger laws or more police stop and search intervention might solve. It is deeply concerning that, to the extent that youth violence is construed as a 'law and order' problem, other potentially more effective and enduring policy responses tend to become sidelined in a self-defeating rush to 'police' the crisis, 'enforce' order and 'punish' the already marginal. In the face of complex problems, difficult evidence or even gaps in the evidence, commentators sometimes opt for the comfort of simple solutions – especially in a mediated political culture where the soundbite is king. (Squires et al. 2006: 6)

However, most approaches to the problem of 'gangs' remain heavily enforcement related. The Criminal Justice Act 2003 established mandatory, five-year minimum sentences for the illegal possession of a prohibited firearm when previously average custodial sentences had stood at eighteen months. The maximum sentence for carrying a bladed weapon was also doubled from two to four years and cautions withdrawn for any 16 and 17 year olds caught in possession of a knife ensuring that all such young people would have to face a court. According to the Street Weapons Commission 'people carrying a knife are now three times more likely to go to prison as ten years ago (up from 6 per cent in 1996 to 17 per cent in 2006) and the average sentence has increased by a third over the same period' (2008: 82).

## Concluding comments

The continuing addition and extended use of powers to control and take action against organised and disorganised offenders and the targeting of groups which this chapter outlines appears in many respects to represent a focused and deliberate policy trajectory, but the fact that it has been so incremental and sustained over a lengthy period of time suggests that it may be the consequence instead of a strengthening internal philosophy which has become ever more entrenched in government attitudes to dealing with any behaviour considered to be problematic. This attitude seems to stem from a fundamentally pessimistic attitude not only towards those individuals who become involved in such 'problem' behaviour but also to the 'broken society'[6] at large which is unable to mend itself and further more may be beyond rehabilitation. It is a perspective which sees Britain as faced with incorrigible criminality and the prospect of an unstoppable slide into disorder (at least in some sections of society and within particular neighbourhoods) in which the government cannot intervene positively to change people's lives so must show through punishment and condemnation that bad behaviour will be dealt with severely. People's attitudes, it posits, will be changed through the application of a moral and punitive external force which requires a different model of behaviour to prevail. This perspective was amply demonstrated by Jack Straw back in 1997 when he condemned the practice of protecting young people from the criminal courts in the hope that 'they would grow out of it' (Squires and Stephen 2005: 89) and instead insisted on the application of punitive discourse and practice. Anything else was seen as continuing to allow young offenders to act with impunity and encouraged the idea that they were above the law and could not be touched by it (Campbell 2002). However, as Squires and Stephen explain – using Cohen's dispersal of discipline thesis – the reconsideration of less serious offences by young people as worthy of a great deal more punitive attention and casting petty offenders as persistent and impervious to advice and support leaves no space for a more compassionate view of more serious offenders. These latter are considered to be 'hard core' and irredeemable. As such those involved in more serious offences are cast as 'evil', almost naturally so and consequently without much personal worth. If young people involved in less serious crimes can internalise punitive and condemnatory discourses to self-define as embedded in criminal ways of life (Jamieson 2006) and thereby see themselves as beyond redemption, how much more so must those young people who stray into more serious and persistent criminality.

## FURTHER READING

Pitts, J. (2008) *Reluctant Gangsters: The Changing Face of Youth Crime.* Cullompton, Devon: Willan Publishing.
Woodiwiss, M. and Hobbs, D. (2009) 'Organized evil and the Atlantic Alliance: moral panics and the rhetoric of organized crime policing in America and Britain', *British Journal of Criminology*, 49: 106–28.

## NOTES

1  Nick Clegg, then home affairs spokesperson for the Liberal Democrat Party described Britain thus in 2007 adding 'The government should ask itself why the prisons are at bursting point and yet the level of several crimes are still higher than elsewhere in the EU. The present strategy must be rethought urgently' (*Guardian* 2007j).

2 For example in 2009 television and radio presenter, Joan Bakewell, was appointed 'champion of the elderly' by Minister for Women, Harriet Harman and entrepreneur and media celebrity, Alan Sugar, was brought in as the government's 'enterprise champion'.

3 The Liberal Democrat home affairs spokesperson at the time, Chris Huhne, likened this policy to a reintroduction of the village stocks (*Guardian* 2008e).

4 Other organisations with automatic access to this information included the UK Atomic Energy Constabulary, the Scottish Drugs Enforcement Agency, the Maritime and Coastguard Agency, Financial Services Authority, Office of the Police Ombudsman for Northern Ireland and the Radiocommunications Agency.

5 In the online version of the paper at http://www.independent.co.uk/news/uk/crime/helen-and-sylvia-the-new-face-of-terrorism-472993.html (accessed 13.07.06).

6 The use of this term to describe British society was popularised by David Cameron in 2007 after Iain Duncan Smith MP chaired a report by the party's Social Justice Policy Group. This highlighted the 'problems' of decline in the popularity of marriage as well as binge-drinking and youth violence as characterising the state of Britain.

# 10

# The changing face of crime prevention

The last quarter of the twentieth century saw crime prevention emerge 'as a major focus of public policy and criminological research' (Tilley 2002: 13). However, its journey in reaching this position was not straightforward, linear or forged in a constantly progressive direction. Tilley identifies three distinctive, but overlapping periods through which crime prevention developed. In the first period, 1975–90, crime prevention initiatives and activities were acknowledged as a valid and serious endeavour. In the second, 1985–2000, an accepted body of crime prevention knowledge gained institutional recognition and was co-opted wholesale into mainstream practice but in this shift any radical agendas which had begun to inform its practice were lost as crime prevention became a largely technical and professional affair. In the third phase, 1995–2010 (and here Tilley engaged in some prediction based on policy movements up to 2001) the newly established ways of working to reduce crime were cut free from the largely public institutions which had previously made them their own and crime prevention practice was thrown up in the air once again to find a new balance and focus under a myriad of 'owners' which have turned out to be public, private, voluntary and even commercial. In these latter changes various commentators writing around the turn of the century have identified what Hughes has termed an 'epochal shift' (2007: 8) taking place in considerations of what to do about the problem of crime. Perhaps the most influential of these works has been Garland's meta-analysis of contemporary crime control in the UK and the USA published in 2001. In Garland's words a new criminology of control has emerged which, while still concerned with the reduction of crime, has been animated by much wider concerns and considerations.

The micro-analysis of the crime prevention agenda in the UK offered in this book confirms that it has undergone radical alterations since the turn of the century. When the Conservative government lost office in 1997 crime prevention was still a largely parochial and localised endeavour concerned with the management of crime at the micro-level within problem neighbourhoods, communities and streets. A growing body of crime prevention professionals was active, designing and managing projects which hoped to make an impact at the level of the individual and the community. These projects reflected an interventionist and largely positive programme which rested on the assumption that crime prevention could have significant impacts locally and that community structures were such that any success in deterring target groups from individual acts of crime, however this was achieved, would be transmitted across the neighbourhood and result in reduced levels of crime from which all could adduce some benefit. Over the next decade, as we have seen, the practice and intended targets of crime prevention activity began to move out of this enclave and into new terrains.

## Co-opting the local to the agenda of crime control

While I have argued that crime prevention under New Labour moved from its preoccupation with the local to cover a much wider area of concern, the prevention of crime at local level was never abandoned and continued to exercise the work of the local Crime and Disorder Reduction Partnerships (CDRPs) set in place after the Crime and Disorder Act of 1998 came into force. The 1998 Act was designed precisely to counter what was perceived to be rising levels of crime and disorder at the local level and the structures which it put in place to combat anti-social behaviour and to restrain young people's 'problematic behaviour' remain on the statute books, are widely used and have laid firm foundations for subsequent crime control measures which have extended and strengthened the provisions of the 1998 Act. In the beginning New Labour appeared to accept that it should listen to and take advice from experts, practitioners, academics and the public alike but it has since proved very selective in what it heard and what it acted upon. For after all New Labour was intensely ideological in nature and wedded to its Third Way philosophy, rejecting traditional Labour values in favour of pushing through a 'modernising' reform agenda.

In the end, Gilling has argued, local crime control under Labour proved to be decidedly 'top-down' in nature, formed from the centre and pushed downwards from Labour's political elites to infuse governance at every level. While different consultative and delivery structures were put in place at different levels between the centre and the neighbourhood he argues that Labour did not relinquish attempts to manage and control the population, but attempted 'to shape the actions, and the governing mentalities, of those agencies and individuals involved in exercising governmental power over the population' (2007: 212) and to co-opt them into the New Labour agenda. As a consequence while the state appeared to be in some sense stepping away from its role as manager of social order and handing this over to local actors it was at one and the same time careful to ensure that its own agendas were clearly outlined, through numerous policy pronouncements and legislative changes, and through its policy of micro-managing local initiatives through detailed administrative requirements and outcome-based measures of performance. Through these processes the state has maintained a heavy hand on activities on the ground while professing to merely offer 'light touch' support to CDRPs, local strategic partnerships and communities.

New Labour's modernisation of the local control agenda was not always clear-cut. Even in the close scrutiny to which Gilling has subjected local crime control measures throughout the course of his book he found a clear and consistent approach to local crime control was difficult to discern in the New Labour project. This was in some ways unsurprising given the constant interventions which were made by successive government ministers into the workings of the systems of criminal justice and crime prevention. This 'initiativitis', together with the interlinking (or 'joining up) of criminal justice and crime prevention with other services as diverse as education, housing, family policy, policing and health, all with their own specialist agendas too, has meant a complicated array of inter-ventions, policy initiatives and changes which is sometimes difficult to clearly trace. It can be nigh on impossible in times of rapid and remorseless change to pick out the wood from the trees. However, Gilling has detected a continued politicisa-tion of crime prevention and a steer from the centre which has been driven by the desire to build and maintain neo-liberal forms of governance while on the other hand appearing to offer more social explanations and solutions for the problem of crime. For Gilling, however, the neo-liberal project has won out and local crime control became less about the reduction of crime and more about 'inducing "free" neo-liberal subjects to govern themselves and their families' (2007: 215) and to participate in the governing of their own communities. This was not so different in many respects from then Prime Minister Thatcher's famous dictum that 'there is no such thing as society', reproduced below:

> I think we've been through a period where too many people have been given to understand that if they have a problem, it's the government's job to cope with it. 'I have a problem, I'll get a grant.' 'I'm homeless, the government must house me.' They're casting their problem on society. And, you know, there is no such thing as society. There are individual men and women, and there are families. And no government can do anything except through people, and people must look to themselves first. It's our duty to look after ourselves and then, also to look after our neighbour. People have got the entitlements too much in mind, without the obligations. There's no such thing as entitlement, unless someone has first met an obligation. (Thatcher 1987)

While New Labour called on self-governing communities, Thatcher talked of the importance of neighbourliness, but the simple call to the individual and fam-ily to extricate themselves from dependence on the state and to build independent structures of support is familiar. It was a highly moralising discourse which placed responsibility firmly on local actors rather than state agents. Crime reduction, according to Gilling was a useful tool upon which to build the local strategic partnerships which the government required to shift from a model of centralised government to more disparate and devolved governance without losing the steer from the centre which was, after all, considered vital in maintaining Labour's electoral ascendancy. Crime control could be used as such a political tool precisely because of its normalisation and institutionalisation in previous decades and the acceptance of reduction in crime as a key measure of quality of life, and because feelings of insecurity and fear for the future were growing and extending their reach across different classes and into the fabric of everyday life.

## Crime prevention and securitisation

The recent (re)turn to expert, professional crime prevention practices, the 'what works' agenda and crime science included, together with the rejection of the softer more social and people-oriented experiments which emerged with more radical interpretations within criminology, has been driven by the need to make manageable and knowable the fears, insecurities and threats which dominate life in late-modern societies (O'Malley 2004). These new sets of fears and insecurities are keenly felt but difficult to articulate. Fear of crime, and in particular that which directly affects the individual, has served as a useful proxy for these wider concerns, helping to give indeterminate threats a shape which can be recognised and a form which can be tackled. At the same time economic restructuring left people struggling to make sense of rapidly changing circumstances and has profoundly impacted on people's sense of who they are and what part they play in the world. These threats are more than ever felt in the individual's everyday life where the choices people make – in where to live, how to build an education, where to work, when to start a family – can have major impacts on their future security and well-being. Traditional ways of living have been dismantled and each individual is seen as responsible for building their own successes or failures no longer able to rely on the guiding and supportive hand of the state to help in times of trouble. A burgeoning consumer culture has played a part in helping individuals buy the trappings of success, to appear to the outside gaze to be doing well. The drive to possess more and to be seen to be a success, while driving consumer capitalism has also increased opportunities for crime and selfish (anti-social?) behaviour. Tensions are created between the seemingly successful and the decidedly marginalised and impoverished as the gap between their respective positions widens (Dorling et al. 2008). Even where recorded crime itself appears to be reducing other signs of social disorder and chaotic lifestyles predominate – the heavy drinking culture of some young people, the 'hoodies' at the end of the street, begging in town centres and 'squeegee merchants' have all been identified as signifying chaos and disorder, however, rising house possessions, business collapses, increasing unemployment, lack of affordable housing and deep-rooted poverty could be equally cited as such.

After nearly two decades of state-sponsored evidence-based, 'what works' strategic interventions in preventive policies a solution has not been found to the problem of crime and disorder. Where crime has fallen this appears to be a general phenomenon which is little related to the many and various interventions which have been tried within different nations and appear to be the consequence of a generalised pattern of declining crime rates which has occurred across the liberal democratic states whatever their particular take on the problem of crime and its solutions. Fewer inroads still have been made into reducing the fear of crime which as we have seen has continued to remain high despite the evidence that recorded crime has declined. However, since crime has been accepted as a major concern of national and local politics, governments are expected to understand and address public fears and to put in place policies which will make populations feel more secure and their individual safety assured. With no solutions in sight and unable or unwilling to make the changes which could actually allay the public's fears politicians have had to reassure the public that they have not been forgotten and that something is being done. In order to reassure the public that they understand their fears they pander to them rather than contradict them even where this means mirroring popular but simplistic arguments which do not capture the complex nature of whatever is driving public concerns. The turn to populist pronouncements and solutions can be best understood in these terms.

At the same time as the threats which are experienced in everyday life within late-modernity do not appear to be dissipating, global insecurities have raised significant concerns at the macro-level (Stenson 2005). Constant wars, increased flows of the destitute and the frightened attempting to escape poverty and persecution in their homelands, and since 2001 the increased threat of terrorism, have made a marked impact around the world and are felt at national and at local levels. New global threats are emerging – climate change has destabilised weather patterns and unleashed destructive 'natural' forces, global financial collapse, movements of capital and industry to the new sites of capitalism have led to unemployment, homelessness and despair for many. Increased inequalities between nation-states and regions of the world have fed new forms of crime; people-trafficking, international drug smuggling, identity crime and counterfeiting have all developed to take advantage of growing transnational networks of capital, people and ideas. If public safety and insecurity at the micro-level has previously exercised national governments, forms of international public insecurities are now also of major political concern (Stenson 2005). If the state finds it difficult to allay threats and fears which emerge at the micro-level it has little if no chance of making an impact on forces operating at the macro-level, yet efforts have been made to do just this. In the absence of many effective transnational forms of governance which have the control of crime within their remit it has been left to national governments to take up the fight against international crime and the forces driving this, and to make alliances in this matter wherever possible (Woodiwiss and Hobbs 2009).

The constant search for ways to make populations feel more secure in circumstances over which national governments actually have very little control drives a number of the government's punitive crime control agendas. Under these circumstances attention has to be drawn away from the ineffectiveness of the state in achieving security for its population. This is attempted in a number of ways. First, rather than acknowledge the forces which are fracturing neighbourhoods and rendering individuals helpless it is individuals and 'broken' communities which are blamed for creating their own problems, and are typified as an 'underclass' or as an 'entire social group' which has rejected mainstream values and have chosen to live to a different set of social mores which are destructive to the greater good. They are exhorted to reconsider their actions and to re-engage in the 'good society' and in civic and political life. To this end the government emphasises a moral authoritarian agenda to bring about change. Secondly, agencies other than those sponsored directly by the state are encouraged to take up their hitherto neglected responsibilities – from commercial organisations paying for their own security to social housing projects redesigning physical environments and drawing up probationary tenancies to play their part to reduce crime and anti-social behaviour. This underpins the government's agenda on privatisation and responsibilisation. Then with popular rejection of the idea that rehabilitation of offenders is a realistic possibility more people convicted of crime must be seen to be incarcerated and for longer periods of time, thus pushing up the prison population and pandering to 'penal populism'.

It has been suggested that these policy directions demonstrate the 'hollowing out' or the weakening of the state especially where macro-level forces lie beyond the powers of the nation-state to control (Bottoms and Wiles 1992) but other perspectives suggest that they more accurately reflect a 'dispersal of discipline' (Cohen 1985) where responsibility for social order is passed down from the centre towards greater parts of the population, but still under the guidance of state forces, or that they represent the emergence of a biopolitics of crime control (Stenson 2005) wherein the state has become successful at controlling and regulating more aspects of life than previously but no longer working solely through the traditional institutions of state power but through multiple layers of governance. Rather than weakening the state, crime has, according to Garland, 'come to function as a rhetorical legitimation for social and economic policies that effectively punished the poor and as a justification for the development of [a] strong, disciplinary state' (2001: 102). New forms of public management are subsequently deemed necessary for the state to maintain their overall control of policy direction and to ensure that the periphery does not march to a different tune.

On the level of international insecurities similar attempts at directing attention away from the ineffectual instruments of national government have been constructed. Instead of broken communities, entire states are characterised as 'failing' and in need of intervention and western-style democratisation; commercial organisations and private armies are brought in to rebuild and secure shattered economies (Whyte 2007) and defeated governments. Threats to national security are deemed to emerge from 'foreign' cultures and religious ideologies which are 'anti-western' by nature and a threat to national security. 'Interventions' and invasions are all justified in the name of the west's greater moral authority. Rather than deliver greater security internationally and nationally, however, these foreign policy directions have destabilised global relations and added to global insecurities. In a global 'cumulative feedback loop' (Castells 1997) with terrible consequences they have added more threats and required greater attempts to intervene to neutralise them.

## The globalised nature of threat

While the twentieth century version of crime prevention perceived its threats as emanating from within the nation-state in the twenty-first century there are many more sites from which insecurities and fears emerge which appear to originate outside of national borders. Transnational crimes such as drug smuggling and people-trafficking can be tackled at inter-governmental level using international policing and security organisations such as Interpol or through various arms of the United Nations and the European Commission and using international courts but other sources of insecurity such as the waging of war and banking collapse are not generally cast as 'criminal' issues, although they could and I would argue should be. Other perceived threats, both forced and elective migration, the seeking of political asylum are dealt with as though they were 'criminal' issues and threaten the nation's security although in truth the victims of these global processes are not the receiving nations but the individuals forced to seek sanctity outside their previous homelands.

As we have seen in the later chapters of this book maintaining the security of borders, both physical and metaphorical, has become a major political concern in recent years. The motivation of those crossing British borders is now considered suspect despite the fact that tourism, foreign students and migrant workers add billions of pounds each year to the British economy. Visitors to Britain are subjected to 'criminal-justice style' (Weber 2002) surveillance and monitoring. The over-stayer, the 'foreign' student without the required visas or qualifications, the asylum seeker without papers and the child refugee who cannot prove their exact age are likely to be detained and summarily deported as though a criminal. The very permeability of British culture and the truly multi-cultural nature of many urban neighbourhoods has been cast in an unsympathetic and problematic light. Hybridity, the sharing and swapping of different cultural elements has been framed as an attack on 'British' ways of living rather than an inclusion and enriching of experience and understanding – although what the British way of life is, or has been in the past, is rarely developed or defined. The 'enemy within' is likely now to be framed as a foreign import, the 'home-grown' terrorist formed by dangerous ideas which are alien to British ways of thinking.

As the 'stranger' and 'foreign' become more closely entwined in popular consciousness protectionist discourses grow ever stronger and calls to banish the 'outsider' are increasingly heard. Fortress Britain is constructed to deter those who are outside British borders with thoughts of crossing in, but once inside the borders another system kicks in to deflect thoughts of 'overstaying your welcome'. Even those with permission to stay and work in Britain are subjected to ever more invasive procedures through which they must constantly prove their entitlement to the services which Britain has to offer. The National Health Service used to treat anyone on British soil, whatever their legal entitlement to remain. Now failed asylum seekers are excluded from publicly funded medical services and anyone without British citizenship can be asked to produce their passports when requesting medical attention. Academics and students visiting from abroad must now do the same even if they have contracts of employment within a British institution and if they take up casual or sessional work outside their main place of employment. The treatment of visiting foreigners as 'strangers' easily transfers to others who can be deemed 'not British enough' whatever their legal and citizenship status. The xeno-racism which Fekete (2002) and others have discerned is not based solely on visual differences but on cultural referents too. The old racisms and prejudices have not disappeared but they are joined by even more insidious suspicions, hatreds and fears which are whipped up in the popular press and reflected in the words of politicians.

Globalised fears impact very heavily at the local level. The local remains significant in the majority of individuals' lives. In unequal Britain, where you are born, where you subsequently live, your class position all continue to have huge implications for the way your life develops into the future and the opportunities which present themselves (Wilkinson and Pickett 2009). Cities compete within the global economy to attract private finance and enterprise and to successfully incorporate what are considered to be varied and exciting local amenities. The poor find themselves locked out of these globalised spaces, through lack of economic power, the opportunities and training to access employment or through surveillance and restriction of their movements (Phillips and Cochrane 1988). While the impoverished are separated from the well-heeled even in marginal places, divisions are allowed to develop and become more firmly rooted. Neighbourhoods are set in competition against each other for public funds with which they hope to regenerate and remodel ailing economies. There are winners and there are losers. Where resources are scarce and becoming even more so, old divisions cannot heal and are joined by fresh ones. Newly articulated national threats are played out at the local level, global panics are translated into local fears and the 'others', asylum seekers, migrant workers, Muslims, the not-quite British enough, are all too easily singled out for attention and blame – they take 'our' houses and 'our' jobs and threaten 'our' way of life when in truth past securities in these areas have been removed by political and market forces. Where such fears are played upon and remain unrefuted new and established forms of racism are strengthened and attitudes hardened against Britain's diverse and growing minority populations and while the government plays at building 'community cohesion' at the local level it is all too busy creating the conditions at the international and national level which create divisions locally.

## The management of risk – are we all suspects now?

Where the problem of crime can no longer be eradicated, or the political will to 'solve' it is not present, then it must be managed. As the 'problem of crime' moves into new terrains then the management of crime must move into these spaces too. As more actions are made criminal and actions which are not criminal are dealt with as though they were, then more and more behaviour must be managed. To manage a problem involves first and foremost the collection of information about that problem and as more information is sought this requires taking monitoring and surveillance of the population to a new level. In previous periods those who transgressed the law might be subjected to close monitoring and surveillance either for purposes of detection or after guilt was established lest they fall into crime again. However, in the present period there is a marked tendency to closely monitor and check the veracity of the majority rather than just the minority. Anyone who has had to recently open a bank account, claim welfare benefits or put their child's name down for a popular school will know how closely scrutinised everyday transactions can be. In order to prevent the commission of crime, control is embedded 'in the fabric of normal interaction' (Garland 2001: 129) to create what Garland has termed 'a criminology of everyday life' (Garland 1996, 2001) and no one is immune from the criminological gaze.

The new checks and restrictions which are now part of everyday life create the impression that we are all under suspicion and that anyone might take the opportunity presented to them to make a false or fraudulent claims for their own benefit. This is the rational choice theory applied not to individuals, or indeed 'entire social groups' but to the public as a whole. It returns to a discredited theory which posits that we are all driven by the drive to maximise our own good, that we will push legal boundaries or break the law to do so, and that we will do this at the expense of others. We are all potential criminals, are reminded of this in our everyday interactions and are constantly subjected to deterrent measures. This is a profoundly pessimistic view of human nature and removes from humanity all consideration of the socially supportive and collective experiences which have also characterised our history and present. The basis for a mutual, supportive and trusting society is thereby erased from memory and experience. If society itself is not broken it is treated as though it were. Society cannot continue to function in the same way if all citizens must be closely managed and scrutinised in order to prove their innocence and probity. Blair typified this approach when championing summary justice in his launching of the Respect Action Plan in 2006 – the man with thousands in cash in his pocket must prove that he has come about it legally and all those suspected of wrongdoing must accept that it is their responsibility to prove otherwise. All asylum seekers are treated poorly because some of them are classed as 'bogus', all young people hanging out on particular streets or dressed in a particular 'outlawed' style are considered troublesome and the devout Muslim is considered un-British. While certain groups have always been treated with suspicion and mistrust in twenty-first-century Britain the principles of deterrence and incapacitation, having been vigorously applied to the law-breakers, have now reached a level of acceptance and respectability and have been extended and implemented much more widely. Once it is deemed acceptable to subject 'suspect' groups to inhuman and degrading treatment this can be more easily transferred to the population generally in times of generalised mistrust and suspicions.

Since the criminal justice system and the state institutions which underpin it are no longer the sole agents of crime control the necessary monitoring and surveillance of the citizen is passed into the hands of a whole array of private and public institutions. This changes our entire relationship to public and private service deliverers. Perhaps most significant is that the providers of what were once considered to be the institutions of welfare and support in times of need are also co-opted into a monitoring and surveillance mode, fundamentally changing the social contract between provider and the person in need of provision. Stories abound of local authorities 'snooping' on parents whom they suspect of falsifying addresses to get their children enrolled in their preferred schools, of intrusive surveillance of dog owners who let their animals foul public parks and the overuse of the Regulation of Investigatory Powers Act to tap into the communications of individuals who are suspected of what may be considered bad behaviour but is not criminal in intent or in practice. Our relationship with private institutions is altered too as they pick up more of the security roles which the state previously maintained, or provide more public goods and we must give more information to commercial enterprises before we can access common services. And who checks the checkers? In the 'criminology of everyday life' it is the individual's day-to-day behaviour and intention which is called into account not that of the private enterprise or public provider of services. The intentions of these organisations are generally considered trustworthy and are subject to weaker, regulatory powers.

As the general citizen is subject to such checks and suspicion, the treatment of the known offender becomes more extreme still and they are subject to increasing levels of discipline and continued surveillance. This is exacerbated by the abandonment of the rehabilitative model and the expectation that the 'leopard will not change its spots'. If people cannot or will not change then it follows that they must be subject to constant scrutiny in the future. The language of capital, of cost-efficiencies and of loss prevention infuses the management of risk which has become actuarial in tone (Feeley and Simon 1992). Offenders are assessed by calculations of risk, classified, categorised and subjected to depersonalised models of punishment, care and support which they are expected to respond to in accepted ways and time frames.

## Crime prevention in the twenty-first century

This chapter has considered some of the tensions and forces which have characterised the crime prevention agenda in twenty-first-century Britain. It has explored the growing use of criminalisation as a technique of control and ways in which legislation initially designed to prevent particular forms of crime has encroached on the control of the non-criminal. As the practice of crime prevention has widened in recent years to encompass many more activities and groups than previously, its philosophy has narrowed to become overwhelmingly technicist, to look for individualised solutions to social problems and apparently uninterested in the wider and more fundamental questions as to why crime might be committed. In its preoccupation with situational techniques and sidelining of the social, crime prevention has lost any radical focus it might once have had.

The study of crime and its prevention, however, is not divorced from and uninfluenced by wider socio-political issues; indeed it has been profoundly affected by changing political agendas which are exercised by the need to provide security and safety in a changing world. In truth the situational practices of crime prevention have been adopted to monitor, surveil, deter and incapacitate the non-criminal in a variety of ways. Crime prevention remains an important area to study precisely because its techniques are no longer utilised only for the prevention of crime but also to inform other aspects of social control and to exclude and contain 'risky' populations. This exclusion and containment is not only practised by the institutions of the state but also by private security organisations and companies seeking profit maximisation in their vetting of customers and avoidance of 'bad risks'. As the number of risks increases in insecure conditions then more of us are vetted, brought under suspicion and managed accordingly.

The study of crime prevention today is largely a study of professionals. In researching this book I came across little recent research which outlines the work of community-led and managed crime prevention schemes. In putting Crime and Disorder Reduction Partnerships on a statutory footing this may have resulted in the co-option of community activists into more 'professional' structures and taken away from grass-roots and community-led initiatives. The government's Community Crime Fighter Programme typifies an approach whereby individual community activists are asked to join up with professional agencies such as the police, they receive training and support from programmes and staff sponsored and designed by Home Office (now Ministry of Justice) staff. However, when poorly-funded community groups and individuals join with such powerful and well-resourced forces it will be difficult for them to retain their independence of thought and action.

Precisely because the state continues to use the terminology of crime and its prevention in managing populations which it considers a risk, and indeed extends its use to areas which were not previously considered 'criminal' matters, then I would argue that as academics we must continue to critically engage with the subject but place it in its wider political and social context. To talk of crime prevention in the narrow ways in which it has been defined in mainstream criminology and in government circles obscures so much of its current purpose and direction that it becomes a futile endeavour which may sustain a growing industry and keep a number of people in employment but will never tackle the social ills which beset society and immiserate so many.

## Resistance is never futile!

The adaptations and directions which government policy has taken over the preceding period have by no means always been accepted and reflected back at them from below. While I have argued throughout this book that governments have steered local and national crime prevention projects to their own particular ends it would be wrong to suggest that there has not been resistance from various quarters. Community organisations are often born out of adversity and have carved out spaces in which they can make a difference. Sometimes these happily coexist with more formally constituted structures and at other times they may be antagonistic or even present illegitimate opportunity structures (Evans et al. 1996) for their participants and associates. There is some debate as to how far alternative, democratic and oppositional agendas which resist the directions of the New Labour project have been sustained over the last period. Hughes has pointed out, for example, to the persistence of the community safety perspective across Wales where crime and disorder partnerships have not fallen into the narrow confines of crime reduction. He has also drawn attention to research, his own with Gilling and the work of others, which suggests that the 'habitus' of community safety professionals which was formed in an oppositional stance of resistance to the narrow confines of a technicist and risk-oriented crime prevention paradigm, continues to offer a more sociological and radical understanding of the problem of crime. However, the extent to which this perspective can be maintained in the teeth of a continued ideological onslaught and close scrutiny and steering by the engineers of performance management and output-based assessment of worth and quality remains to be seen.

Resistance to the New Labour project has also come through more overtly political avenues. Publications such as Statewatch and Human Rights Watch continue to monitor the performance of government and state-led institutions in their attempts to control the general population and minority groups within it. While few and far between there are some community-based media such as Nerve in Liverpool and Salford Star which unpick the economic and social regeneration policies of their respective cities and give voice to communities and individuals which resist the dominant paradigms coming down from the centre and impacting heavily on the local. The abject poverty and dehumanising treatment to which refugees and asylum seekers are subjected has also fostered many community and church-led support groups which attempt to mediate the worst effects of government policy in this area. Groups such as the Campaign Against the Criminalisation of Communities and the Coalition Against Secret Evidence have questioned the extension of laws to control anti-social behaviour and suspected terrorism. As these groups have become more numerous and vocal, however, the policing of social movements and oppositional groups has also toughened and taken on many of the characteristics of the changing crime prevention agenda which have been explored above. Demonstrators are now routinely photographed and their images uploaded on to a police database. The introduction of the tactic of 'kettling' where the police surround groups of demonstrators and 'incarcerate' them in public places for hours at a time on a suspicion that a crime might be committed bears many of the hallmarks of recent moves in crime prevention policy. It is no longer those perceived as intent on violent protest who are detained in this way but all demonstrators can be subject to this tactic and it represents another facet of over-policing and surveillance of lawful activity. Protest and demonstration, while a confirmed political right in any democracy can also be treated as akin to a criminal activity.

Of course within the academic community too there are many critical voices raised in opposition to current trends and some have even succeeded in stepping out of the narrow confines of criminology to consider issues of social harm and why this matters more than crime (Dorling et al. 2005). It is not difficult to see that policies and practices aimed at the prevention of social harm would look very different from those which follow on from the state's 'obsession' (to use Dorling et al.'s phrase) with crime. This would naturally reignite radical futures for the subject and more easily re-embed our discussions in the promotion of social justice and human rights. In presenting the material in this book, outlining the directions which crime prevention has taken in twenty-first-century Britain and pointing to some of the trajectories of change and consistencies both practical and theoretical I hope to have in a small way added something to the tools which critical criminologists have at their disposal.

# Glossary

**Actuarialism**  A term taken from the insurance industry whereby risks are calculated and their statistical distribution plotted. Certain activities and groups of people are calculated as particularly risky and are managed accordingly. This actuarialist perspective has been carried across to the correctional establishment and increasingly to probation work. An individual's risk of reoffending is calculated using a number of given risk factors in their lives and they are managed accordingly (Feeley and Simon 1992).

**Administrative criminology**  This term is used to describe a criminological perspective which has been linked to the Home Office from the 1970s. A reponse to rising crime levels and the rejection of the search for the causes of crime, administrative criminology set out instead to reduce and control crime mainly through the adoption of situational crime prevention techniques.

**Civil society**  A term from political science, civil society refers to voluntary association and collective action to pursue shared interests, purposes and values, which is distinct from either the state or the market. It is sometimes used interchangeably with the term community but this is a mistaken use of the term as civil society is more focused around more formalised and institutional forms of collectivity.

**Communitarianism**  A philosophical and sociological tradition which advocates maintenance of a social order in which individuals are bound together by common values that foster close communal bonds. It can be both radical or intensely conservative in its outlook.

**Community crime prevention**  A perspective which uses 'community' itself as a tool for crime prevention. It rejects preventive strategies which focus on individual measures to prevent crime and suggests that crime must be tackled in a more collective manner.

**Community safety**  Goes beyond the narrow confines of crime prevention to suggest that quality of life can only be ensured when people feel safe and protected from crime and the social harms which it can produce. Crime is seen in its widest form to include environmental hazards as well as domestic abuse and bullying or harassment. In its most radical form community safety would encompass protection from other social ills which are not generally linked to crime in mainstream understandings.

**Crime science**   Conceived in the 1990s and best represented by the Jill Dando Institute at the University College London, crime science uses a range of scientific methods and disciplines to prevent and reduce the incidence of crime. It sets out to cut crime not to studying its causes and utilises scientific methodology to achieve this rather than social theory.

**Critical criminology**   A perspective which was developed in the 1970s which draws on critical social science and conflict theories such as Marxism and feminism. It focuses on state power, oppression and the role of economic capital in shaping crime which is viewed as a product of social and historical processes related to the workings of capital and the inequalities which it produces.

**Dispersal of discipline**   A thesis developed by the criminologist Stanley Cohen drawing on the work of Foucault in the late 1970s which contends that the mechanisms of social control are dispersed down from state institutions to other social institutions at different levels of society. Social control is thereby practised by society a whole, not only by the state.

**Globalisation**   An ongoing process by which the needs of global economic networks impact on national, regional and local economies and cultures so that they begin to take on more integrated and shared forms. The term can also refer to the transnational dissemination of ideas, languages, or popular cultures.

**Governance**   This term is used to describe a process by which government disperses some of its power and functions to institutions of civil society and grants them authority to govern in particular ways. These may then influence and enact policies and decisions concerning many aspects of public life.

**Hybridity**   A term from biology which concerns the mixing of material, often genetic. It has been used more recently to denote the sharing of cultures which coexist and which often results in new forms which take elements from all to produce something novel.

**Left realism**   Emerged out of critical criminology in the 1980s as a reaction to what was seen as its failure to take the impact of crime on people's lives seriously. It argues that crime disproportionately affects working class people and impacts negatively on their quality of life and must therefore be controlled to improve the lives of the majority.

**Managerialism**   The application of business techniques to improve productivity and efficiency which have increasingly been used in the non-profit sector to drive through efficiency measures and to direct and manage performance in the delivery of services.

**Net-widening and mesh-thinning** Developed by Stanley Cohen in his 1985 work *Visions of Social Control,* Cohen explains the practices by which more people are brought under the net of crime control measures and fewer are allowed to fall through this net to escape criminal justice interventions.

**Penal populism** The increasing recourse to punishment and especially imprisonment rather than rehabilitation and support for offenders. This is linked to the government's need to maintain popularity and its belief that public opinion, often expressed through the mainstream media, demands punitive and visible sanctions.

**Risk society** The thesis developed by Ulrich Beck in the 1990s which maintains that late modern society organises itself in response to growing numbers and varieties of risk and insecurities. It has been further developed by Giddens in the UK.

**Situational crime prevention** Focuses on reducing the opportunity for crime through the management, design or manipulation of the physical environment. It includes 'target-hardening' measures where the targets of crime are protected by security measures such as locks or gates, as well as designing physical environments to make the commission of crime more difficult. It is focused on the defence of property.

**Social crime prevention** Looks at the social environments in which crime takes place and attempts to alter these to make recourse to crime less likely. It includes measures which seek to improve the social conditions in high crime neighbourhoods so is not always explicitly linked to the crime prevention.

**Social exclusion** Social exclusion is a consequence of multiple and variable factors which result in people being excluded from the normal exchanges, practices and rights of modern society. It refers not only to exclusion by poverty but also to discriminatory practices, poor education and lack of knowledge and skills which can shut people out from access to services of all kinds.

**The Third Way** A centrist political philosophy which attempts to forge a path somewhere between capital and labour. It professes to transcend both established left-wing and right-wing politics by advocating a mix of both. It was popularised in the 1990s by President Clinton in the United States, Tony Blair in Britain and by other social democratic party leaders across Europe.

**Underclass** The theory that an underclass existed in society was popularised in the 1980s in the United States and famously brought over to Britain by *Sunday Times* sponsored commentator Charles Murray. The underclass is often characterised as made up of the young and long-term unemployed, the chronically-sick, and single-parent families as well as racialised minorities in poor neighbourhoods who have placed themselves outside the world of work. It is a much contested concept.

**Volume crimes**   Volume crime refers to offences such as theft, burglary, theft from a motor vehicle, criminal damage which are most often recorded in police statistics and are therefore said to have a significant impact on many victims. These are therefore the target of much crime prevention activity. It does not refer to crimes which, while they may actually occur at a higher volume are not so easily recorded.

**What works**   The principle that preventive and rehabilitative measures must be evaluated and demonstrated to have worked before they are rolled out and applied more widely.

# Bibliography

Aas, K.F. (2007) 'Analysing a world in motion: global flows meet "criminology of the other",
*Theoretical Criminology*, 11: 283–30.

Agozino, B. (2000) 'What is institutionalised? The race-class-gender articulation of Stephen
Lawrence', *The British Criminology Conference: Selected Proceedings*. Vol 3. Available at:
https://vital.liv.ac.uk/webapps/portal/frameset.jsp?tab_tab_group_id=_2_1&url=%2Fwe
bapps%2Fblackboard%2Fexecute%2Flauncher%3Ftype%3DCourse%26id%3D_72391_1
%26url%3D (accessed 17.08.00).

Akers, R.L. (1990) 'Rational choice, deterrence, and social learning theory: the path not
taken', *Journal of Criminal Law and Criminology*, 81(3): 653–76.

Arthur, R. (2005) 'Punishing parents for the crimes of their children', *The Howard Journal*,
44(3): 233–53.

Ashworth, A., Gardner, J., Morgan, R., Smith, A.T.H., von Hirsch, A. and Wasik, A. (1998)
'Neighbouring on the oppressive', *Criminal Justice*, 16(1): 7–14.

Audit Commission (1996) *Misspent Youth: Young People and Crime (Summary)*. Abingdon:
Audit Commission Publications.

Bandalli, S. (1998) 'Abolition of the presumption of Doli Incapax and the criminalisation of
children', *The Howard Journal*, 37(2): 114–23.

Barlow, J., Kirkpatrick, S. and Wood, D. (2007) *Family and Parenting Support in Sure Start
Local Programmes National Evaluation Summary*. Available at: http://www.dcsf.gov.uk/
research/data/uploadfiles/NESS2007SF023.pdf (accessed 06.09.08).

Bateman, T. (2001) 'A note on the relationship between the Detention and Training Order and
Section 91 of the Powers of the Criminal Courts (Sentencing) Act 2000: a recipe for injustice', *Youth Justice*, 1(3): 36–41.

BBC News (1997) 'Labour routs Tories in historic election', *BBC News Online*, 2 May. Available
at: http://news.bbc.co.uk/onthisday/hi/dates/stories/may/2/newsid_2480000/2480505.
stm (accessed 12.0.09).

BBC News (2000a) 'Paediatrician attacks "ignorant" vandals', *BBC News Online*, 30 August.
Available at: http://news.bbc.co.uk/1/hi/wales/901723.stm (accessed 16.07.09).

BBC News (2000b) 'To name and shame', 24 July. Available at: http://news.bbc.co.uk/1/hi/
uk/848759.stm (accessed 02.01.10).

BBC News (2006) 'The politics of exclusion, *BBC News* Available at: http://news.bbc.co.uk/1/
hi/uk_politics/4746592.stm (accessed 19.05.08).

BBC News (2009) 'Blair wants gun crime age reduced', *BBC News Online*, 18 February.

Beck, U. (1992) *Risk Society: Towards a New Modernity*. London: Sage.

Bennett, T. (1988) 'An assessment of the design, implementation and effectiveness of
Neighbourhood Watch in London', *The Howard Journal*, 27(4): 241–55.

Bennett, T.H., Holloway, K.R. and Farrington, D.P. (2008) 'The effectiveness of Neighbourhood Watch in reducing crime', *Campbell Systematic Reviews*, 18. Available at: http://www.campbellcollaboration.org/.

BID Bail for Immigration Detainees (2007) *Immigration Detention in the UK – Key Facts and Figures*. Briefing, June.

Blair, T. (2006a) *Respect Action Plan*. London: HMSO.

Blair, T. (2006b) 'PM targets "eradication of anti-social behaviour"'. Available at: www.direct.gov.uk 10.01.06 (accessed 20.01.06).

Blanden, J.A., Gregg, P. and Machin, S. (2005) *Intergenerational Mobility in Europe and North America*. Sutton Trust.

Blunkett, D. (2003) *Active Citizens, Strong Communities: Progressing Civil Renewal*. London: Home Office Communications Directorate.

Bodi, F. (2001) Unpublished report on racism in Oldham based on research and interviews during visit to the town, June. Cited in N.M. Ahmed, F. Bodi, R. Kazim and M. Shadjareh, *The Oldham Riots: Discrimination, Deprivation and Communal Tension in the United Kingdom*. Available at: http://www.mediamonitors.net/mosaddeq6.html (accessed 07.07.2007).

Bosworth, M. (2008) 'Border control and the limits of the sovereign state', *Social Legal Studies*, 17: 199–215.

Bosworth, M. and Guild, M. (2008) 'Governing through migration control security and citizenship in Britain', *British Journal of Criminology*, 48(6): 703–19.

Bottoms, A. E. and Dignan, J. (2004) 'Youth justice in Great Britain', *Crime and Justice*, 31: 21–83.

Bottoms, A.E. and Wiles, P. (1992) 'Explanations of crime and place', in D.J. Evans, N.R. Fyfe and D.J. Herbert (eds), *Crime Policing and Place: Essays in Environmental Criminology*. London: Routledge.

Bottoms, A.E. and Wiles, P. (1995) 'Crime and insecurity in the city', in C. Fijnaut, J. Goethals, T. Peters and L. Waldgrave (eds), *Changes in Society: Crime and Criminal Justice in Europe, Crime and Insecurity in the City*. The Hague: Kluwer Law International, Vol. 1. pp. 1–38.

Bowling, B. (1999) *Violent Racism: Victimisation, Policing and Social Context*. Oxford: Clarendon Press.

Bradford, S. and Morgan, R. (2005) 'Transformed youth justice?', *Public Money & Management*, 25(5): 283–90.

Bridges, L. (2002) 'Race, law and the state', *Race and Class*, 43(2): 61–76.

Bright, J. (1987) 'Community safety, crime prevention and the local authority', in P. Wilmott (ed.), *Policing in the Community*. London: Policy Studies Institute.

Bright, J. (1995) 'Integrative crime prevention'. Unpublished paper presented to the British Criminology Conference, 17 July.

Brown, A.P. (2004) 'Anti-social behaviour, crime control and social control', *The Howard Journal of Criminal Justice*, 43(2): 203–11.

Burnett, J. (2004a) 'Community, cohesion and the state', *Race and Class*, 45(3): 1–18.

Burnett, J. (2004b) 'What lies behind the recent creation by the Metropolitan Police of a South Asian Crime Unit?', *CARF*, 66 (February/March): 3–6.

Burney, E. (2002) 'Talking tough, acting coy: what happened to the anti-social behaviour order?', *Howard Journal*, 41: 469–84.

Burney, E. (2005) *Making People Behave: Anti-Social Behaviour, Politics and Policy*. Cullompton, Devon: Willan Publishing.

Cabinet Office (1997) PM speech on 'Bringing Britain Together', South London, 8 December. Available at: http://www.cabinetoffice.gov.uk/social_exclusion_task_force/~/media/assets/www.cabinetoffice.gov.uk/social_exclusion_task_force/publications_1997_to_2006/pm_speech_seu%20pdf.ashx (accessed 05.07.08).

Campbell, S. (2002) *A Review of Anti-Social Behaviour Orders*. Home Office Research Study No. 236. London: Home Office Research and Statistics Directorate.

Cantle, T. (2001) *Community Cohesion: A Report of the Independent Review Team Chaired by Ted Cantle*. London: Home Office.

Carlile, Lord (2007) *The Definition of Terrorism*. Home Office Report Cm 7052. London: Home Office.

Carson, D. (2008) 'Justifying risk decisions', *Criminal Behaviour and Mental Health* (CBMH), 18(3): 139–44.

Carson, W.G. (2004) 'Is communalism dead? Reflections on the present and future practice of crime prevention: Part Two', *The Australian And New Zealand Journal of Criminology*, 37(2): 192–210.

Casey, L. (2008) *Engaging Communities in Fighting Crime*. London: Cabinet Office.

Castells, M. (1997) *The Power of Identity, The Information Age: Economy, Society and Culture Vol. II*. Oxford: Blackwell.

Chahal, K. (1999) 'The Stephen Lawrence Inquiry Report, racist harassment and racist incidents: changing definitions, clarifying meaning?', *Sociological Research Online*, 4(1). Available at: http://www.socresonline.org.uk/socresonline/4/lawrence/chahal.html (accessed 04.03.04).

Chapman, T. and Hough, M. (1998) *Evidence-Based Practice: A Guide to Effective Practice*. London: Home Office/HM Inspectorate of Probation.

Clarke, R.V. and Cornish, D.B. (1983) *Crime Control in Britain: A Review of Policy and Research*. Albany: State University of New York Press.

Clarke, R.V. and Cornish, D.B. (1985) 'Modelling offenders' decisions: a framework for policy and research', in M. Tonry and N. Morris (eds), *Crime and Justice. Vol. 6*. Chicago: University of Chicago Press.

Clarke, R.V., Brantingham, P., Brantingham, P., Eck, J. and Felson, M. (1998) *Designing Out Crime*. London: HMSO.

Coaffee, J. and Deas, I. (2008) 'The search for policy innovation in urban governance: lessons from community-led regeneration partnerships', *Public Policy and Administration*, 23: 167–88.

Coaffee, J. and Rogers, P. (2008) 'Rebordering the city for new security challenges: from counter-terrorism to community resilience', *Space and Polity*, 12(1): 101–18.

Cohen, L.E. and Felson, M. (1979) 'Social change and crime rate trends: a routine activity approach', *American Sociological Review*, 44: 588–605.

Cohen, S. (1980) *Folk Devils and Moral Panics: The Creation of Mods and Rockers*. New York: St Martin's Press.

Cohen, S. (1985) *Visions of Social Control: Crime, Punishment and Classification*. Cambridge: Polity.

Coleman, A. (1985) *Utopia on Trial*. London: Hilary Shipman.

Coleman, R. (2004) *Reclaiming the Streets: Surveillance, Social Control and the City*. Cullompton, Devon: Willan Publishing.

Commission for Integration and Cohesion (2007) *Our Shared Future*. Available at: http://collections.europarchive.org/tha/20080726153624/http://www.integrationandcohesion.

org.uk/~/media/assets/www.integrationandcohesion.org.uk/our-shared-future%20pdf. ashx (accessed 03.05.07).

Communities and Local Government (2006) 'Launch of the Commission on Integration and Cohesion'. Speech by Ruth Kelly MP, 24 August. Available at: http://www.communities.gov. uk/speeches/corporate/commission-integration-cohesion#Page (accessed July 2007).

Cooper, D. (2004) *Challenging Diversity*. Cambridge: Cambridge University Press.

Cornish, D. and Clarke, R.V. (1986) *The Reasoning Criminal*. New York: Springer-Verlag.

Cowan, D., Pantazis, C. and Gilroy, R. (2001) 'Social housing as crime control: an examination of the role of housing management in policing sex offenders', *Social and Legal Studies*, 10: 435–57.

Cowell, D., Jones, T. and Young, J. (eds) (1982) *Policing the Riots*. London: Junction Books.

Crawford, A. (1997) *The Local Governance of Crime: Appeals to Community and Partnerships*. Oxford: Clarendon Press.

Crawford, A. (1998) *Crime Prevention and Community Safety: Politics, Policies and Practices*. London: Longman.

Crawford, A. (2001) 'Joined-up but fragmented', in R. Matthews and J. Pitts (eds), *Crime, Disorder, and Community Safety: A New Agenda*? London: Routledge.

Crawford, A. (2002) *Crime and Insecurity: The Governance of Safety in Europe*. Oxford: Willan Publishing.

Crawford, A. (2006) 'Fixing broken promises? Neighbourhood wardens and social capital', *Urban Studies*, 43: 957–76.

Crawford, A. and Jones, M. (1993) 'Inter-agency co-operation and community-based crime prevention: some reflection on the work of Pearson and colleagues', unpublished paper presented at the British Criminology Conference, Cardiff, July.

Crawford, A., Jones, T., Woodhouse, T. and Young, J. (1990) *The Second Islington Crime Survey*. Middlesex: Centre for Criminology, Middlesex Polytechnic.

CRE (1993) *Formal investigation into Oldham Local Authority's Housing Allocations in 1991*. London: Commission for Racial Equality.

Creaton, J. (2003) 'Modernizing the courts and the legal profession', *Contemporary Politics*, 9(2): 115–26.

CRESR (2005) *Research Report 17 New Deal for Communities 2001–2005: An Interim Evaluation*. November. Sheffield: Sheffield Hallam University.

CRESR (2008) *New Deal for Communities: A Synthesis of New Programme Wide Evidence: 2006-07 NDC National Evaluation Phase 2 Research Report 39*. January. Sheffield: Sheffield Hallam University.

Crime Concern (1993) *A Practical Guide to Crime Prevention for Local Partnerships*. London: HMSO.

*Daily Mail* (1997) 'Benefit revolt test for Blair', 8 December: 6.

*Daily Telegraph* (2001a) 'Crime detection rates plunge to their lowest ever', 19 July: 4.

*Daily Telegraph* (2001b) 'Ill-chosen word fuels claims of intent to wage war on Islam', 18 September: 10.

*Daily Telegraph* (2001c) 'Short attacks Bush for "crusade" quote', 21 September.

*Daily Telegraph* (2009) 'Forest Gate anti-terror raid brothers to get £60,000 compensation', 16 May.

Davies, A. (1992) *Leisure, Gender And Poverty: Working-Class Culture in Salford and Manchester, 1900–1939*. Buckingham: Open University Press.

DCLG (2006) *Strong and Prosperous Communities: The Local Government White Paper.* London: HMSO.

DCLG (2007) *Preventing Violent Extremism.* Pathfinder Fund Guidance Note for Government Offices and Local Authorities in England. London: HMSO.

DCLG (2008) *Strong and Prosperous Communities.* London: HMSO.

DCSF (2006) '£115m funds will go direct to young people for the first time – Hughes', Department for Children, Schools and Families Press Notice, 8 March.

DCSF (2007) *The Children's Plan: Building Brighter Futures,* Cm 7280. London: HMSO.

DCSF (2008) *The Impact of Sure Start Local Programmes on Three Year Olds and Their Families.* March. Available at: http://www.dcsf.gov.uk/research/data/uploadfiles/NESS2008SF027.pdf.

Department of Health (1999) *Convention on the Rights of the Child: Second Report to the U.N. Committee on the Rights of the Child by the United Kingdom.* London: TSO.

DETR (1998) *New Deal for Communities: Phase 1 Proposals: Guidance for Pathfinder Applicants.* London: HMSO.

DETR (2001) *Local Strategic Partnerships Government Guidance.* London: HMSO.

DLC (1998) 'About the Third Way', Democratic Leadership Council. Available at: http://www.ndol.org/ndol_ci.cfm?kaid=128&subid=187&contentid=895 (accessed 09.07.08).

Dorling, D., Ballas, D., Vickers, D., Thomas, B. and Pritchard, J. (2008) *Changing UK: The Way We Live Now.* Report commissioned by the BBC. Available at: http://sasi.group.shef.ac.uk/research/changingUK.html (accessed 02.12.08).

Dorling, D., Wheeler, B., Shaw, M. and Mitchell, R. *Life in Britain: Using millennial Census Data to Understand Poverty, Inequality and place.* Bristol: The Policy Press.

Driver, S. and Martell, L. (1997) 'New Labour's Communitarianism', *Critical Social Policy,* 17(3): 27–44.

DSS (1998) New Ambitions for Our Country: A New Contract for Welfare, Cm 3805, London: HMSO. Available at: http://www.dss.gov.uk/hq/index.htm (accessed 01.12.98).

Eades, C., Grimshaw, R., Silvestri, A. and Solomon, E. (2006) *Knife Crime: A Review of Evidence and Policy.* 2nd edn. London: Centre for Crime and Justice Studies, King's College London. Available at: http://www.crimeandjustice.org.u/opus439/ccjs_knife_report.pdf (accessed 17.07.07).

Eagle, A., Duff, L., Tah, C. and Smith, N. (2002) *Asylum Seekers' Experiences of the Voucher Scheme in the UK: Fieldwork Report.* London: Home Office Research, Development and Statistics Directorate.

Edwards, A. and Hughes, G. (2008) 'Resilient Fabians? Anti-social behaviour and community safety in Wales', in P. Squires (ed.), *ASBO Nation.* Bristol: Policy Press.

Evans, K. (1997) '"It's alright' round here if you're local" – Community in the inner-city', in P. Hoggett (ed.), *Contested Communities.* Bristol: Policy Press.

Evans, K. (2002) 'Crime control partnerships: who do we trust?, *Criminal Justice Matters,* 50(Winter 2002/3): 12–14.

Evans, K. (2004) *Maintaining Community in the Information Age: The Importance of Trust, Place and Situated Knowledge.* Basingstoke: Palgrave Macmillan.

Evans, K., Fraser, P. and Walklate, S. (1996) 'Grassing. Whom do you trust in the inner-city?', *Sociological Review,* (44)3: 361–80.

*Evening Standard* (1998) 'Blunkett to shame schools that expel underachievers', 11 May: 5.

Fabricant, M.B. and Burqhardt, S. (1992) *The Welfare State Crisis and the Transformation of Social Service Work.* Armonk, NY: M.E. Sharpe.

Farrall, S. D. (2007) 'Experience and expression in the fear of crime', Paper presented to GERN Interlab, University of Keele, 23 March.

Farrall, S.D., Jackson, J. and Gray, E. (2009) *Social Order and the Fear of Crime in Contemporary Time*. Oxford: Oxford University Press.

Farrell, A. (1992) *Crime, Class and Corruption: The Politics of the Police*. London: Bookmarks.

Farrell, G. and Pease, K. (1993) *Once Bitten, Twice Bitten: Repeat Victimisation and its Implications for Crime Prevention*. Crime Prevention Unit Series Paper No. 46. London: Home Office.

Farrington, D.P. (2006) 'Childhood risk factors and risk-focussed prevention', in M. Maguire, R. Morgan and R. Reiner (eds), *The Oxford Handbook of Criminology* (4th edn). Oxford: Oxford University Press.

Farrington, D.P., Coid, J.W., Harnett, L.M., Jolliffe, D., Soteriou, N., Turner R.E. and West, D.J. (2006) *Criminal Careers up to Age 50 and Life Success up to Age 48: New Findings from the Cambridge Study in Delinquent Development*, Home Office Research Study 229. London: Home Office.

Feeley, M. and Simon, J. (1992) 'The new penology: notes on the emerging strategy of corrections', *Criminology*, 30(4): 449–74.

Fekete, L. (2002) 'The emergence of xeno-racism', *Race & Class*, 43(2) 23–40.

Fekete, L. (2003) 'Analysis: Deaths during forced deportation', Independent race and refugee news network. Available at: http://www.irr.org.uk/2003/january/ak000003.html (accessed 03.11.08).

Fekete, L. (2009) *A Suitable Enemy: Racism, Migration and Islamophobia in Europe*. London: Pluto Press.

Ferguson, I. (1994) 'Containing the crisis: crime and the Tories', *International Socialism Journal*, Issue 62 (Summer).

Fielding, N. (1991) *The Police and Social Conflict: Rhetoric and Reality*. London: Athlone Press.

Fitzgibbon, D.W. (2008) 'Deconstructing probation: risk and developments in practice', *Journal of Social Work Practice*, 22(1): 85–101.

Foley, P. and Martin, S. (2000) 'A new deal for the community? Public participation in regeneration and local service delivery', *Policy & Politics*, 28(4): 479–91.

Follet, M. (2006) 'The local politics of community safety: local policy for local people?', in P. Squires (ed.), *Community Safety: Critical Perspectives on Policy and Practice*. London: Policy Press, pp. 95–110.

Foster, J. and Hope, T. (1993) *Housing, Community and Crime: The Impact of the Priority Estates Project*, Home Office Research and Planning Unit Research Study no. 131. London: Home Office.

Franklin, J. (ed.) (2002) Report by London South Bank University for BID. Available at: http://www.biduk.org/pdf/res_reports/main_contact.pdf (accessed 23.10.08).

Furniss, J. and Nutley, S. (2000) 'Implementing what works with offenders: the effective practice initiative', *Public Money and Management*, 20(4): 23–8.

Gangs in London (2009) *Gangs in London*. Available at: http://www.piczo.com/gangsinlondon?cr=2 (accessed 02.07.09).

Garland, D. (1994) 'Thinking about punishment', in R.A. Duff and D. Garland (eds), *A Reader on Punishment*. Oxford: Oxford University Press.

Garland, D. (1996) 'The limits of the sovereign state: strategies of crime control in contemporary society', *British Journal of Criminology*, 36: 445–71.

Garland, D. (2001) *The Culture of Control*. Oxford: Oxford University Press.

Gibson, M. and Hahn-Rafter, N. (2006) *Criminal Man by Cesare Lombroso; translated and with a new introduction*. Durham, NC and London: Duke University Press.

Giddens, A. (1984) *The Constitution of Society: Outline of the Theory of Structuration*. Berkelay: University of California Press.

Giddens, A. (1990) *The Consequences of Modernity*. Cambridge: Polity Press.

Giddens, A. (1998) *The Third Way: The Renewal of Social Democracy*. Cambridge: Polity Press.

Gillies, V. (2008) 'Pespectives on parenting responsibility: contextualising values and practices', *Journal of Law and Society*, 35(1): 95–112.

Gilling, D. (2001) 'Community safety and social policy', *European Journal on Criminal Policy and Research*, 9: 381–400.

Gilling, D. (2007) *Crime Reduction and Community Safety: Labour and the Politics of Local Crime Control*. Cullompton, Devon: Willan.

Gilroy, P. (1987) *There Ain't No Black in the Union Jack*. London: Routledge.

Golden, S., Bielby, G., O'Donnell, L., Walker, M., Morris, M. and Maguire, S. (2008) *Outcomes of The Youth Opportunity Fund/Youth Capital Fund*. DCSF Briefing Note -RB046. Available at: http://www.dcsf.gov.uk/research/data/uploadfiles/DCSF-RB046.pdf (accessed 09.09.08).

Goldson, B. (ed.) (2000) *The New Youth Justice*. Dorset: Russell House.

Goldson, B. (2002) 'New punitiveness: the politics of child incarceration', in J. Muncie, G. Hughes and E. McLaughlin (eds), *Youth Justice: Critical Readings*. London: Sage, pp. 386–400.

Goode, E. and Ben-Yehuda, N. (1994) *Moral Panics: The Social Construction of Deviance*. Oxford: Blackwell.

Green, P. and Grewcock, M. (2002) 'The war against illegal immigration: state crime and the construction of a European identity', *Current Issues in Criminal Justice*, 14(1): 87–101.

*Guardian* (1993a) 'Street Values', 23 June.

*Guardian* (1993b) '"Deportation Squad" Inquiry Tests Race Pledge', 4 August.

*Guardian* (1997a) 'Labour toes Thatcher line to aid poor', Home Page, 15 August: 4.

*Guardian* (1997b) 'Poverty and social exclusion: outsiders' chance', *Society*, 1 October: 2.

*Guardian* (1997c) 'Robin Cook's speech on the government's ethical foreign policy'. Available at: http://www.guardian.co.uk/world/1997/may/12/indonesia.ethicalforeignpolicy (accessed 23.10.08).

*Guardian* (1997d) 'Analysis: ethnic equality: a beacon burning darkly', 2 October.

*Guardian* (1998a) 'Labour targets lazy parents', 16 January: 1.

*Guardian* (1998b) 'Irvine urges young to turn away from "don't care" culture; Citizenship: Lord Chancellor wants response from voters', 28 January: 9.

*Guardian* (1998c) 'Budget: Families: Welfare to work: Young or old, incentives flow; Help for over 50s and the disabled', City Page, 18 March: 15.

*Guardian* (1998d) 'Truants' parents risk benefit cut', 25 March: 5.

*Guardian* (2006a) 'Kelly urges random drug tests for al pupils after successful trial', 14 April.

*Guardian* (2006b) 'Victims have to be paramount – PM', *Guardian website*, 3 April. Available at: http://www.number10.gov.uk/Page9274 (accessed 07.07.06).

*Guardian* (2006c) 'Terror Law is an affront', 13 April: 1–2.

*Guardian* (2006d) 'Muslims have lost faith in police – poll', 27 June: 4.

*Guardian* (2006e) 'Anti-terror laws alienate Muslims says top policemen', 7 August: 2.

*Guardian* (2006f) 'Radical Muslims must integrate, says Blair', 9 December: 4.

*Guardian* (2006g) 'Victims have to be paramount – PM', 3 April.

*Guardian* (2007a) 'Unborn babies targeted in crackdown on criminality', 16 May.

*Guardian* (2007b) 'Every child to be screened for risk of turning criminal under Blair justice plan', 28 March.

*Guardian* (2007c) 'Four choices on detention but 28 days is not an option', 26 July: 4.

*Guardian* (2007d) 'Terror suspects' control order face new court challenge', 28 January.

*Guardian* (2007e) 'Terror suspect who went on the run cleared of control breach', 14 December.

*Guardian* (2007f) 'Mistake to curb liberties in response to 7/7, says minister', 27 September: 14.

*Guardian* (2007g) 'Anti-terror rhetoric to be softened', 20 November: 8.

*Guardian* (2007h) 'Blair blames spate of murders on black culture', *Guardian Online* 12 April.

*Guardian* (2007i) 'Police fear lurid terror briefings used to divert attention from Whitehall problems', 3 February.

*Guardian* (2007j) 'Britain named as one of Europe's crime hotspots', 6 February.

*Guardian* (2008a) 'Brown told detention is excessive and out of step with Europe', 2 June: 2.

*Guardian* (2008b) 'Smith strengthens rules on banning extremists', 28 October: 10.

*Guardian* (2008c) 'New plan to tackle violent extremism', 3 June: 4.

*Guardian* (2008d) 'MPs seek answers on torture "outsourcing"', 21 July: 12.

*Guardian* (2008e) 'Brown books centre-fighting ideas to counter public cynicism', 19 June: 17.

*Guardian* (2008f) 'Schools may be judged on teenage pregnancy rates and drug problems: plan to include 18 social targets in Ofsted reports: teaching unions reject proposals as madness', 30 April: 1.

*Guardian* (2009a) *Anti-terrorism, Crime and Security Act 2001*. Available at: http://www.guardian.co.uk/commentisfree/libertycentral/2009/jan/13/anti-terrorism-act (accessed 02.02.09).

*Guardian* (2009b) 'Police accused of abusing powers as stop and searches triple', 1 May: 15.

Guilfoyle, M. (2008) 'A probation officer's story', in P. Squires (ed.), *Community Safety: Critical Perspectives on Policy and Practice*, London: Policy Press, pp. 149–58.

Hancock, L. (2001) *Crime, Disorder and Community*. London: Palgrave.

Hall. S, Critcher, C., Jefferson, T., Clarke, J. and Roberts, B. (1978) *Policing the Crisis: Mugging, the State and Law and Order*. London: Macmillan.

Hansard (2002) *Written Answers to Questions*, Vol No 391, 22 October. Available at: http://www.publications.parliament.uk/pa/cm200102/cmhansrd/vo021022/text/21022w25.htm:Column234W22nd October.

Hansard (2005) *Debate on Immigration, Nationality and Asylum Bill*, 5 July. Available at: www.publications.parliament.uk/pa/cm200506/cmhansrd/vo050705/debindx/50705-x.htm (accessed 24.03.06).

Heal, K. and Laycock, G. (1986) *Situational Crime Prevention: From Theory into Practice*. London: Home Office.

Heal, T. (2007) 'UK approach to counter-radicalisation', *Countering Radicalisation: Perspectives and Strategies from Around the Globe*, October. Conference in The Hague, Netherlands.

Hewitt, D. (2007) 'Bovvered? A legal perspective on the ASBO', *Journal of Forensic and Legal Medicine*, 14(6; August): 355–63.

Hine, J. and Williams, B. (2007) *DfES Youth Strategy Review. Youth Crime and Offending*. Leicester: Youth Affairs Unit, De Montfort University. Available at: http://www.dmu.ac.uk/Images/11%2E%20Youth%20Crime%20and%20Offending_tcm6-11010.pdf (accessed 05.09.08).

Hirschfield, A., Yarwood, D. and Bowers, K. (2001) 'Crime pattern analysis, spatial targeting and GIS: the development of new approaches for use in evaluating community safety initiatives', in M. Madden and G. Clarke (eds), *Regional Science in Business*. Berlin: Springer-Verlag, pp. 323–42.

HM Government (2006) *Countering International Terrorism: The United Kingdom's Strategy*. Cm 6888. London: HMSO.

HMSO (2005) *Report On The Operation in 2004 of the Terrorism Act 2000 By Lord Carlile Of Berriew Q.C.* Available at: http://security.homeoffice.gov.uk/news-publications/publication-search/terrorism-act-2000/terrorism-act-report.pdf (accessed 01.03.09).

HM Treasury (1998) 'Statement by the Chancellor of the Exchequer on the Comprehensive Spending Review – 14 July 1998'. Available at: http://www.hm-treasury.gov.uk/spend_csr98_statement.htm (accessed 24.09.01).

Holdaway, S. (1999) 'Understanding the police investigation of the murder of Stephen Lawrence: a "mundane sociological analysis"' *Sociological Research Online*, 4(1). Available at: http://www.socresonline.org.uk/socresonline/4/lawrence/holdaway.html (accessed 03.03.04).

Home Office (1993) *Safer Cities Progress Report 1992/3*. London: HMSO.

Home Office (1997a) 'Blair's speech at the launch of the Social Exclusion Unit'. Available at: http://www.number10.gov.uk/Page6 (accessed 02.03.02).

Home Office (1997b) *No More Excuses: A New Approach to Tackling Youth Crime in England and Wales*. Available at: http://www.homeoffice.gov.uk/documents/jou-no-more-excuses?view=Html#named1 (accessed 25.07.08).

Home Office (1997c) *Tackling Delays in the Youth Justice System*. London: HMSO.

Home Office (1998) *Joining Forces to Protect the Public Prisons-Probation, A Consultation Document*. London: Home Office.

Home Office (2002a) *Secure Borders, Safe Haven: Integration with Diversity in Modern Britain*, Cm. 5387. London: Home Office.

Home Office (2002b) Criminal Refugees To Be Removed from Country: Blunkett'. Press Release, 24 April. Available at: http://nds.coi.gov.uk/content/detail.asp?ReleaseID=29464&NewsAreaID=2&NavigatedFromSearch=True (accessed 21.08.08).

Home Office (2003) *Respect and Responsibility – Taking a Stand Against Anti-Social Behaviour*. London, Home Office.

Home Office (2004a) 'Strengthening Security, Protecting Identity: Home Office Publishes Identity Cards Bill', Press Release, 29 November. Available at: http://press.homeoffice.gov.uk/press-releases /Strengthening_Security,_Protecti?version=1 (accessed 21.02.09).

Home Office (2004b) *Building Communities, Beating Crime*. London: Home Office.

Home Office (2005a) *Controlling our Borders: Making Migration Work for Britain: Five Year Strategy for Asylum and Immigration*. Cm. 6472. London: Home Office.

Home Office (2005b) 'Asylum applications continue to fall'. Press Release, 23 August. Available at: www.homeoffice.gov.uk/about-us/news/asylum-applications-fall?version=2 (accessed 21.02.09).

Home Office (2005c) *Preventing Extremism Together. Working Groups, August to October 2005*. London: Home Office.

Home Office (2007a) *Delivering Safer Communities: A Guide to Effective Partnership. Working Guidance for Crime and Disorder Reduction Partnerships and Community Safety Partnerships*. London: Home Office Police and Crime Standards Directorate.

Home Office (2007b) *Control of Immigration: Statistics United Kingdom 2006*. Cm 7197. London: Home Office.

Home Office (2007c) *Asylum Figures Lowest Since 1993*. Press Release 27 February. Available at: http://www.homeoffice.gov.uk/about-us/news/asylum-quarter-report? version=1 (accessed 07.03.07)

Home Office (2007d) *The Governance of Britain*. Cm 7170. London: HMSO.

Home Office (2007e) 'Understanding the prolific and other priority offender programme', Crime Reduction Unit Leaflet, Ref: 282156.

Home Office (2008a) *UK Border Agency*. Available at: http://www.ukba.homeoffice.gov.uk/aboutus/[.]

Home Office (2008b) *Tackling Violent Crime Programme*. Available at: http://www.crimere-duction.homeoffice.gov.uk/tvcp/tvcp01.htm#purpose (accessed 02.07.09).

Home Office (2009) *Crime in England and Wales 2008/09, Volume 1: Findings from the British Crime Survey and Police Recorded Crime*. Alison Walker, John Flatley, Chris Kershaw and Debbie Moon (eds). London: HMSO.

Home Office Communication Directorate (2003) *Active Citizens, Strong Communities: Progressing Civil Renewal*. London: Home Office.

Hope, T. (1995) 'Community crime prevention', in M. Tonry and D.P. Farrington (eds), *Building a Safer Society – Strategic Approaches to Crime Prevention: Crime and Justice*, Vol. 19. Chicago: University of Chicago.

Hope, T. (1996) 'Communities, crime and inequality in England and Wales', in T. Bennett (ed.), *Preventing Crime and Disorder: Targeting Strategies and Responsibilities*. Cambridge: Institute of Criminology.

Hope, T. (2001) 'Community crime prevention in Britain: a strategic overview', *Criminal Justice*, 1(4): 421–39.

Hope, T. and Foster, J. (1992) 'Conflicting forces: changing the dynamics of crime and community on a "problem" estate', *British Journal of Criminology*, 32(4): 488–504.

Hope, T. and Hough, M. (1988) 'Area, crime and incivility: a profile from the British Crime Survey', in T. Hope and M. Shaw (eds), *Communities and Crime Reduction* London: HMSO.

Hope, T. and Shaw, M. (eds) (1988) *Communities and Crime Reduction*. London: HMSO.

Hough, M., Clancy, A., McSweeney, T. and Turnbull, P.J. (2003) 'The impact of Drug Treatment and Testing Orders on offending: two-year reconviction results', *Home Office Findings*, No. 184. London: Home Office.

House of Commons (1998) *The Crime and Disorder Bill [HL], Bill 167 of 1997–98: Anti-Social Neighbours, Sex Offenders, Racially Motivated Offences and Sentencing Drug-Dependent Offenders*, Research Paper 98/44. 6 April.

House of Commons Committee of Public Accounts (2004) *An Early Progress Report on the New Deal for Communities Programme*, Thirty–eighth Report of Session 2003-04, HC 492. London: The Stationery Office.

House of Commons Home Affairs Committee (2007) *Young Black People and the Criminal Justice System Second Report of Session 2006–07*, Vol. I. London: HMSO.

House of Lords and House of Commons (2007) *Government Response to the Committee's Tenth Report of this Session: The Treatment of Asylum Seekers. Seventeenth Report of Session 2006–7*, HL Paper 134, HC 790. London: The Stationery Office.

House of Lords and House of Commons Joint Committee on Human Rights (2007) *The Treatment of Asylum Seekers. Volume I and II. Tenth Report of Session 2006–7*, HL Paper 81-1 and II, HC 60-1 and II. London: The Stationery Office.

Hudson, B. (2003) *Justice in the Risk Society: Challenging and Re-affirming Justice in Late Modernity*. London: Sage.

Hughes, G. (1996) 'Communitarianism and law and order', *Critical Social Policy*, 16: 17–41.

Hughes, G. (1998) *Understanding Crime Prevention: Social Control, Risk and Late Modernity*. Buckingham: Open University Press.

Hughes, G. (2007) *The Politics of Crime and Community*. Basingstoke: Palgrave-Macmillan.

Hughes, G. and Edwards, A. (2002) *Crime Control and Community: The New Politics of Public Safety*. Cullompton: Willan Publications.

Hughes, G., McLaughlin, E. and Muncie, J. (eds) (2002) *Crime Prevention and Community Safety: New Directions*. London: Sage.

*Independent* (1994) 'Police attack proposals for volunteer street patrols: Home Office scheme for citizens' army will put untrained people in danger' 16 August.

*Independent* (1997a) 'Labour taskforce to help underclass', 14 August.

*Independent* (1997b) 'Harman plans work-ethic route to welfare reform', 14 November: 4.

*Independent* (1997c) 'Blair puts parents in firing line over school attendance', 9 December: 7.

*Independent* (1998a) 'Let school-shy begin work at 14, MPs urge MPs', 7 April: 7.

*Independent* (1998b) 'Brown swoops to save doomed estates', 6 February: 1.

*Independent* (2000) 'Tony Martin, the harmless eccentric whose obsession made him a killer', 20 April. Available at: http://www.independent.co.uk/news/uk/this-britain/tony-martin-the-harmless-eccentric-whose-obsession-made-him-a-killer-721200.html (accessed 02.01.10).

*Independent* (1994) 'Police condemn council estate patrols', 25 August: 1.

*Independent* (2006) 'Helen and Sylvia, the new face of terrorism', 6 April.

IPPR (2006) *Freedom's Orphans: Raising Youth in a Changing World*. London: IPPR.

James, A.L. and James, A. (2001) 'Tightening the net: children, community, and control', *British Journal of Sociology*, 52(2): 211–28.

Jamieson, J. (2005) 'New Labour, Youth Justice and "Respect"', *Youth Justice*, 5(3): 180–93.

Jamieson, J. (2006) 'New Labour, youth justice and the question of respect', *Youth Justice*, 5(3): 180–93.

Jan-Khan, M. (2003) 'The right to riot?', *Community Development Journal*, 38(1): 32–42.

John, P., Margetts, H., Rowlands, D. and Weir, S. (2006) *The British National Party: The Roots of its Appeal*. York: Joseph Rowntree Charitable Trust.

Johnston, L. and Shearing, C. (2003) *The Governance of Security: Explorations in Policing and Justice*. London: Routledge.

Johnston, V., Shapland, J. and Wiles, P. (1993) 'Developing the role of the Crime Prevention Officer', Unpublished paper presented to the British Criminology Conference, July.

Jones, D.W. (2001) 'Questioning New Labour's Youth Justice Strategy: a review article', *Youth Justice*, 1: 14.

Keith, M. (2004) 'The Thames Gateway paradox', *New Economy*, 11(1): 15–20.

Kershaw, C., Nicholas, S. and Walker, A. (2008) *Crime in England and Wales 2007/08: Findings from the British Crime Survey and police recorded crime*. London: Home Office Statistical Bulletin 07/08.

Khan, U. (1998) 'Putting the community into community safety', in A. Marlow and J. Pitts (eds), *Planning Safer Communities*. Lyme Regis: Russell House Publishing, pp. 33–41.

Kinsey, R., Lea, J. and Young, J. (1986) *Losing the Fight Against Crime*. London: Blackwell.

Klein, M. (1996) 'Gangs in the United States and Europe', *European Journal of Criminal Policy and Research*, 4(2): 63–80.

Knepper, P. (2007) *Criminology and Social Policy*. London: Sage.

Kundnani, A. (2007) *The End of Tolerance: Racism in the 21st Century*. London: Pluto Press.

Kundnani, A. (2009) *The BNP's Success Reflects the New Racism of Our Political Culture*, Institute of Race Relations. Available at: http://www.irr.org.uk/2009/june/ha000028.html (accessed 01.07.09).

Labour Party (1997) 'New Labour because Britain deserves better', Labour Party Manifesto. London: Labour Party.

Laming, H. (2003) *The Victoria Climbié Inquiry Report Of An Inquiry By Lord Laming*, CM 5730. London: HMSO.

Lavalette, M. and Ferguson, I. (2007) 'Democratic language and neo-liberal practice: the problem with civil society', *International Social Work*, 50: 447–59.

Lawless, P. (2004) 'Locating and explaining area-based urban initiatives: New Deal for Communities in England', *Environment and Planning C: Government and Policy*, 22: 383–99.

Laycock, G. and Clarke, R.V. (2001) 'Crime prevention policy and government research: a comparison of the United States and the United Kingdom', *International Journal of Comparative Sociology*, XLII (1–2): 235–55. Special Issue: *Varieties of Comparative Criminology*. Ed. Gregory Howard and Graeme Newman. Leiden: Brill.

Laycock, G. and Tilley, N. (1995) 'Implementing crime prevention', *Crime and Justice*, 19: 535–84.

Laycock, G. and Tilley, N. (undated) 'Policing and Neighbourhood Watch: strategic issues', *Police Research Group – Crime Detection & Prevention Series paper No. 60*. London: Police Research Group.

Lea, J. and Young, J. (1984) *What is to be Done about Law and Order*. London: Pluto Press.

Levitas, R. (2005) *The Inclusive Society? Social Exclusion and New Labour*. Basingstoke: Macmillan.

Levitas, R., Pantazis, C., Fahmy, E., Gordon, D., Lloyd, E. and Patsios, D. (2007) *The Multidimensional Analysis of Social Exclusion*. London: Social Exclusion Task Force.

LGA (2002) *Guidance on Community Cohesion*. London: LGA Publications.

Liberty (2009) *Identity Cards: Fiction and Fact*. Available at: http://www.liberty-human-rights. org.uk/publications/pdfs/id-cards-fact-and-fiction.pdf (accessed 11.02.09).

*London Evening Standard* (1997) '"Charles got cracking, now we will work with him"; Mandelson goes to war on "scourge" Of Britain's underclass', Patrick Hennessy, 14 August: 4.

Long, J. and Bramham, P. (2006) 'Joining up policy discourses and fragmented practices: the precarious contribution of cultural projects to social inclusion?', *Policy & Politics*, 34(1): 133–51.

McAra, L. (2008) 'Crime, criminology and criminal justice in Scotland', *European Journal of Criminology*, 5: 481–504.

McCahill, M. and Norris, C. (2002) 'CCTV in Britain', Working Paper 3, Urban Eye. Available at: www.urbaneye.net/results/euwp3.pdf (accessed 01.07.04).

McGhee, D. (2006) 'Community safety and lesbian, gay, bisexual and transgender communities', in P. Squires (ed.), *Community Safety: Critical Perspectives on Policy and Practice*. London: Policy Press, pp.181–97.

McKnight, J. (2009) 'Speaking up for Probation', *The Howard Journal*, 48(4): 327–43.

McLaughlin, E. (2002) 'The crisis of the social and the political materialization of community safety', in G. Hughes, E. McLaughlin and J. Muncie (eds), *Crime Prevention and Community Safety: New Directions*. London: Sage.

McLaughlin, E. (2007) *The New Policing*. London: Sage.

McLennan, D. and Whitworth, A. (2008) *Displacement of Crime or Diffusion of Benefit: Evidence from the New Deal for Communities Programme*. London: Department for Communities and Local Government.

Macdonald, S. (2007) 'ASBOs and Control Orders: two recurring themes, two apparent contradictions', *Parliamentary Affairs*, 60(4): 601–24.

Macpherson, W. (1999) *The Stephen Lawrence Inquiry Report Of An Inquiry By Sir William Macpherson Of Cluny*, CM 4262-I. London: TSO.

Maguire, M. (2004) 'The crime reduction programme in England and Wales: reflections on the vision and the reality', *Criminal Justice*, 4(3): 213–37.

Malik, K. (2005) 'Born in Bradford', *Prospect*, October. Available at: http://www.kenanmalik.com/essays/bradford_prospect.html (accessed 01.09.2009)

Malloch, M.S. and Stanley, E. (2005) 'The detention of asylum seekers in the UK: representing risk, managing the dangerous', *Punishment Society*, 7: 53–71.

Mandelson, P. (1998) 'Welfare should mean a hand-up not a handout, says Mandelson', Speech to Annual General Meeting of the Big Issue, *Scotsman*, 3 February: 8.

Mandelson, P. and Liddle, R. (1996) *The Blair Revolution: Can New Labour Deliver?* London: Faber.

Mares, D. (2000) 'Globalization and gangs. The Manchester case', *Focaal*, 35: 151–69.

Martinson, R. (1974) 'What Works? Questions and answers about prison reform', *The Public Interest*, 35: 22–54.

Matthews, R. (1992) 'Replacing "broken windows": crime incivilities and urban change', in R. Matthews and J. Young (eds), *Issues in Realist Criminology*. London: Sage.

Matthews, R. (2009) 'Beyond "so what?" Criminology: rediscovering realism', *Theoretical Criminology*, 13(3): 341–62.

Matthews, R. and Young, J. (eds) (1992) *Issues in Realist Criminology*, London: Sage.

Measor, L. (2006) 'Young women, community safety and informal cultures', in P. Squires (ed.), *Community Safety: Critical Perspectives on Policy and Practice*. London: Policy Press, pp. 35–51.

Miles, R. (1982) *Racism and Migrant Labour*. London: Rouledge and Kegan Paul.

Misztal, B.A. (1996) *Trust in Modern Societies*. Cambridge: Polity Press.

Morenoff, J., Sampson, R.J. and Raudenbush, S. (2001) 'Neighborhood inequality, collective efficacy, and the spatial dynamics of urban violence', *Criminology*, 39: 517–60.

MORI (2006) *MORI Five-Year Report: An Analysis of Youth Survey Data*. London: Youth Justice Board for England and Wales.

Movement for Justice (1999) 'Submission to Part 2 of Sir William Macpherson's inquiry'. Available at: http://www.users.globalnet.co.uk/~justice/submission.htm (accessed 05.11.08).

Mulgan, G. (2003) in M. Taylor (ed.) *Public Policy in the Community*. London: Palgrave.

Muncie, J. (1999) 'Institutionalized intolerance: youth justice and the 1998 Crime and Disorder Act', *Critical Social Policy*, 19: 147–75.

Muncie, J. (2000) 'Decriminalising criminology', in G. Lewis, S. Gerwitz and J.Clarke (eds), *Rethinking Social Policy*. London: Sage/Open University.

Murray, C. (1990) *The Emerging British Underclass*. London: Institute for Economic Affairs.

Mythen, G., Walklate, S. and Khan, F. (2009) '"I'm a Muslim but I'm not a terrorist." Victimisation, risky identities and the performance of safety', *British Journal of Criminology*, 49: 736–54.

Nash, M. and Ryan, M. (2003) 'Modernizing and joining-up government: the case of the prison and probation services', *Contemporary Politics*, 9(2): 157–69.

National Gang Research Center (2004) *Frequently Asked Questions About Gangs*. Available at: http://www.nationalgangcenter.gov/About/FAQ#q4 (accessed 13.05.2005).

National Literacy Trust (2009a) 'Literacy Changes Lives', National Literacy Trust Website. Available at: http://www.literacytrust.org.uk/Database/Exclusion.html (accessed 01.07.09).

National Literacy Trust (2009b) Website comment: Early Years. Available at: http://www.literacy trust.org.uk/early_years (accessed 19.12.09).

NCIS (2000) *The National Intelligence Model*. London: National Criminal Intelligence Service.

Neighbourhood Renewal Unit (2008) *Social Exclusion Unit*. Available at: http://www. neighbourhood.gov.uk/page.asp?id=630 (accessed 19.05.08).

Nellis, M. (1999) 'Towards "the field of corrections": modernizing the probation service in the Late 1990s', *Social Policy & Administration*, 33(3): 302–23.

*New Statesman* (1998) 'Interview of Jack Straw by Steve Richards', 4 March, 127(4379): 14.

Newbury, A. (2008) 'Youth crime: whose responsibility?', *Journal of Law and Society*, 35(1): 131–49.

Newman, O. (1972) *Defensible Space – Crime Prevention Through Urban Design*. New York: Macmillan.

Nixon, J. and Hunter C. (undated) 'Taking a stand against anti-social behaviour? No, not in these shoes.' Centre for Research in Social Inclusion, Sheffield Hallam University. Available at: http://www.york.ac.uk/inst/chp/hsa/papers/spring%2004/Nixon&Hunter.pdf (accessed 30.07.08).

O'Malley, P. (1992) 'Risk, power and crime prevention', *Economy and Society*, 21: 252–75.

O'Malley, P. (2004) *Risk, Uncertainty and Government*. London: Cavendish Press/Glasshouse.

*Observer* (1998) 'Labour stirs from its slumber on poverty', 25 January: 26.

Office for the Commissioner for Human Rights (2005) *Report By Mr Alvaro Gil-Robles, Commissioner For Human Rights, On His Visit To The United Kingdom*, 4–12 November 2004. Available at: http://www.statewatch.org/news/2005/jun/coe-uk-report.pdf (accessed 20.08.10).

Office of the Deputy Prime Minister (undated) *Factsheet 15: Community Cohesion and Neighbourhood Renewal*. London: ODPM.

Office of the Deputy Prime Minister (2002) *Neighbourhood Renewal Fund: Race Equality Action Plan*. London: Office of the Deputy Prime Minister.

OJJDP (2009) 'Youth Gang Prevention Initiative', Office of Juvenile Justice and Delinquency Prevention website. Available at: http://ojjdp.ncjrs.org/programs/antigang/index.html (accessed 01.06.09).

Operation Trident (undated) 'What is Trident?', Operation Trident. Available at: http://www. stoptheguns.org/whatistrident/index.php (accessed 01.07.09).

Osborne, D. and Gaebler, T. (1992) *Reinventing Government: How the Entrepreneurial Spirit is Transforming the Public Sector*. Reading, MA: Addison-Wesley.

Patrick, J. (1973) *A Glasgow Gang Observed*. London: Eyre Methuen.

Paylor, I. and Simmill-Binning, C. (2004) 'Evaluating youth justice in the UK', *The American Journal of Evaluation*, 25(3, Autumn): 335–49.

Pearson, G. (1983) *Hooligan: A History of Respectable Fears*. London: Macmillan.

Phillips, S. and Cochrane, R. (1988) 'Crime and nuisance in the shopping centre', *Crime Prevention Series Paper 16*. London: Home Office.

Pitts, J. (2001) *The New Politics of Youth Crime: Discipline or Solidarity*. Lyme Regis: Russell House Publishing.

Pitts, J. (2008) *Reluctant Gangsters: The Changing Face of Youth Crime*. Cullompton, Devon: Willan Publishing.

Whyte, D. (2007) 'The crimes of neo-liberal rule in occupied Iraq', *The British Journal of Criminology*, 47: 177–95.

Whyte, D. (2008) 'Market patriotism and the War on Terror', *Social Justice*, 34: 111–31.

Wilkinson, R. and Pickett, K. (2009) *The Spirit Level: Why More Equal Societies Almost Always Do Better*. London: Allen Lane.

Wilmott, D. (1986) *Social Networks, Informal Care and Public Policy*. London: Policy Studies Institute.

Wilson, J.Q. and Kelling, G. (1982) 'Broken windows: the police and neighbourhood safety', *The Atlantic Monthly*, March: 29–37.

Woodiwiss, M. and Hobbs, D. (2009) 'Organized evil and the Atlantic Alliance: moral panics and the rhetoric of organized crime policing in America and Britain', *British Journal of Criminology*, 49: 106–28.

Yates, S. (2008) *Youths' career aspirations and socioeconomic outcomes in adulthood: A literature review*. Available at: http://www.learningbenefits.net/Publications/DiscussionPapers/Youth%20aspirations%20and%20outcomes%20literature%20review%2008-02.pdf (accessed 05.09.08).

YJB (2007) 'Tackling Gangs Action Programme', Youth Justice Board. Available at: http://www.yjb.gov.uk/en-gb/ (accessed 05.05.07).

Young, J. (1971) *The Drugtakers*. London: Paladin.

Young, J. (1999) *The Exclusive Society: Social Exclusion, Crime and Difference in Late Modernity*. London: Sage.

Yuval-Davis, N. (1999) 'Institutional racism, cultural diversity and citizenship: some reflections on reading the Stephen Lawrence inquiry report', *Sociological Research Online*, 4(1).

Yuval-Davis, N., Anthias, F. and Kofman, E. (2005) 'Secure borders and safe haven and the gendered politics of belonging: Beyond social cohesion', *Ethnic and Racial Studies*, 28(3, May): 513–35.

Pitts, J. and Hope T. (1997) 'The local politics of inclusion: the state and community safety', *Social Policy and Administration*, 31(5): 37–58.

Plowden, P. (1999) 'Love thy neighbour', *New Law Journal*, 2 April and 9 April, 479 and 520.

Power, M. (1997) *The Audit Society*. Oxford: Oxford University Press.

Raco, M. (2007) 'Securing sustainable communities: citizenship, safety and sustainability in the new urban planning', *European Urban and Regional Studies*, 14: 305–20.

Ray, L. and Smith, D. (2001) 'Racist offenders and the politics of "hate-crime"', *Journal of Law and Critique*, 12: 203–21.

Ray, L., Smith, D. and Wastell, L. (1999) 'The Macpherson Report: a view from Greater Manchester', *Sociological Research Online*, 4(1). Available at: http://www.socresonline.org.uk/socresonline/4/lawrence/ray_smith_wastell.html.

Reiner, R. (2007) *Law-and-order: An Honest Citizen's Guide to Crime Control*. Cambridge: Polity Press.

Ritchie, D. (2001) *Oldham Independent Review Report 2001*. Available at: http://image.guardian.co.uk/sysfiles/Guardian/documents/2001/12/11/Oldhamindepentreview.pdf (accessed 08.01.2003)

Roe, S. and Ashe, J. (2006) 'Young people and crime: findings from the 2006 Offending, Crime and Justice Survey', *Home Office Statistical Bulletin 09/08*. London: Home Office.

Roe, S. and Ashe, J. (2008) *Young People and Crime: Findings from the 2006 Offending, Crime and Justice Survey*. London: Home Office Statistical Bulletin 09/08.

Rose, N. (1999) *Powers of Freedom: Reframing Political Thought*. Cambridge: Cambridge University Press.

Safe Neighbourhoods Unit (1986) *The Safe Neighbourhoods Unit Report 1981–1986*. London: NACRO.

Sanders, B. (2005) *Youth Crime and Youth Culture in the Inner City*. London: Routledge.

Scarman, Lord (1981) *The Brixton Disorders 10–12 April 1981. Report of an Enquiry*. Cmnd 8427. London: HMSO.

Scraton, P. (1997) (ed.) *Childhood in 'Crisis'*. London: UCL Press.

*Scotland on Sunday* (1997) 'Blair's £200m bid to beat truants', 7 December: 1.

*Scotsman* (1997) 'Academics rebuff Blair's social vision', 2 October: 5.

*Scotsman* (1998) 'Welfare should mean a hand-up not a handout, says Mandelson', 3 February: 8.

*Scotsman* (2005) '"Confession" lifts lid on London bomb plot', 31 July.

SEU (2000) *Report of Policy Action Team 12: Young People*. London: SEU.

SEU (2004) *Breaking the Cycle: Taking Stock of Progress and Priorities for the Future*, September. London: Office of the Deputy Prime Minister.

Shaftoe, H. (2004) *Crime Prevention: Facts, Fallacies and the Future*. Basingstoke: Palgrave Macmillan.

Shropshire, S. and McFarquhar, M. (2002) *Developing Multi Agency Strategies to Address the Street Gang Culture and Reduce Gun Violence Amongst Young People*. Briefing No 4. Manchester: Steve Shropshire and Michael McFarquhar Consultancy Group.

Simon, J. (1997) 'Governing through crime', in L. Freidman and G. Fisher (eds), *The Crime Conundrum*. Boulder, CO: Westview Press, pp. 171–89.

Sivanandan, A. (1990) *Communities of Resistance: Writings on Black Struggles for Socialism*. London: Verso.

Sivarajasingam, V., Moore, S. and Shepherd, J.P. (2007) *Violence in England and Wales 2007: An Accident and Emergency Perspective*. Violence and Society Research Group, Cardiff University, Heath Park, Cardiff. Available at: http://www.cardiff.ac.uk/dentl/resources/Trends_in_violence_2007.pdf (accessed 01.09.08).

Smith, D.I. (2007) *An Overview of Transitions and the Contribution of Recent Research*. Youth Affairs Unit, De Montfort University, Leicester. Available at: http://www.dmu.ac.uk/Images/2%2E%20An%20Overview%20of%20Transitions%20and%20the%20Contribution%20of%20Recent%20Research_tcm6-10998.pdf

Smith, M.J. and Tilley, N. (2005) *Crime Science: New Approaches to Preventing and Detecting Crime*. Cullompton, Devon: Willan Publishing.

Smith, R. (2001) 'Foucault's Law: The Crime and Disorder Act 1998', *Youth Justice*, 1(2): 17–29.

Smithers, R. and Woodward, W. (2001) 'Action zones do not make much impact, says Ofsted Flagship initiative fails to raise standards, watchdog warns', *Guardian Unlimited Education*, Tuesday 6 March. Available at: http://www.guardian.co.uk/uk/2001/mar/06/ofsted.education (accessed 04.08.08).

Social Exclusion Unit (1998) *Bringing Britain Together: A National Strategy for Neighbourhood Renewal*. Cm 4045. London: HMSO.

Social Exclusion Unit (2000a) *National Strategy for Neighbourhood Renewal Report of Policy Action Team 8: Anti-social behaviour*. London: Cabinet Office.

Social Exclusion Unit (2000b) *National Strategy for Neighbourhood Renewal Report of Policy Action Team 8: Young People*. London: Cabinet Office.

Social Exclusion Unit (2001) *A New Commitment to Neighbourhood Renewal: National Strategy Action Plan*. London: Cabinet Office.

Solomos, J. (1999) 'Social Research and the Stephen Lawrence Inquiry', *Sociological Research Online*, 4(1).

Spalek, B. (2008) *Ethnicity and Crime: A Reader*. Milton Keynes: Open University Press.

Spalek, B. and Lambert, R. (2008) 'Muslim communities, counter-terrorism and counter-radicalisation: a critically reflective approach to engagement', *International Journal of Law, Crime and Justice*, 36: 257–70.

Spangenburg, S. (2001) 'The political economy of a British stakeholder society', *Briefing notes in Economics*, 47, December 2000/January 2001: 1–9.

Squires, P. (ed.) *Community Safety: Critical Perspectives on Policy and Practice*. London: Policy Press.

Squires, P. and Stephen, D.E. (2005) *Rougher Justice: Anti-social Behaviour and Young People*. Cullompton, Devon: Willan Publishing.

Squires, P., Silvestri, A., Grimshaw, R., Solomon, E. (2008) *Street Weapons Commission: Guns, Knives and Street Violence*. London: Centre for Crime and Justice Studies.

Statewatch (2005) *News Online*, February. Available at: http://database.statewatch.org/protected/article.asp?aid=26323 (accessed 18.11.08)

Stenson, K. (2005) 'Sovereignty, biopolitics and community safety in Britain', *Theoretical Criminology*, 9(3): 265–87.

Stenson, K. and Edwards, A. (2003) 'Crime control and local governance: the struggle for sovereignty in advanced liberal politics', *Contemporary Politics*, 9(2): 203–17.

Stoker, G. (2004) *Transforming Local Governance: From Thatcher to New Labour*. Basingstoke: Palgrave Macmillan.

Sveinsson, K.P. (ed.) (2009) *Who Cares about the White Working Class?* London: The Runnymede Trust.

Taylor, M. (2003) *Public Policy in the Community*. London: Palgrave.

Taylor, I. (1995) 'Private homes and public others: an analysis of talk about crime in suburban South Manchester in the mid-1990s', *British Journal of Criminology*, 35(2): 263–85.

Taylor, I., Evans, K. and Fraser, P. (1996) *A Tale of Two Cities: Global Change, Local Feeling and Everyday Life in the North of England. A Study in Manchester and Sheffield*. London: Routledge.

Taylor, I., Walton, P. and Young, J. (1973) *The New Criminology For a Social Theory of Deviance*. London: Routledge and Kegan Paul.

Thatcher, M. (1987) *Women's Own Magazine*, 31 October.

TIAG (undated, a) 'Foreword' *Operation Trident*. Available at: http://www.stoptheguns.org/working together/independentadvsiorygroup.php (accessed 01.07.09).

TIAG (undated, b) *London Against Gun and Knife Crime*. Available at: http://www.london.gov.uk/gangs/projects/cross-borough/project-05.jsp (accessed 14.07.09).

Tilley, N. (1993) 'Crime prevention and the safer cities story', *Howard Journal*, 32(1): 40–57.

Tilley, N. (1994) 'Towards a discipline of crime prevention: a systematic approach to its nature, range and concepts', Paper presented to the 22nd Cropwood Conference 'Preventing Crime and Disorder', September.

Tilley, N. (2002) 'Introduction: analysis for crime prevention', in N. Tilley (ed.) *Analysis for Crime Prevention*, Crime Prevention Studies Series, Vol. 13.

*The Times* (1997) 'Blair launches One Nation taskforce', 9 December: Features Section.

van Dyk, J., Manchin, R., van Kesteren, J., Nevala, S. and Hideg, G. (2007) 'The Burden of Crime in the EU Research Report: A Comparative Analysis of the European Crime and Safety Survey (EU ICS) 2005'. Available at: http://www.gallup-europe.be/euics/Xz38/downloads/EUICS%20-%20The%20Burden%20of%20Crime%20in%20the%20EU.pdf (accessed 01.07.09).

Waiton, S. (2006) 'Antisocial behaviour: the construction of a crime', *Spiked*, 19 January.

Walker, A., Flatley, J., Kershaw, C. and Moon, D. (eds) (2009) *Crime in England and Wales 2008/09*. Volume 1: *Findings from the British Crime Survey and police recorded crime*. London: Home Office.

Walklate, S. and Evans, K. (1999) *Zero Tolerance or Community Tolerance: Managing Crime in High Crime Areas*. Aldershot: Ashgate.

Walsh, C. (2002) 'Curfews: no more hanging around', *Youth Justice*, 2(2): 70–81.

Webber, F. (2006) 'From deterrence to criminalisation', *European Race Bulletin*. Institute Race Relations, No. 55.

Weber, L. (2002) 'The detention of asylum seekers: 20 reasons why criminologists should card', *Current Issues in Criminal Justice*, 14(1): 9–30.

Weber, L. and Bowling, B. (2008) 'Valiant beggars and global vegabonds: select, eject, immobilize', *Theoretical Criminology*, 12(3): 355–75.

Webster, C. (2008) 'Marginalized white ethnicity, race and crime', *Theoretical Criminology*, 293–312.

Werber, P. (2005) 'The translocation of culture: "community cohesion" and the force of multiculturalism in history', *Sociological Review*, 53: 745–68.

Whyte, D. (2004) 'All that glitters isn't gold: environmental crimes and the production of criminological knowledge', *Crime Prevention and Community Safety*, 6(1): 165–85.

# Index

Please note – where page numbers are in italics these index to footnotes rather than main text.